TRACKING THE AUDIENC

In *Tracking the Audience: The Ratings Industry from Analog to Digital*, author Karen Buzzard examines the key economic, political, and competitive factors that have influenced the dominant ratings methods in each of the markets for radio, TV, and the Internet.

Beginning with the birth of the industry in 1929, *Tracking the Audience* traces the establishment of a standardized ratings "currency" as it evolved to meet the needs of the analog broadcast system and explores the search for new gold standards necessitated by the devastating effects of the digital revolution. Buzzard examines key challenges to the established system by discussing the movement from traditional sampling methods to new, more transparent measurements. More than a history of the ratings industry itself, it also tracks the evolving business model for the broadcast industry.

Tracking the Audience: The Ratings Industry from Analog to Digital shows how the development of conceptual tools designed to measure and package radio, TV, and Internet audiences is the result of a variety of historical factors. With a detailed examination of ratings providers, their methods, and their attempts to adjust to meet new demands in a digital age, this volume explains how a standardized broadcast system of audience measurement ratings has evolved and where it is going in the future.

Karen Buzzard is professor of media, journalism, and film at Missouri State University and is internationally acclaimed for her seminal scholarship in the area of ratings history and practice. She is the author of several works on the ratings industry and has published in professional journals such as the *Journal of Radio Studies* and the *Journal of Media Economics*. Her scholarship has resulted in solicitation by legal scholars, industry professionals, journalists, and business start-ups.

TRACKING THE AUDIENCE

The Ratings Industry from Analog to Digital

Karen Buzzard

Routledge
Taylor & Francis Group

NEW YORK AND LONDON

First published 2012
by Routledge
711 Third Avenue, New York, NY 10017

Simultaneously published in the UK
by Routledge
2 Park Square, Milton Park, Abingdon, Oxon OX14 4RN

Routledge is an imprint of the Taylor & Francis Group, an informa business

© 2012 Taylor & Francis

Library of Congress Cataloging in Publication Data
Buzzard, Karen.
Tracking the audience : the ratings industry from analog to digital/ by Karen Buzzard.
    p. cm.
    1. Television programs–United States–Rating–History. 2. Radio programs–United States–Rating–History. 3. Television viewers–United States–Measurement–History. 4. Radio audiences–United States–Measurement–History. 5. Analog electronic systems. 6. Digital electronics. I. Title.
    HE8700.66.U6B895 2012
    384.55′443–dc23   2011041079

ISBN: 978-0-8058-5851-8 (hbk)
ISBN: 978-0-8058-5852-5 (pbk)
ISBN: 978-0-203-14949-2 (ebk)

Typeset in Bembo
by HWA Text and Data Management, London

SFI Certified Sourcing
www.sfiprogram.org
SFI-00453

Printed and bound in the United States of America
by Edwards Brothers, Inc.

For Steve

CONTENTS

ACKNOWLEDGMENTS

This book is a continuation of a long journey, a journey that began with my dissertation research on audience ratings in 1985 at the University of Wisconsin-Madison and has continued. It is dedicated to all the ratings pioneers who shared this journey with me through their stories and memories, some of whom have now passed on: Archibald Crossley, who greeted me warmly at his home in Princeton, who provided the first ratings service and also the term "ratings" for the industry to come; Arthur Nielsen, Jr., for his continuing support and gracious hospitality during the times we met at his office and in his home near Chicago, and for sending copies of my first book to all his industry colleagues for comments; Mary Glaze Seiler, for opening her door to me to share in her husband's treasure trove of belongings and her kindness in sharing her own story; Hugh M. Beville, former head of research at NBC, for meeting with me at his home on Long Island while he was writing his own book on ratings; John Landreth, Bill Harvey, and Norm Hecht, all formerly with Arbitron, and Jack Hill, formerly senior vice president at Ogilvy and Mather, who all provided important pieces of the story for this and earlier books on ratings; to current executives at Nielsen, such as Paul Donato, executive vice president and chief research officer, as well as those at Arbitron, who took time from their busy schedules to be interviewed. Their graciousness, openness, and responsiveness to historical researchers, such as myself, should not be taken for granted and hopefully is a tradition that will be passed, through their examples, to their successors in new emerging digital industries.

This book is also dedicated to my life partner and husband, Steve Sullam, who has provided a different type of journey; to my brother Clyde Buzzard, who has provided the benefits of his editing expertise throughout the years; and to my three sisters, Beverly, Shirley, and Sharon, who have provided emotional sustenance along the way. To all, I wish to say, thank you.

A version of Chapter 1 "Establishing the Analog Currencies for Network Radio Audiences: The Telephone Recall, the Telephone Coincidental, and the Household Meter Initiatives" was published as "Radio Ratings Pioneers: The Development of a Standardized Ratings Vocabulary," *Journal of Radio Studies* (1999) 6(2), 287–306.

Chapter 2 "Establishing the Analog Currency for Local Radio and TV Audiences: The Diary Initiative" is an adaption of two earlier articles: "Ratings Forgotten Pioneer: James Seiler of the American Research Bureau" (now Arbitron), *Journal of Radio Studies* (2003) (10)2: 186–201; and "Radio Ratings Pioneers: The Development of a Standardized Ratings Vocabulary," *Journal of Radio Studies* (1999) 6(2) 287–306.

A version of Chapter 3 "Establishing the Analog Currency for Network TV Audiences: The People Meter Initiative" was first published as "The Peoplemeter Wars, A Case Study of Technological Innovation and Diffusion in the Ratings Industry," *Journal of Media Economics* (2002) 15(4), 273–291.

A version of Chapter 6 "Establishing the Digital Currency for Internet Audiences: The Software Meter Initiative" was first published in *New Media: Theories and Practices of Digitextuality*, Anna Everett and John T. Caldwell (eds), New York: Routledge, 2003.

INTRODUCTION

Audience Ratings in the Twenty-First Century: The Digitalization of Media Audiences

The efficient and effective operation of the TV, radio, and Internet marketplace requires information (ratings) that both buyers and sellers agree to use, known as *currency*. Currency, as used here, has a double meaning. First, it refers to what method is currently in use by the dominant ratings services, but it also refers to the use of ratings as a form of currency or money by which to buy and sell an otherwise invisible product. The buyer's (advertisers, agencies, media buyers) goal in the TV marketplace is to move products and services through the use of advertising as effectively and efficiently as possible. The seller's (programmers and media such as network, station, syndicators, cable, and the Internet) goal is to maximize revenue and profits by maximization of the audience size, especially in highly sought-after demographic groups, sometimes known as "commodity audiences." (See, for example, a range of scholars, including Murdock (1978); Jhally (1982); and Meehan (1993)) on what has become commonly known as the "Blindspot Debate" sparked initially by Dallas Smythe's seminal essay (1977) that urged scholars to focus on the economic dimensions of media industries in capitalism and suggested that audiences are the main commodity manufactured by these industries (see also Ettema and Whitney (1994). More recent scholars, such as Fernando Bermejo, have extended this debate to understanding audience exposure (listening and watching) as not only products packaged and sold by ratings services but audience's participation by offering their labor through responding, leading to a commodification of "interactivity" (Bermejo, 2009).

The ratings marketplace for radio and television has historically been divided into two markets (or samples). One sample is drawn for the networks and their national audiences and one gathered for the local marketplace for radio and TV. Since 1987, the Nielsen Company, the sole provider of TV ratings for network television, has employed the National People Meter as the currency method at the national or network level and is presently implementing the same method, the people meter, in the local television market level, but here known as the Local People Meter (LPM). Arbitron held a similarly dominant position in radio measurement, except it traditionally employed a diary method to gather information about its local radio audiences until it more recently introduced a method known as the Portable People Meter (PPM). The people meter in its various forms was the latest evolution of a body of audience measurement methods and tools that came to define the twentieth-century TV and radio marketplace.

It should be noted that Arbitron also is the sole provider and currency for national ratings for network radio, known as RADAR (Radio's All Dimension Audience Research). This service measures 56 individual radio networks (in 2011), merging respondent data with some 3 million "clearances" (when commercials air). However, I have elected not to cover RADAR as a separate chapter in this book for a number of reasons. First, it draws a nationally representative subsample from Arbitron's local market samples and therefore is not a stand-alone service. Second, it continues to use Arbitron's Radio Listening Diary although these data are now supplemented with PPM data. Last, because it is a quarterly service, rather than a daily syndicated service, which provides cumulative ratings—ratings that indicate who was in an overall listening audience by station typically over one month rather than by specific program or time period.

The body of conceptual tools designed to measure and package radio and TV audiences are the result of a variety of historical factors, including changes in the needs of marketing and advertising, changes in the broadcast marketplace itself due to technological or legal factors, and the competitive conditions of the rating services. I have written two other books about the ratings industry in the United States, one that details a history of their development—*Chains of Gold: Marketing the Ratings and Rating the Markets* (Scarecrow Press, 1990)—and *Electronic Media Ratings: Turning Audiences into Dollars and Sense* (Butterworth, 1992), which examines how the ratings are gathered, packaged, and sold.

In this book, *Tracking the Audience: The Ratings Industry from Analog to Digital,* I examine the major players in the ratings industry. Part I looks at the broadcast analog ratings system from its beginnings in 1929 through the present currency system; in Part II, I examine the ratings industry as it attempts to attune its methods and tools to twenty-first-century digital technology.

Part I: The Analog Era and the Currency Market in Ratings

Prior to the 1930s, knowledge of media audiences consisted primarily of subjective impressions such as anecdotes, postcards mailed in by audiences, and other schemes conceived of by advertisers. The sales departments in print advertising were among the first pioneers in the field of marketing research, conducting what became known as "pantry" studies—door-to-door interviews to collect data about household purchases. Advertising historian Roland Marchand argues that, in practice during this period, advertisers conceived of the public in two broad groups: mass and class (Marchand, 1985). This rather impressionistic and relaxed view of the audience was upset by the rapid growth of radio. As radio became commercialized, many advertisers worried about a backlash. Research entrepreneurs such as Paul Lazarsfeld at the Bureau of Applied Social Research at Columbia University were pioneers in developing new research methods and answering the elusive questions of who the audience was and how it responded to specific programs, information desired by customers, such as the government and private businesses (Converse, 1987; Fleming and Bailyn, 1969; Douglas, 1999).

However, the absence of a regular industry source of audience data was about to change with the collaboration of both broadcasters and advertisers who formed a collective known as the Cooperative Analysis of Broadcasting and hired a noted polling expert, Archibald Crossley, to carry out the research. This new service began in 1929 and was one of many services throughout the history of broadcast media audience measurement, including C. E. Hooper Inc., A. C. Nielsen, Inc., the American Research Bureau (now Arbitron), and more recently Internet services, such Media Metrix, comScore, and Nielsen NetRatings, who contributed to the statistical vocabulary, methods, and conceptual tools that were developed and continue today.

In the first section of the book, I examine how a standardized broadcast system of audience measurement ratings evolved. In Chapter 1, "Establishing the Analog Currencies for Network Radio Audiences: The Telephone Recall, the Telephone Coincidental, and the Household Meter Initiatives" I examine the ratings pioneers who contributed significantly to the development of a body of ratings tools to measure the mass audiences characteristic of radio in the 1930s and 1940s and television during the 1950s. It was these pioneers, namely Archibald Crossley, C. E. Hooper, and A. C. Nielsen, who developed the basic vocabulary, such as the terms *ratings*, *share*, and *Households Using Television* (HUTs), and such buying yardsticks as cost per thousand, and reach and frequency, and developed important methods.

By the late 1950s and 1960s, the emphasis of marketing had changed—from a focus on mass production to an age of distribution, with the burden on advertisers and marketers to move a growing body of products from factories to homes. To do this more effectively, raters moved beyond the mass tools of the first era to more refined tools to measure audiences at local levels. More than seven rating companies competed during this early period but, by the late 1960s, the number of services had thinned to two major services: the American Research Bureau and A. C. Nielsen, Inc. Advertisers now desired better tools to target audiences at the local level, such as demographic and geographic data, which required different methods and sampling techniques. Rather than buying audiences by cost-per-thousand, cost-per-point became the norm as advertisers and broadcasters sought to refine their tools to better pinpoint their customers (Buzzard, 1990; Turow, 1997). In Chapter 2, "Establishing the Analog Currency for Local Radio and TV Audiences: The Diary Initiative," I explore the significance of the American Research Bureau (now Arbitron) under the pioneering efforts of James W. Seiler, its founder, in establishing a body of local market research tools using the diary method.

By the end of the 1960s, the ratings marketplace has settled into an oligopoly with Nielsen Media Research, the monopoly provider in the TV marketplace, and Arbitron, the sole provider of radio audience measurement, but splitting the local TV marketplace with Nielsen. This oligopoly structure at the network level was to continue until the 1980s, until the entry of a new player from Great Britain, known as Audits of Great Britain (AGB) with its people meter technology.

The people meter technology led to a series of competitive battles among various ratings rivals, which I detail in Chapter 3, "Establishing the Analog Currency for Network TV Audiences: The People Meter Initiative." The dynamics of the ratings industry can be gleaned by examining the four rival firms who attempted to enter the market with their own versions of the people meter. Audits of Great Britain and Arbitron made unsuccessful attempts to enter the national ratings marketplace with national services but withdrew in 1987 and 1992, respectively. A significant impact of the battle was the withdrawal of Arbitron from the local television ratings marketplace and from the national one. Another rival, Statistical Research (or SRI), funded by the broadcast networks, attempted to operate SMART (The System for Measuring and Reporting Television Statistical Methods in Audience Research for Television), and used a small sample in Philadelphia to create a national TV ratings lab. During the testing period, SMART sought financial support from major media companies and other investment sources but concluded its operation in 1999 having failed to find the necessary funding (Buzzard, 2002). As the air cleared after the battle, Nielsen was the only competitor left standing. Despite attempts by various ratings rivals, Nielsen's monopoly control of the TV ratings business was to continue until the present.

Part II: The Digital Era and the Search for New Gold Standards

In 2009, the Federal government mandated that the transition from analog to digital broadcasting be complete, ushering in profound changes in the former analog-based broadcasting industry and reshaping the media landscape not only for consumers but for government regulators and the buyers and sellers in the industry. The impact of digital technology forced businesses in the former broadcasting industry to create new business models to keep pace with rapid changes. For those in the TV advertising business, the digital revolution was characterized by three primary factors: increasing audience segmentation due to increasing numbers of channels and technological innovations; increasing shifting of program viewing away from linear programming, known as time shifting, made possible by TiVo and other digital video recorders; and growing portability or mobility of the medium as it moved to iPods, cell phones, and other portable devices, a phenomenon known as *place shifting*.

Not only was the industry transformed but the very ways in which consumers used media were revolutionized. The once-passive, captive, network family audience who sat around the family console was no more. Television was now received on multiple screens and offered the consumer more control over what to watch, when to watch, and where to watch, sometimes called the "user revolution." The newly liberated viewer no longer was forced to sit through an endless barrage of commercials, forcing both advertisers and broadcasters to rethink former models of advertising. However, digital technology also offered the industry the ability to better reach target audiences, and a more transparent measure of the effectiveness of their advertising.

Key market forces in the analog TV industry, which continued to exercise great influence in the new digital industry, were technology, regulation, and competition. From the regulation of telephone and cable companies, through setting of content and technological standards, government regulation affected the structure, content, and adoption of technology. The 1996 Telecommunications Act launched a free-for-all in the TV marketplace because regulation was lifted that had been in place for decades. Broadcasters, cable TV operators, and local and long distance phone companies were now permitted to increase their market power within their traditional markets and to enter one another's markets. The result of this legislation led to mergers and restructuring that reshaped the industry and continues to do so.

However, it was the application of digital technology to TV and the technological and regulatory underpinnings that supported it that has led to the most dramatic and sweeping impact on the industry. The convergence, or collision, of data/voice/video/networking (i.e., computers with TV) altered the TV landscape radically. It represented the single most important change in the delivery and capabilities of TV in fifty years. Television usage changed as viewers were offered more options, greater interactivity, and increasing customization. These changes in the markets squeezed profit, heightened competition, intensified the battle for market share, and increased pressure for accountability, making it more difficult to succeed in all the former core businesses of television—the networks, the stations, advertisers and agencies, and the ratings providers themselves. The movement to digital technology increased the pace of change, the number of competitors, and the risks associated with each marketplace as each player competed with new business infrastructures and new ways of offering programming and content.

With the advent of digital cable and satellite TV, TV ratings for the top ten programs declined as more choices allowed people to be more selective in viewing. Cable and satellite companies used technology to offer more channels, telephony, high-speed data, video-on-demand, subscription music services, and more. *Business Week* magazine called the new digital era the "end of TV (as we know it)" (*Business Week*, 2008).

The use of new technology, such as digital video recorders, digital set-top boxes, and handheld mobiles led to more control and personalization, including time shifting, message avoidance, and customerized uses, such as information, games, e-commerce; and electronic communities and affinity groups. Media players needed to find new ways to deliver content and messages, new methods to transact with the active consumers, and countermeasures to maintain advertising effectiveness.

The major upheaval resulting from the digital revolutions in the ratings industry was that Nielsen was no longer assured its people meter method would be the currency. By 2009, the U.S. advertising business was worth more than $6 billion annually with Nielsen's profits in the neighborhood of $60 million or 1 percent annually. Yet, in a customer satisfaction survey executed in 2002, Nielsen came in 13 of 13 among the world's ratings services (*Manneer Report*, 2002).

In an effort to continue to be relevant in the new digital marketplace, Nielsen made major changes in its data delivery. The Active/Passive (AP) meter was implemented to better sample what Nielsen considered to be technically difficult homes (homes with TiVo, satellite television, digital video recorders, video-on-demand, etc.) despite the fact that it failed to receive the approval of the ratings industry accreditation agency, the Media Rating Council (MRC), by the time of its launch in 2005. This meter, promised ten year earlier, was feared by the industry to be an example of a lack of investment by Nielsen in research and development to resolve sample representativeness, a problem addressed too little, too late, and too expensive but resulted in additional surcharges paid by Nielsen customers.

After years of complaints by the industry, in 2007, Nielsen agreed to release more granular data in the form of what were known as C3 ratings, minute-by-minute commercial audience ratings that included three days of viewing recorded for playback. C3 ratings, a compromise between the advertising and broadcasting communities, resulted in the industry's begrudgingly agreeing to an incremental cost of $4 million, an increase that the American Association of Advertising Agencies considered predatory pricing because the data had already been paid for once by the licensees. This type of granular level of data had become common in the rest of the world in all the major countries with the exception of the United States and Canada and offered at minimal costs. Three years after the national advertising currency had shifted to C3 ratings as the *de facto* currency, the industry self-regulatory watchdog—the MRC—finally accredited Nielsen's commercial estimates (Mandese, 2010).

In a digital era, one thing was clear: the diary method, which had served as the basis for demographic information for Nielsen and Arbitron, was grossly ineffective in measuring radio and TV audiences in a 100+ channel environment. Thus, both companies began aggressive campaigns to introduce newer people meter methods into local markets. Nielsen, for its part, determined to use its National People Meter, which it had used at the national level since 1987, in the local TV markets but here called the LPM, with the goal of replacing the diary altogether. Nielsen's LPM initiative is the subject of Chapter 4, "Establishing the Digital Currency for Local TV Audiences: The Local People Meter Initiative."

By the twenty-first century, many in the TV and radio industry questioned Nielsen's use of both the National People Meter and the LPM as gold standards in either market to measure the vastly changing digital marketplace. Rather, they saw the people meter method as one held in place simply due to Nielsen's lack of spending in research and development and its lethargy due to its lack of competitors. Of particular concern for the local TV marketplaces that employed the new local people system was that local broadcast stations lost significant portions of their program audiences while cable companies saw significant increases. Nielsen's decision to roll out its people meter technology at the local level without MRC accreditation also resulted in much industry controversy.

Many broadcasters, such as Fox TV, along with local TV stations and minority interest groups resisted the LPM services, decrying the inadequacy of the LPM in measuring minority audiences. Fox TV, for its part, helped to fund and enflame minority interest groups, such as "Don't Count Us Out," which brought the LPM to the attention of policy makers and members of Congress, leading to a congressional investigation (Bachman, 2004b; see Napoli, 2008, 2010 for a more detailed study of policy issues surrounding this matter). At the same time, a Florida station owned by Sunbeam TV Corp, having lost a significant share of its audience and thus overall value as a result of Nielsen's shift to the LPM, filed a complaint against Nielsen Media Research accusing it of violating federal and state antitrust laws, violating Florida's unfair trade practices, and breaching its contract with Sunbeam (United States District Court Southern District of Florida, 2009). By 2011, a federal judge dismissed these charges and stated that while Nielsen may be anti-competitive and there was evidence of exclusionary contracting practices, but Sunbeam had failed to establish the existence of a willing and able competitor as required by antitrust law. Sunbeam, according to the judge, had failed to provide a better way to compile TV ratings than with the PPM or that such ratings would benefit Sunbeam (Garvin, 2011).

Others in the industry complained loudly about what they saw as Nielsen's abuse of its monopoly position to raise product prices. Given its monopoly status, many in industry were no longer sure what the cost for its products should be as prices had been held to an artificial standard. At the same time, most agreed that the people meter, even if executed to the minimum standard at the local market level, was superior to the set-meter/diary method used in larger and medium-size markets or the diary-only approach used in smaller markets. Some called Nielsen a *de facto* monopoly and wondered whether it had lived up to the legacy of the Harris Commission (1963), a Congressional investigation that had put into place the ratings industry oversight group, the MRC. (See the following for more on the Harris Hearings: Buzzard, 1990, 2002.) Many felt that Nielsen's history of ignoring the MRC's accreditation decisions (such as Nielsen's recent decision to deploy its

LPM despite a lack of accreditation) indicated that Congress needed to strengthen oversight to ensure responsiveness to the concerns of the marketplace. Others felt that Nielsen needed some form of a shake-up. Some, such as ABC's Head of Research, Alan Wurtzel, called for some form of a joint industry committee, used in other major countries, which could oversee such concerns as media surveys, the use of data, contract terms, and competitive bidding (Wurtzel, 2009).

Still others felt that the industry itself was, in part, to blame for failing to support competitive TV measurement opportunities, such as Arbitron's ScanAmerica, AGB's people meter and SRI's SMART, and even Arbitron's PPM initiative. Even newer smaller competitors, such as erinMedia, which planned to compete using set-top box data, found significant barriers to entry due to start-up costs and infrastructure and failed to gain the support it needed to become a viable business. Other barriers to entry were the long-term staggered contracts signed by Nielsen's largest clients—Viacom, Disney/ABC, Fox, and NBC—that effectively tied them exclusively for a period of years to Nielsen, thereby preventing competition. According to Frank Maggio, CEO of erinMedia and ReacTV, who filed an antitrust lawsuit in 2005 against Nielsen (U.S. District Court Southern District of Florida, 2005), subsequently settled out of court in 2008:

> Our suit initially addresses two potentially illegal antitrust behaviors by Nielsen: the use of long-term staggered contracts to ensure competition cannot get a toehold and the acquisition of competitors. As we dig deeper we expect that we may find other antitrust behavior. The use of long-term staggered contracts was an insidious and extremely devious way that monopolies can entrench themselves. They do so by taking the biggest customers out of the market for long periods of time, and the effect is to keep the industry as a whole from moving away from the monopoly without vast penalties and disruption.
>
> (Leahy, 2005; Hinman, 2008)

Nielsen, for its part, felt that, as the umpire, it was being blamed for reporting on changes in the marketplace, such as the increase in cable viewing and the decrease in traditional broadcast viewing, brought about because of changes wrought by the impact of the new digital technology. In truth, the industry no longer knew what a competitive price would be for television audience measurement in what was considered the five critical areas: enumeration, sampling, data collection, data processing, and analysis tools.

Arbitron also arrived at the same conclusion regarding the obsolescence of its method, the diary, and began an introduction of a new people meter methodology, known as the PPM. Chapter 5, "Establishing the Digital Currency for Local Radio Audiences: The Portable People Meter Initiative," discusses the controversy around this new device. Many questioned Nielsen's decision to stall on a possible business partnership with Arbitron to introduce the PPM for television measurement and instead used a four-year decision-making impasse to continue its LPM push, thus effectively restraining competition in local TV measurement. By comparison, the PPM had been embraced in areas of Canada and Europe as early as 2004 as the currency for TV and radio. When Nielsen refused to test the LPM and PPM side by side, the industry was particularly mystified as the PPM was considered a more twenty-first-century technology in measuring the out-of-home audiences, now considered essential for both radio and television. Moreover, the PPM device used a superior method in that it was passive and did not require user input. By comparison, the LPM did not move beyond the older at-home active model, which some saw as rooted in an older era (Pellegrini, 2004). To keep pace with the new digital marketplace, raters and the media industry now found it urgent to think beyond the former core model, sometimes known as the CPM/Currency model, and the methods used to sustain it.

A key driver of what promised to be a paradigmatic change in audience measurement was the tremendous growth of the Internet as an advertising medium. In Chapter 6, "Establishing the Digital Currency for Internet Audiences: The Software Meter Initiative," I explore the development of a new system of ratings for the Internet and how broadcast and Internet ratings have influenced each other. Though Internet ratings were originally modeled on the older system of ratings, gradually the transparency provided by Internet audience research methods led broadcasters and advertisers to seek the same transparency in the older system.

In the digital era, Nielsen faced a new set of challenges. Key challengers to the Nielsen monopoly and what some saw as its reliance on traditional sampling methods and cruder methods, such as ratings and share, included old foe Arbitron, and smaller outlying challengers, such as TiVo, Google, and even cable companies, as they attempted to move TV audience research closer to the models of transparency provided by the Internet. Foreign-based companies, such as Nelson Sofres Taylor, who had made major footholds in the field of media audience measurement in Europe and Asia, were also planning challenges. In particular, the use of broadband cable and its use of digital set-top boxes, which provided actual measures of audience viewing rather than estimates, seemed promising as a measurement method. In Chapter 7, "Exploring New Digital Currencies for TV, Cable, and Internet Audiences: Digital Cable and STB Data Initiative," I examine the digital set-top box ratings marketplace and the various competitors. By 2007, Nielsen formally had thrown its hat into the proverbial ring and announced its "anytime anywhere initiative," known as A2/M2, which included researching whether digital set-top data was a viable method of TV measurement in smaller markets.

The key methodological changes occurring in the current ratings marketplace—the LPM, the PPM, panel-based software measurements, and digital cable set-top box data—today are all attempts to measure changes in the digital audience. The fundamental message behind all these new devices is that digital technology was not only splintering audiences but allowing them to skip the commercials that were the foundation of the industry's business model. Even more alarming was the possibility that the television networks, the oldest of television's business models, may be out of the broadcasting business altogether as NBC, CBS, and Fox sold off their local TV stations and explored other models to send TV programs directly to the viewer, such as through Hulu.com and as cable empires rethought older delivery systems and sought to purchase former broadcast networks, such as Comcast's announced purchase of NBC.

Even the cable business model that was based on subscription fees and advertising, was threatened as more and more subscribers cut the cord because of skyrocketing cable bills. Because cable and satellite companies were monopolies, higher costs were due to lack of competition, together with the higher costs of programming, such as local stations demanding carriage fees. In addition, both TV and cable were squeezed by lower advertising income due to the economic meltdown and were passing the costs on to the consumer.

The new cord-cutting model had stimulated the development of an entire new marketplace in set-top boxes that allowed consumers to bypass cable altogether and led to new hardware and software methods of content and program distribution, as set-top box devices, such as Roku, Boxee, AppleTV, eyeTV hybrid, and Sony Media Player, provided Web interfaces for programming services and sites such as NetFlix, Hulu, YouTube, and iTunes.

The switch to digital technology presented measurement issues that challenged traditional audience measurement data and its body of established knowledge. In many instances, former analog business models and their beliefs about the audience were called into question. Advertisers needed new measures to better comprehend the effectiveness of ads in a digital multi-channel, non-linear world. Digital reception and increased data storage allowed traditional TV to be accessed on an ever-growing number of devices, while content providers had the ability to access many more windows than traditional TV through the use of cell phones, IPods, and broadband. Viewers were increasingly turning to TiVo and other digital video recorders rather than watching programs as they aired. In some areas, DVD usage jumped as much as 50 percent with the switch-over from diary/meter to the people meter. Shows scheduled at 10 PM were plummeting in ratings as people watched shows they taped earlier. Because DVR watchers skipped commercials, networks and advertisers were exploring new ways for advertisers to reach viewers, such as product placement. Many former business models had been upended and new ones were being explored as we enter the twenty-first century.

PART I

Analog

1

ESTABLISHING THE ANALOG CURRENCIES FOR NETWORK RADIO AUDIENCES

The Telephone Recall, the Telephone Coincidental, and the Household Meter Initiatives

Introduction

Pioneer radio ratings services were the first to establish a more tangible measure to estimates of otherwise intangible broadcast audiences. Unlike the print media, which used circulation figures as a measure of mass eyeballs, radio advertisers had no way of knowing how many listeners they were reaching through their sponsored programs. The Cooperative Analysis of Broadcasting (CAB), C. E. Hooper, and A. C. Nielsen entered the field of radio audience measurement in 1929, 1934, and 1942, respectively, to provide an answer to this problem. Each research firm made significant advances in research methods and developed conceptual standards that were to continue throughout the history of broadcast audience measurement. In particular, the first generation of audience research pioneers established uniform industry standards to eliminate the chaotic use of varied techniques all resulting in different and often incomparable size estimates. (This chapter is a summary of the conclusions of my earlier work. For more detail on marketing and advertising as they influenced the rise of ratings, see Buzzard, 1990, 2002.)

The Need for Audience Measurement

Early radio, similar to the Internet, had originally floundered about in search of a viable business model. Eventually a business model was advanced—one known as radio networking, whose origin was in chain-stores marketing. The resulting chain of centralized outlets or network chain empowered the national advertiser, who became the main financial underpinning for the newly commercial radio system. Because, during most of this period, commercial success meant network affiliation, the drive to create a regular syndicated system of audience measurement initially was tied to the needs of national or network radio advertisers. By late 1938, the four major national networks—NBC Blue, NBC Red, CBS, and Mutual Broadcasting System—had affiliated with all but two of the fifty-two clear-channel stations (a regulatory category of AM broadcast stations with the highest protection from interference from other stations, particularly concerning night-time skywave propagation) and had ties with regional stations and lower-power stations. Network affiliation rose from 60 percent of all stations in 1940 to 95 percent in 1945 (Sterling and Kittross, 2002). Never before or after was radio so dominated by networks.

Because the national advertiser dominated radio advertising, it was perhaps not surprising that the Association of National Advertisers (ANA), through its Radio Commission, made the first attempt to answer the basic questions regarding radio's anonymous audience and the national advertiser's possible customers. As the advertiser created the program and purchased time from the network, the first question that served as the focus for the first generation of audience research was the relative network program popularity. In other words, what network programs were the most popular (i.e., drew the largest audience, relative to other programs). This question served as the focus of the first "rating" company, the CAB. Although A. W. Lehman was the formal president of the CAB, Archibald Crossley of Crossley, Inc., a private marketing firm, was hired to carry out the technical end of the research (Crossley, 1983).

Archibald Crossley and the Cooperative Analysis of Broadcastings

Archibald M. Crossley had started his own research organization, known as Crossley, Inc., in 1918 and was one of three major organizations, beside Roper and Gallop, which engaged in political polling. Similar to how ratings were to be used, political polling results were ranked by percentage points.

The ANA hired Crossley to undertake an advertising audit to determine whether the ads that advertisers paid for were actually played on various stations across the country (Crossley, 1983). When the ANA returned to him to repeat this audit, Crossley suggested that instead he study radio's listening audience and their program preferences, thereby providing the first network program rating services. Crossley, in fact, coined the term *rating* (Crossley, 1983). Though the Radio Committee of the ANA decided not to finance the study, they did agree to endorse the study provided Crossley underwrote it.

By 1929, Crossley had gained endorsement from thirty sponsors and, by 1930, he began field work. As Crossley's service was directed toward national advertisers and agencies, it initially served only the thirty-three cities where the networks had outlets. During the first four operating years, the service belonged to Crossley, Inc. With the entry of the American Association of Advertising Agencies (AAAA) in 1934, Crossley turned over his service to a jointly financed cooperative venture consisting of national advertisers and agencies. By 1936, the CAB included the National Association of Broadcasters and, by 1945, the four major networks (Nye, 1957). Though operating as a non-profit, the CAB became the first formal rating company to provide regular studies of the radio audience on a continuing basis.

The CAB was not only a ratings service but a marketing research organization because it studied not only radio listening but what advertisers, in general, got out of advertising and the best way of selling products. During this period, radio advertisers were also program producers purchasing time periods from the radio networks and filling these periods with their own programs. Many sponsors oversaw program production and sat behind a sponsor's booth during the program. Radio program ratings provided an answer to the question of how large an audience radio advertisers received for the money invested to help them analyze their program development and time period purchases. Sponsors used the information to build a program that attracted the type of listeners most likely to buy their products. As radio audiences were broadly based and were not predetermined, as were magazines by editorial policy, most advertisers concentrated on merely attracting numbers, or mass circulation. For this measure, the program rating sufficed.

Crossley's Method: the Telephone Recall and Innovations

Although Crossley used a variety of techniques for different clients, including printed roster, mechanical recorder, personal interview, and telephone coincidental, he selected a simple "next day" recall telephone method to provide the first regular measure of network program audiences. His technique was to dial a telephone-based list and interview respondents about their previous day's listening. During this time period, multiple telephone-homes and unlisted numbers did not pose a problem.

Crossley chose the telephone recall as a method for four primary reasons. First, radio and telephone ownership had originally exhibited a high degree of congruence. Second, telephones covered a wide area quickly. Third, recall meant that a great deal of information about viewership could be collected at little expense. And last, sponsor identification was an important concern during the period so this method could elicit from listeners if they recalled the sponsor. As Daniel Yankelovitch (1963) writes, for many years the advertiser held the belief that recall or registration was the most useful index to advertising effectiveness. As most early sponsors or agencies typically developed their own programs, or at least sponsored an entire program, advertisers sought to know the degree of registration between the program and their product.

The foundation of Crossley's survey technique originally was based on a survey technique known as *quota sampling*. Quota sampling was a method in which desired sample sizes, or quotas, were established for various subclasses, such as age, gender, and income, to ensure that the characteristics of the sample were distributed in the same proportion as the characteristics of the population. The researcher established what proportion of the population was, for example, eastern, urban, White, Black, and so forth, and these subsets had to be kept up to date. However, unlike true random sampling, the probability of selecting any one household was unknown. The quota method assumed that if a sample's known characteristics were current, its unknown characteristics were automatically correct. This was a dubious but an economic and practical assumption. Crossley later changed to random sampling in response to competition by Hooper to be sure that bias was minimized and sampling error estimates could be calculated.

During the early thirties, survey researchers were still perfecting their techniques, but the belief in survey research techniques already was established. In 1916, the *Literary Digest* had begun the first of many presidential polls culminating in the infamous *Literary Digest* poll of 1936 that, in spite of its size, proved biased and incorrect (*Printer's Ink,* 1938). Using a sampling of 10 million, the poll had predicted that Al Landon would beat Franklin D. Roosevelt in the 1936 election. However, the *Digest* had sampled mostly Republicans as it used its own subscribers and lists of automobile owners and telephone users, all groups with higher-than-average income. Thus, its techniques were discredited when Roosevelt won in a landslide, winning all but two states. Using a smaller but more representative and random sample of 50,000, George Gallup correctly predicted the results of the election. The debacle led to a considerable refinement of public opinion polling techniques and was largely regarded as spurring the beginning of the era of modern scientific public opinion research. By 1922, important forerunners in sampling had appeared through the impetus of the U.S. government. Herbert Hoover reorganized the Bureau of Foreign and Domestic Commerce to act as a medium of exchange for market information (*Printer's Ink,* 1938). The statistical needs of the government had increased tremendously as a result of the Depression and the New Deal.

C. E. Hooper and Hooperatings

In 1934, Crossley's major competitor entered the field of radio measurement. The original team of Clark-Hooper, Inc. was encouraged by a group of magazine publishers who desired to set up a more valid measure of radio's advertising effectiveness. These publishers were convinced that Crossley's ratings overstated the actual number of radio homes. Under Crossley's rating system, more popular programs would achieve ratings as high as 40 to 60 percent of the radio audience. To make matters worse, despite that Crossley merely provided a rating index (figures in an index are comparable but as they are not random they cannot be projected to a total universe of listeners), many broadcasters persisted in projecting CAB ratings to total radio homes, resulting in an astronomical number of radio homes. The reason for this rating inflation was that Crossley initially used only the "identified listening audience," or what is now called the *share*, as the base for his ratings (Nye, 1957). All of these factors hurt magazines' advertising sales by inflating the size of the radio audience and were factors that the early team of Clark–Hooper undertook to correct. While a group of magazine publishers encouraged the service, they did not provide underwriting. Thus, Hooper was free to sell his subscriptions as an independent service, making his service the first commercial venture in the field of radio ratings.

Hooper's Method: the Telephone Coincidental and Its Innovations

By 1938, the team of Clark–Hooper, Inc. had split, with Hooper continuing alone in the field of radio measurement, which, at that time, consisted almost entirely of radio networks. Like the CAB, the early service only covered sponsored network programs on NBC-Blue, NBC-Red, CBS, and Mutual.

In entering the radio field, the company pioneered a method that was to become an industry standard throughout the heyday of radio network programming: the telephone coincidental. Hooper heard about the coincidental method from George Gallup and elected to adopt it for his radio ratings service. The coincidental technique represented a step forward in radio measurement as the interview was placed simultaneously with the broadcast or while the program audience was still an audience. In the struggle between CAB and Hooper, the coincidental method was the only method that measured the "available audience" during the broadcast of the actual program. Both the daypart recall used by the CAB and printed roster methods, used by such research firms as the Pulse, a smaller New York-based service during this period, sampled only the population at home during the time of the call.

This available audience, a unique feature of Hooper's telephone coincidental method, resulted in a more reliable and standardized base. Hooper was able to compile all those listening to a specific time period, dividing viewing into percentages based on programs/station viewed. Each program/station rating was a percentage of the entire viewing only during that time period. By comparison, the CAB had used the total radio homes as its base, including all those who were in the radio universe regardless of whether they were available to watch. As a result, Hooperatings were half the size of Crossley's ratings (*Advertising and Selling,* 1949). The available audience estimates, both for Hooperatings and subsequent rating services, were the most important element for comparing ratings as the attraction value of a program was equal to the percentage of the available audience. Each station was provided with an estimate of the total viewing audience during a time period, known as *Household Using TV* or HUTs, and viewing to its station was a percentage of the HUT or share. This innovation meant listening could be compared year to year and program to program. While the HUT levels could rise and fall, a station's share of viewing should remain the same unless it was gaining or losing audience.

In addition, Hooper's coincidental method supplied the average audience rating rather than the total program listeners, characteristic of the CAB method. An average audience rating was a program's total audience divided by the time intervals. The average audience rating was comparable from one program to another and from one time to another, as the base was the same for each program. Crossley's method, conversely, presented the total listeners to a given program in a sample or only the program's total audience.

Furthermore, the coincidental technique eliminated another major flaw with the recall method—the memory factor. The recall method was subject to a number of influences that could affect memory: the intensity and vividness of the program; the use of stars, novelty, contests, and distinctive program names; familiarity with a program, or its duration or repetition; listener occupation at the time of the call; the limitation to telephone homes that by 1940 comprised less than half of the radio homes and were centered in the upper economic strata; memory loss in reporting program listening; influence of telephone answerers; length of time elapsed before the interviewer call; and, last, but not least, the brand name effect of being more heavily advertised and better known. Because network programs were more heavily promoted and made more of an impression, telephone respondents more frequently recalled network programming. A program's higher ratings could be based on a factor that influenced recall or memory rather than based in actual viewing.

The Battle to Be the Currency System: CAB versus Hooperatings

By 1944, the CAB's telephone recall method had lost ground to the coincidental method despite a valiant attempt to address Hooper's attacks in a number of areas. In 1940, the CAB had shifted from "next day" recall to two-hour interviews to address the problem of memory. In 1944, the CAB shifted to an overlapping technique in which interviews were given at half-hour intervals to attempt to equalize the length of time between the program broadcast and the recall measurement. However, Hooper attacked this overlapping technique as the final percentage of set owners reported was a composite of four samples thus hiding reactions to specific broadcasts (Womer, 1941).

The CAB's next sign of weakness was its expansion into the field of coincidental research, which, according to A. W. Lehman, president of the CAB, functioned as a two-way check on the radio audience. The CAB planned to continue with its recall method providing two sets of ratings for programs. In doing so, Lehman maintained that recall measurement was still valuable as it measured conscious impression, or those who remembered the programs to which they listened. The CAB would also furnish coincidental ratings and be able to supply an average audience rating to answer those critics who attacked it for lack of a stable base (*Business Week*, 1942; *Broadcasting*, 1942).

However, from the very beginning of audience ratings, this dual rating system was not particularly loved by industry as it only added confusion to the area of buying, a criticism that was to ring throughout the history of ratings as new companies attempted to enter the field. Eventually in 1945, after one-and-a-half years of this dual system, the CAB dropped recall ratings altogether, moving entirely into the field of coincidental measurement. This decision resulted after a vote by subscribers determined a preference for a single base. Whereas the CAB recall measurement service was based on thirty-three cities linked by networks, the new coincidental technique was based on interviewing eighty-one cities to provide a more accurate national cross-section including urban areas not served by the networks. The dropping of recall measurement left only an average audience rating based on eighty-one cities and therefore did not provide sufficient product differentiation from its competitor (*Broadcasting*, 1942).

In the battle for ratings supremacy, the insurmountable problem for the CAB, however, was not only its recall method but a number of other areas that Hooper criticized. Although the CAB and Hooper both used a telephone-based interview method to measure the radio program's audience, the comparative size of their ratings varied drastically. The size of the program audience or ratings was affected by differences in tabulation procedures, the phrasing of questions asked, and in sample distribution methods, so reports simply were not comparable.

CAB reports were primarily available to the buyers of advertising time and, consequently, reports were guarded. Hooper took a different strategy and managed to make himself and his reports newsworthy, as he openly courted the press. His name appeared in a vast assortment of newspapers and trade magazines, even garnering a feature article in *Saturday Evening Post* (Beville, 1983; Small, 1945). Hooperatings soon began to provide the humor for syndicated cartoons, and he began the tradition of releasing the "first fifteen" evening programs and the "top ten" daytime programs to the press. Fans watched the Hooperuppers and Hooperdowners of such favorite programs as "Fibber McGee and Molly," "Edgar Bergen," "Amos 'n Andy," "Hopalong Cassidy," and "Fred Allen." The press had a field day attaching Hooper's name to such derivatives as Hooperatingitis, Hoopermania, and Hooper Happy. Publicity surrounding Hooperatings rode such a crest that Crossley was later to remark that his defeat could be traced to the fact that his name did not rhyme with anything (Crossley, 1983).

Whereas Crossley's reports aided the advertising community, Hooper worked the other side of the street, the networks and the stations, by introducing services specifically designed to aid stations and networks. By 1940, Hooper introduced its national station reports and branched into six available reports before its conclusion (*Broadcasting*, 1942; Hooper, 1949).

Furthermore, as part of his regular service and as a byproduct of all these reports, Hooper accumulated a great deal of data. By packaging the findings, he could constantly market new features. A particularly ingenious marketing feature was his introduction of the pocket piece that allowed a market's major statistics to be carried conveniently around in the shirt pocket, of considerable value to those who sold or purchased station availabilities.

The year 1944 marked a major battle in the Hooper and CAB battle for survival as Hooper applied another last spin to his momentum. He had, by this time, demonstrated the defects of the recall method. In response, the CAB had switched to coincidental ratings, had increased its sample size from thirty-three to eighty-one cities, had tripled the number of phone calls from 2.1 million to 6.3 million, had increased its yearly reports to ninety-four, and had extended its survey to distribution to nine geographical areas all in an attempt to keep up with Hooper (Nye, 1957; *Broadcasting*, 1942). Hooper furthermore revealed the inadequacy of the CAB base. As a result, the CAB switched to a random sample and to using "average audience" as a base. Hooper's next move was a report geared to local radio broadcast stations, known as Station Listening Area Reports, quickly signing up 205 local markets to the CAB's none, with stations assuming 44.5 percent of Hooper's cost of operation. Though Hooper was weakest in advertising clients, the community sponsoring the CAB, the move to local market reports, together with Hooper's open press policy, made a major impact on the advertising community. Moreover, in 1944, Hooper and Dr. Matthew N. Chappel published *Radio Audience Measurement,* a book presented to CAB subscribers, which detailed the rationale of Hooper's methods and made a solid impression (Hooper and Chappell, 1944).

The effect of the ratings warfare on the industry was one of growing dismay. With both services using the coincidental method, with growing costs, and with increasing numbers of interviews yet different results, industry executives began to argue that two services were repetitive and wasteful. Agencies began to cry out for more qualitative data, data that provided more information about the purchasing habits of radio listeners rather than two men with the same set of figures. As the radio industry had begun to realize, qualitative data were best suited to other methods such as panel diary, automatic recorder, and personal interviewing rather than a coincidental-based method. Thus, in its attempt to combat Hooper, the CAB had become superfluous and forced into the corner of either ceasing operations or moving into another area.

As the authority of CAB was whittled away by a compiler of a more convincing set of statistics, backers of the CAB became alarmed because Hooper began to acquire substantial subscribers. The final straw for the CAB was the financial withdrawal of ABC, CBS, and NBC, leaving the Mutual Broadcasting System as the only radio network member. The four networks had provided 40 percent of the total cost. The three advertising association backers—the Association of National Advertisers, the American Association of Advertising Agencies, and the National Association of Broadcasters—were left holding the proverbial bag. The CAB made an attempt to cover the remaining operating costs through increasing dues and assessment but, by 1945, they decided to throw in the towel after ceding more and more ground to Hooper. In that year, CAB membership considered a recommendation to quit and invited Hooper and a young upstart, A. C. Nielsen (who had begun operation in 1942), to present proposals for carrying out subscriber agreements. The sentiment was that the CAB be discontinued. By June 1946, the CAB had suspended its seventeen-year service. As a result, Hooper inherited 102 subscribers (*Broadcasting,* 1946).

Run as a cooperative membership organization, the CAB was operated by a board of governors consisting of advertisers, agencies, and broadcasters. A crucial difficulty that had impaired the CAB was this cooperative structure, hindering its efficient operation and making it much less responsive to the marketplace than Hooper. The committee's divergent idea and politics often led to a bureaucratic situation that Crossley called "too many chiefs" (Crossley interview, 1983). Its committee structure meant that decisions were long in the making; decisions were typically compromises on decisions; and decisions were tied to self-interest rather than economic considerations; furthermore, results were not measured in terms of profits or losses in the marketplace. Hooper's private enterprise, conversely, was conscious of cost, was keenly aware of its degree of acceptance from its clients, and was more responsive in general to the marketplace. As Hugh Beville, then NBC director of research, later remarked, Hooper moved on a dime while the CAB was more like a tire (Beville interview, 1983).

As Frank Nye points out in his book, *Hoop of Hooperatings*, the odds had been against Hooper, an unknown, selling a deflationary method to those who wanted optimum figures based on a technique one-third more costly and pitted against a service backed by three powerful associations (Nye, 1957). Whereas the CAB had been developed to serve the advertising community, Hooper had marketed its services to stations in sixty cities and their rep firms. By 1945, Hooper made his reports available to advertisers, agencies, and networks. This strategy of including local stations as a vital part of his service resulted in economic and methodological advantages. The economic results were to increase the scope of Hooper's service without excessive financial burden to any one subscriber. In this sense, Hooper operated the first radio pool, made up of the commercial interests in radio, a precedent that became an industry norm.

Although industry had attacked the CAB in particular, in general telephone-based methods were coming under closer scrutiny. In 1929, 10.25 million radio homes existed compared to 12.4 million telephone homes (Hooper and Chappell, 1945). However, the situation changed rapidly when the number of radio homes began to grow substantially ahead of telephone homes, raising the question of the representativeness of a telephone-based sample to measure radio. Homes with telephones were primarily upper income, and geography restricted many small towns and farms. As a result, even with random measurement, telephone-based methods distorted measurement, placing too many telephone calls in an urban, higher-income bracket.

As radio went into World War II, radio homes were approaching saturation and were estimated to reach a national average of 85 percent of all homes, far in excess of telephone homes. The radio industry was beginning to grumble about the exclusion of listeners on farms, in small towns, and in areas remote from transmitters. This concern also extended to urban homes without a telephone. Furthermore, telephone homes were limited in providing ratings for all of the broadcast day as calls only proved efficient between 8:00 AM and 10:30 PM.

Though it had proven the winner over Crossley's recall method, the telephone coincidental required a large number of telephone calls for a reliable sample and gathered this information at a much less efficient rate than the recall method. Furthermore, it produced limited qualitative information about radio listeners. The handwriting was on the wall: the telephone coincidental was expensive and increasingly failed to produce the complete picture.

Nielsen Ratings and A. C. Nielsen Sr.

Thus, the scene was set for the entry of the next major competitor in the field of radio ratings—A. C. Nielsen. The year was 1948, a year that brought attack on two key fronts of the established Hooperatings by the up-and-coming A. C. Nielsen. These two fronts were projectable ratings, ratings projectable to a true national cross section, and TV ratings.

A. C. Nielsen played a pioneering role in advancing the science of marketing and advertising by aiming his service at reducing the cost of moving goods from factory ultimately to the consumer. He had begun by conducting "performance surveys" that he sold to industrial manufacturers. These surveys provided independent and technical analyses of manufacturers' products in the plants of their customers, the retailers. Based on objective analysis of information, Nielsen could aid the manufacturer in developing products that were the most desired by consumers and promoted their sales in the most efficient way. In 1933, A. C. Nielsen expanded this service by launching a continuous market research service, the Nielsen Drug Index (Nielsen, 1964). In measuring the flow of goods off retail store shelves, such precise data helped to better align production with distribution.

Nielsen was part of a rapidly growing sector of the economy known as the "information" industry, which helped to align production, distribution, and consumption in a changing industrial society. The single largest category of data provided by the information industry was research on the marketing of products, including the use of the various advertising media to accelerate sales. This new information industry, of which broadcast audience research was a sector, was derived from primary sources, was numeric, and was in database form. These databases were furnished to subscribers on a continuing syndicated basis in a variety of modes. Marketing research for consumer and industrial products provided information to guide manufacturers or retailers in marketing decisions.

Marketing as a means of maximizing efficiency came into its own as the cost of distribution now exceeded production. Reductions in the cost of distribution produced larger sales and profits for manufacturers and lower costs to consumers.

The development of data on retail purchases aligned production more carefully with distribution as actual consumer purchases were measured rather than factory shipments. The function of these systems of audits provided by firms such as Nielsen, then, was to allow for a more efficient distribution process. It allowed manufacturers to decide on products to be produced, to better select salable package sizes and types, to price products advantageously, to select more effective channels of distribution, to avoid overproduction, to determine advertising budgets, and to reduce business depressions by tying production to consumer sales.

Key to Nielsen's success was his belief in sampling, a theory that he employed in many of his businesses. For a business to succeed, decisions should be based on facts. He believed much waste could be reduced if data could be provided that permitted products to be sold at lower cost, thereby increasing a person's standard of living. Pertinent facts, expressed by a number, he believed, could be obtained from small samples that, if systematically and continuously collected, could provide a "moving picture" of a market. Furthermore, using numbers he gathered, he was able to convert the data into a specific plan of conduct for a client's business. Because most business executives in the thirties and forties were unfamiliar with statistical methods and unaware that small samples could produce reliable data, his was a tough sales pitch but one that eventually led to his company's success.

Nielsen's businesses developed a form of sampling known as *stratified sampling*. Stratified sample applied random sampling not to the total sample but to subdivisions in it. Internal consistency was achieved by scientifically controlling eight dimensions of the radio audience sample in proportion to their actual numbers in the population: the number of radio homes; the geographical location; the size of each locality; and the size of families, their occupation, their income, their race, and their telephone ownership.

Another of Nielsen's major contributions to the science of marketing was the concept of share of the market—a measure of a company's overall competitive performance in the market (comparable to cost-per-thousand for rating(s)). This idea came from his early experiences with factories where he developed a ratio of performance for different machines to determine which machine produced the most widgets per hour at the lowest cost. Out of this experience came a company's or program's share of the market as a measure of marketing performance. If the manufacturer's product and marketing plan worked, its share of the market should increase.

Although Nielsen began in the drugs retail industry, he soon branched into food, cosmetics, and other household supplies, the majority of markets for radio (and soon television) use. Many advertisers and agencies subscribed to the Nielsen Food-Drug Index. Because the food and drug industries were major users of sponsored radio time and the Depression was a rapid period of growth for radio advertising, Nielsen's expansion into radio research was requested by his clients who found it profitable to have Nielsen's Food and Drug Index guide their marketing opportunities and who desired guidance to determine a more effective indicator of the success of their programs for their broadcasting activity. Nielsen writes:

> And it was logical for these advertisers to suggest that, having placed other phases of their marketing operation on a factual basis, we should endeavor to develop a factual method of solving their radio problems.
>
> (Nielsen, 1942)

Although ratings were about 10 percent of his total marketing business, they were to become the best known of all Nielsen services. Ratings aided the advertiser in attracting viewers who were the best prospects for products. Thus, the Nielsen Radio Index (NRI) gained immediate acceptance from the industry served by Nielsen Food and Drug Index. The NRI addressed itself to problems that could not be solved through the use of telephone-based techniques.

Nielsen's Methods and Innovations

Nielsen pioneered a mechanical recording device that he called the *Audimeter*, a device that made an electrical recording or graphic record on a photographic tape when connected to a radio receiver and thereby provided a continuous record of set tuning measuring when the set was turned off and on, the time of day, the length of time, and the station to which the set was tuned for a period of one month. Early recorders were time clocks that rotated on tapes recording dial changes.

Establishing the Audimeter on a commercial scale was a risky venture, one that only companies with capital assets such as A. C. Nielsen were prepared to undertake. Nielsen had purchased the rights to the Audimeter, which initially used a wax tape to make a record of the stations to which a set was tuned, from the faculty at Massachusetts Institute of Technology in 1936. Though he acquired the patent right and trade registration, the system for decoding the tapes had yet to be worked out as was how to reduce the speed of delivery. Though Hooper reports were produced much faster, Nielsen early reports could take as long as eleven weeks after the broadcast. It took six years to improve the Audimeter and to develop the necessary device that could decode the wax tape on which the tuning data were recorded.

The Audimeter was a mechanized audience feedback system, similar in concept to a gas or water meter. It reported program ratings primarily in terms of average audience estimates. To calculate a measure of average tuning, all the time lines indicating tuning would be added together and divided by the number of intervals.

From 1939 to 1942, Nielsen conducted a three-year pilot operation offering the NRI to clients for the first time in August 1942. In introducing his Audimeter-based service, Nielsen wrote in the *Journal of Marketing*,

There is no denying the fact that mechanization had effected remarkable reduction in the cost of producing goods. However, continued improvement in the American standard of living requires substantial reductions in the cost of distributing goods from the manufacturers to the consumer, and I have long suspected that in the distribution field, too, the principle of mechanization could be applied with telling effect.

(Nielsen, 1942b)

The problem of gaining acceptance for Nielsen's work in developing a viable ratings service proved far more difficult than his other services. Broadcasters, magazine publishers, and others disparaged his method for using a small sample of only 1,500 households to accurately measure the listening behavior of hundreds of millions of people. Because the radio signal was broadcast into the air, no empirical means of verifying the accuracy of Nielsen ratings was possible. Consequently, other cheaper services, such as gathering listening data through door-to-door interview and telephone calls, were preferred. Nielsen, a skilled statistician, believed that numbers were more reliable, and so he persevered, losing money on his service for the first seventeen years.

His company's use of stratified sampling also was criticized. Though stratification facilitated representative sampling, a smaller sample meant a higher standard error. For example, a sample of 300 with a 10-percent tune-in rate meant that thirty individuals served as the base for determining tune-in. Furthermore, Nielsen originally intended to fix his sample to retain repeated information from the same sources over time, which opened the door to questions concerning representativeness. How long was a fixed sample representative? Who permitted a recorder to be attached to their sets? How did an Audimeter influence viewing behavior?

Both Crossley (calling his the Radio-Graph) and Hooper (calling his the Programeter) had experimented with early forms of meters but had dropped them when studies indicated that set tuning was measured when no one was listening. In other words, the Audimeter failed to provide available audience information. Another major drawback was the absence of people's listening data as an Audimeter recorded set tuning rather than who was listening.

A further disadvantage was that meters were costly and slow as the tape was initially picked up by Nielsen personnel before tabulating. Nielsen's Audimeter tapes were shipped to a Chicago plant where they were decoded on specially designed machines. By 1946, Nielsen had introduced the mailable Audimeter to help speed delivery of ratings and to render the personal visits by staff, characterizing the early Audimeter, unnecessary. In addition, the mailable meter lowered the cost of metering multiple homes, permitting both FM and TV measurement whereas only AM had been measurable previously. The mailable meter contained a small magazine mailed at regular intervals. Each time a new cartridge was inserted, a quarter was discharged. Each magazine contained a roll of sixteen-millimeter film capable of recording minute-by-minute listening over four receivers for two-week periods.

However, its advantages were many if a sample could be developed sufficiently large to measure total tuning homes. Unlike the coincidental, the Audimeter was equally applicable to all broadcasts and all programs. It provided a measure of public dissatisfaction in short-term tuning. It also provided a measure of frequency and length of tuning, not to mention audience flow and duplication between programs. For an advertiser, the Audimeter provided an estimate of the size of the program audience during the commercial break as an advertiser could determine the average minute and compare the ratings to the time the commercial ran. A single Audimeter, according to Nielsen, provided the same amount of information as 500,000 coincidental telephone calls (Nielsen, 1950). Not to mention, the Audimeter's efficiency in collecting information was an automatic feature that eliminated response errors and other human factors. Furthermore, the Audimeter was not restricted to telephone homes so was not subject to their bias during this period. In fact, in using a sample stratified to represent the entire U.S. listening audience, it could provide projectable ratings, ratings able to be projected to produce actual size figures rather than the former indices used by earlier pioneers. If Audimeter homes were carefully selected and spread over the United States, they could furnish a more accurate cross-section of the entire radio listening audience.

By 1945, freed of wartime restriction of radio stations, Nielsen moved ahead. He continually expanded his sample to represent a more accurate national audience and, in doing so, gained a growing number of clients, not the least of whom was Frank Stanton, who had played an early role in the development of the Audimeter. Hooperatings soon began to feel the effect of this new competition.

The Battle to Be the Currency System: Hooperatings versus Nielsen Ratings

Indeed, Hooper was facing aggressive and comprehensive competition. His Program Hooperatings were merely an index and were not projectable to total U.S. homes. It became increasingly apparent that his telephone-based Hooper service was doomed without developing a national sample. Because projectable ratings required a sample representative of national radio homes, Hooper's key challenge was to develop a representative sample.

His introduction of his projectable service, called U.S. Hooperatings, in 1948 were an attempt to achieve this national cross-section by adding a diary method to his coincidental method to measure non-telephone homes. Hooper planned to use the coincidental measurements as a base and project them to a national total through information collected from diaries and therefore to provide a projected coincidental system. He planned to charge a separate fee to subsidize this new service and to operate it on a regular basis if enough subscriptions were found—especially what he considered to be his primary clients, the networks.

However Nielsen integrated projectable ratings as a feature of his service with no extra charge. In addition, by March 1948, Nielsen had expanded his sample to a national basis, thereby producing the total number of homes each network delivered and reporting total homes in thousands and in ratings. Thus, both Hooper's extra cost and his technique came under attack. Nielsen criticized Hooper's national ratings as synthetic ratings that attempted to combine old apples with fresh oranges. Moreover, the telephone coincidental measured only one minute of the broadcast whereas Nielsen's Audimeter measured the actual program length (deducting five minutes for short-term listening). Nielsen thus charged that the coincidental method expressed the program audience in terms of equivalent full-time listeners based on short-term sampling rather than in terms of actual number of homes reached during the broadcast. Nielsen claimed that his fixed sample was superior in providing a measure of U.S. radio homes (Nielsen, 1949).

Until ratings could be projected, the bottom line was that they were indices of arbitrary value. Nielsen thus offered a significant product-innovation through the development of projectable ratings. Nielsen's projectable ratings offered both a pricing advantage and a superior method. Both strategies resulted in an eventual defeat of Hooperatings. U.S. Hooperatings, as a result, were not well received, and Hooper failed to achieve enough subscriptions to launch his projectable rating service as a regular feature.

Besides aggressive competition from Nielsen on projectable ratings front, a second major event in 1948 was to lead ultimately to Hooper's confinement to this period of network radio. This new development was the rise of a new advertising medium: television. A key force in the development of television as a commercial medium was NBC's head of research, Hugh Beville, who turned to Hooper to develop a TV rating service. As television penetration was limited to urban areas, NBC had decided that Hooper's random telephone method was the most efficient method. In 1948, 37.6 million radio homes existed compared to 995,000 estimated TV homes (Nye, 1957). An initial difficulty, according to Beville, was selling the idea to Hooper. Hooper was, at this time, busy trying to launch his projectable rating service. As he had not seen television, Hooper was invited by Beville to NBC-TV studios to watch a baseball game. Hooper was so fascinated he stayed for the entire game. The next day, Hooper called Beville to report that he had reconsidered the idea of starting a TV rating service (Beville interview, 1983).

A critical problem in developing a TV rating service was discovering how many TV homes existed. Just compiling a list of set owners was difficult. NBC had acquired a list of TV set owners from those who requested a schedule. RCA distributors also provided NBC with warranty lists. These lists were turned over to Hooper. After a few months, Hooper abandoned his fixed lists of radio owners supplied by NBC and took his own measure of TV audiences as a by-product of his telephone interviews conducted for radio.

Furthermore, not many national advertisers were interested in television at the time. A number of factors initially had discouraged advertiser interest. Many advertisers doubted that people would be willing to give the sort of attention that TV demanded. Furthermore, early TV programming was spotty because its development had been arrested by the war. And this was an era of print, whose mass circulation magazines decorated the coffee tables of many households during the period.

With NBC's encouragement, Hooper's TV ratings reports were available by September 1949 and provided three key figures: program ratings, audience composition (men, women, children, and total lookers per set), and program share. Originally these figures were based on a random sample of thirty-one TV cities that could be expanded to one hundred cities as TV grew (Hooper, 1949).

However, the unexpectedly rapid growth of television devastated Hooper's network radio service. Hooper was accused of shortchanging and deflating radio's audience and brought him under attack by the very radio constituency where once he was king. Rather than creating a separate sample, Hooper merely added TV viewing questions to his radio interview. The questions now read: Was anyone at home looking at TV or radio? What station/program? Is someone using another set? Do you own a TV set? The last question was used to obtain a base for TV sets-in-use.

Hooper had based his network program ratings wholly on telephone homes in the urban areas where television had made the greatest inroads. As a result, his sample was attacked for overweighing the influence of TV on radio listenership. To make matters worse, telephone subscribers were found to be a disproportionate number of TV owners when compared to non-subscribers.

The radio industry, not to mention the magazine industry, was critical of any research that reflected the growth of TV between 1946 and 1949. Compared to radio, TV already had more people per set. Furthermore, fewer stations and programs resulted in less competition and higher TV ratings. The result was TV ratings sometimes exceeded radio ratings. Although this condition would correct itself as TV grew in population and program availability, Hooper had lost ground by attempting to straddle both TV and radio under extraordinary conditions.

In February 1950, Hooper sold his national ratings television and radio rating services to A. C. Nielsen, Inc. Hooper cited three factors in his decision. First, the number of sponsored network radio programs on the air had dropped 40 percent in three years. Thus, his radio network service had declined due to the flight of advertisers to network TV. Second, Hooper noted the increased competition from Nielsen. According to Hooper, without Nielsen competition, he would have continued his network Hooperatings "riding the radio curve down and the television curve up." However, with the growing revenue split between Hooper and Nielsen, even the network TV rating business did not bring the total network ratings to a profitable level. Revenue had dropped from $40,000 in January 1949 to $25,000 by January 1950 (Hooper, 1949). Third, Hooper stated that television had so changed listening habits in cities with TV service that the averaging of listeners in cities with TV and without TV was no longer plausible (*Broadcasting*, 1950).

The fundamental assumption of thirty-six city-based network Hooperatings had been that conditions under which measurements were taken remained relatively constant, and consequently the change in the rating index or rank was a valid indication of change in popularity. This assumption, with the advent of television, was no longer valid. National Hooperatings indices were no longer comparable and had become essentially meaningless.

According to A. C. Nielsen, the steady cancellation of Hooper's network account was due to the big impetus of television. The Hooper network service covered only the larger urban areas with telephone homes, representing 20 percent of the country. Television had hit these urban areas the hardest and had made the most impact in cities where Hooper had based his radio rating service. In other words, while radio was going to pieces in the areas measured by Hooper's network service, it was not going to pieces in 80 percent of the nation's homes. Thus, according to Nielsen, it was utterly unrealistic for Hooper to ignore TV's impact in his network radio cities (*Broadcasting*, 1950; *Advertising Age*, 1950).

Although Hooper quit the national rating business, he planned to continue at the local level with city Hooperatings, city teleratings, area coverage indices, and sales impact ratings. These local markets were now where Hooper was getting two-thirds of his profits. In a prophetic statement, Hooper argued that the shift in their packaging was away from one average index to analytic reports of individual markets and differences between markets. Hooper left the national ratings field for TV and radio to A. C. Nielsen, Inc. and his Audimeter. As a result of his sale, national ratings were sold continuously for five decades by a single firm, although this time the victor was not Hooper. Oddly enough, Hooper's defeat lay in the timely limitations of the telephone coincidental method he had championed. The Nielsen Television Index (NTI), based on a representative sample of U.S. television homes, was to become as influential to network TV as Hooperatings had been to network radio.

Conclusions: Contributions to a Ratings Vocabulary

Three pioneer radio rating services, each associated with strong individuals, contributed to the development of basic measurement concepts that have become part of a standardized ratings vocabulary. Archibald Crossley invented the concept of program ratings and gave to radio and later TV measurement its most basic term, *rating* (although Crossley used only the actual number of listeners as the base for his ratings, what today is known as the share). Claude E. Hooper made Hooperatings a part of the nation's vocabulary and gave the ratings' system solidity and comparability by introducing the *available audience base* and the *average minute rating*. Arthur C. Nielsen,

Sr. took the ratings higher-tech through his electronic method that enabled him to design a probability sample for the first time that incorporated non-telephone home and rural areas. In the long term, Nielsen's most important contribution that shaped the entire system was his projectable ratings. Prior to Nielsen's development of *projectable ratings*, earlier ratings services measured only urban areas due to the limitations of their telephone-based methods in an era of limited telephone penetration. Their ratings indices were comparable to other figures of the same sort but were not pertinent to size. As a result, Nielsen championed *CPM* (cost per thousand) *theory* that tied advertising prices to audience size and made ratings the medium of exchange (although in practice, tying advertising prices to delivery by rating points became more widely used). However, the notion of using ratings as a form of currency medium for the industry became embedded. Nielsen also was the first to provide a wealth of analytical detail, such as *reach, frequency*, and *audience flow* as his method provided measure of the average minute audience, the total audience, and could be extended to twenty-four hours a day.

2

ESTABLISHING THE ANALOG CURRENCY FOR LOCAL RADIO AND TV AUDIENCES

The Diary Initiative

Introduction: the Transformation of Radio

The company now known as Arbitron began in 1949 as the American Research Bureau, a name that was changed in 1964 due to concern that its surveys might be confused as an arm of the American government. While originally entering as a television measurement service, in the 1960s, Arbitron diversified into radio measurement and customized marketing services after Nielsen withdrew from measuring radio altogether. As radio morphed from the discrete program units characteristic of the Golden Age of Radio during the thirties and forties into continuous sound, composed of music, news, talk, and sports, it also became mobile—acquiring a new audience—the out-of-home listening audience that would require a new method capable of measuring radio's soon-to-be highest rated time periods, morning and evening drive-time. This need to measure this new type of audience meant that an opening in the market emerged for new challengers, such as the American Research Bureau. The American Research Bureau was and remains one of Nielsen's most formidable challengers and was deemed by Arthur Nielsen, Jr. to have been one of Nielsen's best competitors (Nielsen interview, 2001).

The forties and fifties were times of great competition in the ratings industry prompted by both the challenges of measuring radio as it transitioned to a entirely new medium and the entry of television as a new advertising medium. By the sixties, the dust had settled, with the ratings industry forming an oligopoly structure with Nielsen the sole provider of national TV ratings, Arbitron, the sole provider of radio ratings, and together dividing the field of local TV measurement. They held this position until 1992 when Arbitron abandoned its measurement of local television audiences, leaving its rival Nielsen to dominate both national and local markets for television. Arbitron's decision to exit the field of local TV measurement, in part, was determined by its costly and unsuccessful battle to introduce people meter ratings tied to product purchasing, a service known as ScanAmerica, and, in part, by the decision by many local stations to opt for a single rather than two local market services during this time period, resulting in an enormous loss of revenue.

Throughout this next period, as Hooper prophesized, the trend in marketing was toward local market measurement because, as the saying went, all buys are local ones. The cost of the television medium together with the rise of automation and computerization accelerated a new marketing emphasis on consumerism or using marketing information to more precisely pinpoint individual consumers. The previous marketing era had focused on opening wider channels of distribution and moving products along these channels, and advertisers had characterized their approach as a buckshot approach, targeting a broad audience in the hope that individuals interested in any particular product would be blanketed. Now advertisers became concerned about more precisely pinpointing their perspective customers to eliminate reaching and paying for audiences who were not likely prospects for their products.

Marketing and advertising switched its emphasis accordingly from targeting by sheer masses of undifferentiated viewers and listeners to more precision instruments, such as demographic and geographic targeting. Though the early radio pioneers—the CAB, Hooper, and Nielsen—had introduced many of the tools by which the national market was measured, Arbitron was to be an innovator in introducing the body of tools desired by advertisers to measure the efficiency of their buy at the local level. To gather this more detailed information, Arbitron helped to pioneer the diary method that it championed until its recent foray in a digital era into the portable people meter method detailed in Chapter 5.

During the waning of network radio and the early days of television, both radio and TV surveys reported audiences by program, a measurement unit that was quickly becoming obsolete with the transformation of network radio into a local advertising medium. More and more radio stations abandoned the discrete programs characterizing the Golden Age of Radio as they moved to music and talk formats. Nielsen had exercised major influence in the radio ratings field in the forties and fifties until out-of-home listening (not covered by the meter) became too great (Buzzard, 1990, 1999; Seiler, 1981). Similarly, the Hooper method was not designed to measure this new audience. This left the door open to new competitors in the measurement field.

Competitors in the Field of Radio and TV Ratings

As television's popularity skyrocketed in the late forties, advertisers, agencies, and stations became more interested in knowing the audience drawn to this medium.

By the fifties, the broadcast ratings industry had many newcomers. Aside from what were to become the Big Four—James Seiler and the American Research

Bureau (with a diary method); Sidney Roslow and Pulse (with a personal interview method); A. C. Nielsen and A. C. Nielsen, Inc. (with a mail-in household meter method); and C. E. Hooper (with a telephone coincidental method)—three new competitors entered the marketplace: Allan V. Jay and Videodex (with a diary method); A. C. Sindlinger and Sindlinger (with hour-long telephone interviews and Radox, an electronic meter method); and Edward G. Hynes and Trendex (with a telephone coincidental method and a meter method (Hines, 1960; Conte, 1983).

With all seven firms providing different estimates, many in industry grumbled about duplication of services and lower standards and lack of consensus among the various methods. What the industry needed, some argued, was a shake-out leaving those with the best methods to survive. This concern was to come to a head in 1963, when Representative Oren Harris of Arkansas chaired a House committee on the methodology, accuracy, and use of ratings in broadcasting (Buzzard, 1990; Harris Commission, 1963), detailed later.

Besides Hooper, the other major radio ratings service during the heyday of network radio was known as the Pulse (Seiler personal papers, n.d.(a)). In 1941, Dr. Sidney Roslow had founded the Pulse, a service that used a personal interview method to obtain radio listening during the past twenty-four hours from those he interviewed. As a method, the personal interview offered significant advantages. It included out-of-home listeners (e.g., radios in automobiles and the workplace) and at hours not covered by Hooper's coincidental (before 8 AM and after 10:30 PM). When respondents were contacted, they were given a list of programs or roster to aid in their recall or listening for the past few hours. Because Hooper's— and later Nielsen's—service concentrated on network ratings, Pulse's local service expanded rapidly to become the dominant source for local radio measurement by 1960. Its reports determined the weekly cume, or a station's cumulative audience for a week, largely because in those years, as car radios became more frequent, neither Hooper's home telephone coincidental nor Nielsen's home-based meter could cover this growing segment of radio listening. The cumulative audience was a measure of a station's weekly circulation figures and was roughly comparable to the figures used by the print media. Pulse was to remain a viable local service until the mid-1960s, when studies by NBC showed that potential respondents were home when the Pulse interviewer called but refused to answer the door, casting doubt on the representativeness of its method (Beville, 1988). By the late sixties, both Pulse and Nielsen had exited the field of radio ratings. However, Arbitron's innovative management team was ready for the challenge that these departures represented and positioned itself as the leader in radio ratings as a result of leaps in product design such as precision geographic and demographic targeting.

James W. Seiler and His Contributions

James Seiler, the founder of the American Research Bureau (ARB), entered the field of ratings research when he wrote a term paper on audience measurement as a student at George Washington University. Seiler's thesis described a method using personal diaries to survey television audiences to find out what they were watching. After he distributed copies of the paper on radio listening to local DC radio stations, he landed his first job beginning as part-time analyst at WRC, an NBC affiliate. After graduation, he was promoted to research and promotion director. According to Hugh Beville, then director of research at NBC, the network closely followed his early ratings experiments (Beville, 1983). Seiler, who lived in Laurel, MD, was subsequently hired by NBC to survey its audiences. In 1949, Seiler decided to form his own company and founded the ARB, the name chosen because it sounded very patriotic after the War. In 1973, Theodore Shaker changed the name to Arbitron Ratings Co. (Buzzard, 1990; Webster & Lichty, 1991) so as not to evoke a Big Brother image. Initially, the ARB consisted of James Seiler, his wife Betty, and eight others publishing a program rating for Washington DC, Baltimore, and Philadelphia, from a room in the National Press Building. The company eventually spread nationally.

Seiler had begun by conducting both radio and TV studies, but it soon became apparent that the new field of television research was where the action was. Here lay the greatest interest and demand. Realizing this need, Seiler introduced the first television household diary study for WRC in 1947. Although Seiler was not the first to experiment with the diary (Garnet Garrison had experimented with it as early as 1937, as had Frank Stanton at CBS in the 1940s), he was the first to introduce it as a principle method. Before long, other broadcasting stations began participating and sharing costs for his studies on the television audience. Soon he made the decision to focus exclusively on television.

Although TV had started as a mass medium, initially only 10% of homes had television, so the bigger radio rating firms during the period (Hooper and Pulse) could not turn out accurate TV ratings because they did not have a large enough sample. Their radio samples were 90 percent radio homes and only 10 percent TV homes (Jim Seiler, Seiler personal papers, n.d). Seiler saw an opportunity to be the only service that focused exclusively on TV ratings, so he replaced the formerly multimedia diary (that recorded both radio and TV audiences) with a TV-only diary. He selected a sample of 500 TV homes in a single market and placed a diary in each of these homes. According to Seiler, "no one had ever heard of us at the time but we were the only game in town" (Jim Seiler, Ratings innovator, ND). By the time the other services reacted, the ARB was too big for them to catch up.

Mergers and Acquisitions: TeleCue

On a trip to the West Coast in 1952, Seiler found a local service, TeleCue, owned by William Coffin, Roger Cooper, and Earnest H. (Hank) Clay, which also used a diary method to measure a one-week period, and decided to merge, moving TeleCue's headquarters to Beltsville, MD. Seiler realized that the FCC freeze had artificially restricted TV development to East Coast cities and that when the freeze was lifted, the number of stations and the need for measurement would spread to the West Coast. The consolidation leveraged the ARB into a stronger position on both coasts. Even with the merger, at this time, the ARB was the smallest of the seven companies in the field and the least well financed (*Advertising Age*, 1955; Conte, 1983).

In addition to new markets and national coverage, the ARB added key personnel as a result of the merger. Ernest Clay became head of development and research, Roger Cooper became station relations manager, and John Landreth, former president of TeleCue, became general manager of the ARB. The new managers were a youthful group (all younger than 40) with the boundless energy and enthusiasm to drive the ARB to new heights. In Landreth, Seiler had found his ideal counterpart. Whereas Seiler's strengths were in salesmanship, policy, and planning, Landreth was skilled in internal organization (Cooper, 1983). Landreth reorganized the ARB into autonomous departments, each with its own profit and loss sheets, modeled on General Motors. Seiler and Landreth were quickly dubbed Mr. Outside and Mr. Inside, respectively (Cooper, 1983; Landreth interview, 2008).

Shortly after the merger, Seiler moved ARB headquarters to a white frame farmhouse with its own barn in Prince Georges County. The dining room was replaced by the clatter of the tabulation center where results were counted by a simple slide rule. The backbone of the company was a female workforce. It was they who made the phone calls, tabulated the results, and did the mailings (McArthur, 1955).

Similar to the informal start-up Internet companies formed today, the ARB with its band of loyal managers and friends was ideally suited to this environment. It competed through offering a different method, through product differentiation, and through expansion of its services into local and national markets. In particular, Seiler and his staff more finely tuned their statistical wares in response to key changes in marketing.

The Diary Method

Seiler was a pioneer in the extensive use and perfection of the diary method, which was not a new idea but an application of an old one. The diary was a questionnaire that initially was sent to 2,200 selected homes. Each member of the family logged in programs viewed during the first week of the month, and diaries were returned to its main office.

Viewer diaries had two salient features that were important to advertisers. Inexpensive, their samples could be changed often. (A sample is a means of obtaining information from a portion of a larger group or population.) In particular, diaries were well suited to measuring local markets where meter coverage was prohibitively expensive. They also provided marketing information of growing importance to advertisers such as gender and age demographic data. Demographic data allowed advertisers and agencies finer and more discriminating tools by which to choose their audiences. Beside audience composition information, diaries provided set ownership histories, could indicate what programs to which the audience was drawn throughout an evening (called audience flow), unlike those services who used the telephone to collect viewing data, could offer measures of early morning and late night viewing, and provided measures of viewing outside the telephone dialing area (*Advertising Age*, 1955). The ARB was noted for being much more supple and flexible in meeting advertising needs and tailoring its services to the advertising community than what some saw as the more conservative and bureaucratic Nielsen.

Like all services during this period, Seiler initially tailored his service to the proverbial nuclear family that served as the target of oceans of merchandise for manufacturers and advertisers choosing the household as the measurement unit. Both the diary and the meter (at this time) were tailored to a lifestyle in which the family gathered around a single huge console radio or television and watched *en masse*. Only one diary was sent to each family, and the assumption was that the housewife would record for the entire family. In an era before it became commonplace for households to have separate sets for family members, rating services mailed a diary or installed meters in the huge family set that dominated most living rooms during the period. Ratings gathered by these instruments were known as "household" ratings in that one set or diary gathered the information for the entire household.

ARB Enters Network TV with Projectable Ratings

In 1950, understaffed and undercapitalized, Seiler decided to take an all-or-nothing gamble by coming out with a national rating. Whereas local ratings used samples drawn to represent each local market, a national rating drew a sample from a nationally located population to provide estimates of viewing for advertisers who bought time on television networks (*Sponsor*, 1958). This would prove to be Seiler's first major success. Without national or network ratings, Seiler would later remark, the ARB would have become lost in the crowd (*TV Bureau of Advertising*, 1955). As viewers were measured every quarter hour, an hour-long program could count the same viewer four times. The diary offered advertisers measures of both duplication and overlap in viewing for a given program (also known as gross or frequency) and a measure of how many different people watched a given program, eliminating duplication (known as cumulative audience or reach). As it represented a national cross-section, the ARB's samples were projectable to an estimate of all U.S. TV homes. Only the ARB, Nielsen, and a much smaller rating service called Videodex (whose actual surveys a Congressional investigation later uncovered as a sham) offered projectable ratings.

The American Research Company Grows in Local Research

As Seiler had predicted, the lifting of the FCC freeze led to a demand for services to measure a growing number of markets, as both very high frequency (VHF) and ultra high frequency (UHF) stations were added. As the number of radio and television stations and markets grew after the FCC thaw, former one-station markets faced growing competition and increased demand for local measurement. Because the ARB used diaries for both local and national measurement, its results were comparable as the same methods were employed and measured the same time periods. This comparability was a big selling point for the ARB (*Broadcasting/Telecasting*, 1953). Local market reports proved financially efficient for the ARB, as data from individual market reports could be used again to package its national reports and broaden its clientele base beyond the advertising community.

The year 1955 proved golden for the ARB as a result of its merger and successful new products. That year, the ARB had added reports on 140 "small markets" not previously measured and included UHF stations. It also introduced a blood descendent of the UHF study, called "small market studies," that studied the coverage of all VHF and UHF stations. These reports showed that UHF stations were having an uphill struggle competing in markets with two or more VHF stations and helped advertisers appraise their investments (*Advertising Age*, 1955).

As the ARB gained markets, Hooper began to decline in popularity among advertisers. Although Seiler and Hooper had met to discuss a merger, Hooper was the big name in the business and was not willing to combine with the lesser known ARB. Fate stepped in, and Hooper met an untimely demise in 1955, which led the ARB to purchase his local TV rating service (Conte, 1983).

As Arbitron grew in projects and personnel, so did its need for a new headquarters to keep up with production. In 1959, the ARB moved to a modern two-story headquarters located on eleven acres of farmland specifically designed for its new computer system, Univac, in Beltsville, MD, with four major departments: tabulation, composition, duplication, and mailing.

New Product Features: from Metro Areas to Sweeps

In the early fifties, local TV market measurement was centered on metropolitan areas. Like most other services, the ARB furnished only metro area ratings for its local market reports. Network ratings services also restricted measurement to a similar metro area that they called "areas of equal network opportunity." These areas showed how programs competed in the overlapping part of a market where stations had the same opportunity to reach the same numbers of viewers.

Both network and local market geography had been based on metro area measurement because they traditionally had competed against local metropolitan newspapers. If radio and television advertising were measured by the same geographical areas as newspapers, circulation figures and ratings between the two could be compared by advertisers. This metro geography had also been reinforced by the growth of telephones that were far more common in metro areas. Because power and frequency caused vast differences in station coverage areas, using an area common to all made ratings estimates more comparable. Later, the census bureau slightly enlarged these areas into standard metropolitan statistical areas. Buyers and stations often used the metro ratings to project the household population to the total survey area. Although the formulas used were as much guesswork as mathematics, they provided at least some information in what was otherwise darkness.

By 1959, ARB was to change all this with the introduction of its sweeps reports or what it called its *nationwide simultaneous measurement concept*. Sweeps measured a station's actual coverage area or signal location rather than former artificial metro areas (*Advertising Age*, 1959a, 1959b). Now for the first time in ratings history, the ARB was offering a true national measurement with a standardized base, one that would include all areas, viewers, stations, and programs. The new total homes figures, provided by sweeps, credited each station for all viewership regardless of location and indicated individual station differences in signal strength.

Sweeps periods were to become the key measurement periods used by the broadcasting and advertising community to establish network and station viewership size and rates and became the key tool for comparing local markets and prices. Roger Cooper notes, "We had to take great leaps in concept design and provide what the industry needed so far ahead that it took a while for the others to catch up with us" (Conte, 1983). In part, the sweeps were made possible because of the diary's ability to collect much data in an inexpensive manner.

Another major influence was introduction of the ARB's new Univac computer. The Univac electronic computer added the ability to tabulate the data quickly and efficiently. A computer fed by national sampling data was capable of reporting the exact audience of every one of the 504 national commercial television stations by every U.S. market in fifteen-minute segments. In pre-Univac days, hand-tabulated methods limited reports to metro areas. However, with the computer, the previous seven-week reports now were available in four weeks. Computerized tabulation meant stations could be reported not only by metro area but by entire station coverage areas. Advertisers would no longer need to project metro ratings to guess the total coverage area of a station. Furthermore, audience composition, also formerly confined to metro areas, now was measured for the full coverage area.

County Coverage Studies

A by-product of the enormous amount of data provided by the sweeps was the ARB's country coverage studies. Because sweep surveys asked viewers by county what programming they watched, the data gathered could then be retabulated and viewership be clustered around TV markets. As a result, ARB used the reprocessed sweeps' diaries to produce county coverage studies that determined county viewership by actual measurement rather than projections. This was new; no one offered anything to match it. Although sweeps subsequently became criticized because of the network's practice of hyping (putting on atypical fare to draw viewers), they provided the first and only simultaneous comparison of viewing across all markets. With its sweeps and country coverage studies, the ARB posed the first serious threat to Nielsen, pitting its comprehensiveness against Nielsen. Prior to sweeps, Nielsen Coverage Service had cornered the national coverage field, but these reports were not regular features of Nielsen's service.

With the introduction of computer for tabulation, the early days of the ratings pioneers when estimates were calculated by long hand or slide rule was drawing to an end, and in their place was a future of complex sampling techniques and detailed use of demographic and geographic data. This initial era of computer-delivered estimates was but a Model T by comparison to the enormous changes to come in data gathering and delivery in a digital era.

Four-week Measurement Periods

A second problem that the ARB management sought to address was the one-week measurement periods on which most services had based their reports during the time, through its introduction of the four-week measurement period. One-week periods left the door open for stations to load their program schedules with atypical fare, which advertisers called hyping. ARB's new one-week/four-week ratings were gathered for 101 markets, allowing various weeks to be compared against other weeks. Four-week averages were particularly useful in smaller markets as they surveyed less frequently and allowed network advertisers and spot buyers to study more typical network and local performance. By 1982, Arbitron switched once again from four-week to twelve-week measurement periods for radio measurement again to reduce the influence of promotions, give-aways, and other gimmicks used by radio stations to increase listenership.

A Standardized Market Geography or Areas of Dominant Influence

One effect of regular studies of the station coverage area was to raise industry interest in the issue of station and county overlap when viewers received the signal of more than one station. Simultaneous measurement of all counties or sweeps led to county coverage studies. These, in turn, stimulated industry interest in developing a fixed standardized marketplace geography based on actual measurement of station coverage areas, together with the question of how much viewing spilled in and out of a market from surrounding areas. This concern was to take on greater importance at the ARB by the mid-sixties.

As a result of its sweeps data, the ARB later developed a standardized treatment of market geography called the area of dominant influence (ADI) which became a generic industry tool until Arbitron withdrew from TV measurement in 1993

(*Electronic Media*, 1993; *Broadcasting & Cable*, 1993). It proved so successful that Nielsen was forced to come up with it own fixed geography that it called the designated market area (DMA). Unfortunately Arbitron, unlike its competitor Nielsen, failed to patent one its most successful innovations. The ADI concept divided the United States into just more than 200 markets and assigned each station to only one market where it captured the largest share of audience. The ADI was the first standardized way of defining a TV market, as previously many media planners had used their own ways of defining markets, and there was little industry consistency. It paved the way for demographic targeting as, now that each station had a boundary, its performance could be related to demographics (Harvey, 1983).

The market definitions determined by the ADI were not only used to determine each station's viewing area but were later used by the FCC to determine which TV stations have a right to be carried on which local cable systems. Under the "must-carry" rule as set forth by the 1992 Cable TV Act, broadcasters could opt for a "must-carry" status, which guaranteed a TV station's carriage on its market's local cable system and thus could negotiate additional compensation in return for carriage rights. In March 1992 the FCC announced it would use data supplied by Arbitron to determine radio station ownership limits. The new limits would prevent broadcasters from purchasing a new station if it would give a broadcaster more than 25 percent of the total market, based on audience share, in markets with fifteen or more stations.

Another card in the ARB's winning hand was James Seiler's local market sales strategy. The affable yet intense Seiler was a superb salesman. Though most rating companies had concentrated on national advertisers and agencies, the ARB undertook to educate the local advertising communities and developed regional offices and moved outside the top ten markets where most rating services previously had focused their efforts. Seiler knew that once the advertising community subscribed to a ratings service, stations were compelled to subscribe as buyers placed their orders using a specific service. Local stations could also use these reports to study network affiliation, programming and, of course, station compensation and revenue, increasingly important. Because stations came to pay a huge share of the cost for the ratings reports, 85 percent of the advertising dollar, compared to the 15 percent earned by agencies, station support was crucial.

In fact, it was Seiler who shifted the burden of the expense of ratings reports to broadcasters. When Nielsen had entered the business, he believed the beneficiary of the reports was the advertiser community. He had been encouraged by Lever Brothers to enter the ratings business, and Lever was its first customer. Nielsen had sold its reports to advertisers. As a result, during this time period, advertisers were permitted to show ratings reports to agencies without charge. When Nielsen began to sell to agencies, broadcasters complained because they did not have access to the reports when negotiating with agencies. According to A. C. Nielsen, Jr.,

This was a very tough problem for us. I credit Jim Seiler with solving the problem. His solution was to reduce the price dramatically to agencies, particularly to the five largest agencies that bought most of the broadcast time. He practically gave his reports to them. Once, having done this, he then increased his price to the broadcasters, in effect, loading most of the cost of the service on them. The broadcasters found that in order to negotiate with the agencies, they needed the reports. This is how the broadcaster wound up paying for most of the cost of TV audience research. We soon copied Seiler's system.

(Nielsen interview, 2001)

Seiler proved ingenious in figuring out how to make a profit from local ratings by charging the station community rather than the advertiser.

The ARB Launches Arbitron

In 1959, induced by the networks, Seiler made a dramatic and calculated move in an effort to gain control of the national ratings marketplace. He introduced an instant ratings service that employed an electronic meter, called Arbitron. Similar to Nielsen's Audimeter, Arbitron was an electronic meter attached to TV sets, which registered channel tuning and switching but with an important difference: it provided instantaneous measurement. Telephone lines linked TV sets in sample homes to a central computing office and helped to resolve cost problems as many homes could be linked to a single line.

Ever the salesman, Seiler had an amazing graphic display of his service at his New York headquarters that looked like a mammoth switchboard lighting up every ninety seconds. Each station was represented on a string of electric lights that displayed their current measurement. As viewers switched from one station to another, lights blinked from one row to another. This graphic illustrated that Arbitron could now measure the audience while the program was still on, offering measurement in real time and offered the potential to revolutionize time buying (*Broadcasting*, 1959). The data were sent at ninety-second intervals, and reports were mailed to subscribers the next day.

This new service was a significant advance over both Nielsen's mail-in Audimeter, in use at the time, and the hand-tabulated method of diary analysis. Seiler had launched this metered service in reaction to a major study from the American Research Foundation released in 1959. This study concluded that the best way to measure the TV audience was the electronic meter service, then offered only by Nielsen. At this time, Nielsen was still limited to filmed tapes that were mailed in at seven-day intervals. To counteract the publicity advantage, Nielsen responded by inventing his own meter that measured households simultaneous with viewing.

In addition to using instant ratings as a wedge into Nielsen's market, Seiler hoped to solve several problems for rating-conscious advertisers, agencies, and networks.

Subscribers often had to wait two to four weeks for national ratings. Trendex offered overnight ratings through its telephone coincidental method, but it measured only cities of equal competition during prime-time hours and did not represent a national sample.

Seiler planned to substitute the meter-based reports for the diary service and eventually to build a national service. Although the ARB had produced national reports based on diary measurement since 1952, most advertisers and agencies believed the meter to be the superior method in eliminating "human" errors. Arbitron was launched in New York using a 300-household sample, and Seiler planned to add seven cities to produce a national or multiple city ratings (*Business Week*, 1957/1958). Though given extensive free trials in Chicago, Arbitron's relatively low number of nighttime sets-in-use tabulated and its cost (1,500 a month) kept all but one station from subscribing (*Newsweek*, 1959). By the time he reached the seventh market, he was unable to sell his new meter reports because the amount of advertising revenue received by stations was less in smaller markets. ARB faced a critical problem: Arbitron was expensive and did not provide demographic information. Seiler eventually conceded that individual market meter ratings were economically feasible only for the top fifteen markets. Those who had encouraged him to enter national audience measurement felt they could no longer finance him. In what was to become a familiar story, stations balked at the increased costs compared to diary methods, forcing him to sell his business to the Committee for Economic and Industrial Research (CEIR) as money ran out.

Another drain on Seiler's resources was a lengthy patent infringement suit filed against it by Nielsen, draining it of financial resources at a critical time in which it was trying to start a national ratings service. Soon after Arbitron was introduced in New York in 1958, Nielsen introduced its own instantaneous storage meter and filed a patent infringement suit against the ARB (as well as Radox and Trendex, who also used meters). The settlement involved the ARB's paying Nielsen substantial monthly royalties (at 5 percent of the gross) and licensing any future inventions to Nielsen (at 5 percent of the gross), effectively squeezing out the ARB from the national ratings market (Buzzard, 1990; Harris Commission, 1963).

A crucial legal tactic in the Nielsen repertoire was its arsenal of patents. A. C. Nielsen Sr. had very early on taken a personal interest in patents and, according to a Nielsen official, "it is extremely unlikely that any organization will develop anything important in the field without eventually finding themselves blocked by patents of ours" (Harris Commission, 1963). Nielsen's patent conferred to the company exclusive rights and use of the meter and excluded imitators from using the same method—offering his firm a degree of protection from competition, or monopoly power. As a result, rather than taking a leadership role in innovation, Nielsen followed the business policy, in general, of letting smaller firms initiate innovations and development and then entering in when its own quick research and development produced a knock-off of rivals' products and methods. Because he could suffer losses in the ratings business that could be borne by other parts of the business, Nielsen was better able to bankroll its products through the crucial latter stages—entrepreneurial, investment, and diffusion. The company established the policy of filing a portfolio of numerous patents for any likely innovation, hoping to entangle future competitors, and wrapping up more than 56 patents to ensure its position.

The embattled Seiler also faced Nielsen's other efforts to drive him from the market; for example, in the battle with Arbitron, Nielsen cut its audience composition ratings to one-third of the cost to force Arbitron out of the field (Buzzard, 1990; Harris Commission, 1963).

Seiler Exits the American Research Bureau

In 1961, strapped for money, Seiler decided to merge with the CEIR, a decision that proved to have disastrous consequences for him. The CEIR was a data-processing service that handled the computational needs of the U.S. government on a contractual basis. In doing so, it used large computers capable of processing data at lower costs and faster than could be done on smaller machines. However, when businesses began to acquire personal computers, the CEIR's future was threatened. Soon after the merger, the CEIR's stock dropped to double digits and soon the relationship between Herbert Robertson, head of the CEIR, and Seiler became so strained that Seiler proposed buying the ARB back. Adding to the growing friction was the fact that Robinson did not give Seiler proper credit for his work, as Arthur Nielsen, Jr. notes: "Dr. Robinson did not properly recognize his good work. For example, Robinson never elected Seiler a vice president of his company or mentioned his contributions in the CEIR Annual Report (Nielsen interview, 2001).

By 1964, the last straw for Seiler was when George Dick replaced him as president of the ARB. Seiler left because, at the time of the merger, he understood that he would continue to run the ARB. Arthur C. Nielsen, Jr. noted that Seiler was a "brilliant man...our smartest competitor." "When Robinson fired him, we got rid of a tough competitor who really knew how to run the business" (Nielsen interview, 2001). Seiler's exit resulted in the departure of the entire top echelon of ARB executives who joined Seiler in a new venture. The losses of Seiler and other key management executives left the ARB in serious trouble. Though experienced in computers, Dick was inexperienced in broadcast advertising and, with the original management gone, he was not well received by major agencies (*Broadcasting*, 1964; M. G. Seiler interview, 2000). In May 1966, Dick was replaced with Peter Langhoff, a former vice president of Young and Rubicam. Langhoff, while successful with advertising agencies, did not play well with TV station managers. In 1967, faced with agency and station cancellations, the CEIR sold the ARB to Control Data, a computer manufacturer.

The Harris Hearings

By the late fifties and early sixties, the ratings industry became caught up in the dirty underside of the TV business as rigged quiz shows and payola were all laid at the door of the ratings industry. Critics argued that ratings had been made into false gods and accused the industry reliance on them to be a sign of the softening of moral fiber and creeping mediocrity. The entire industry, critics charged, was hopelessly cowed by sets of cold, unreliable, and totally meaningless numbers. Ratings were condemned on two counts: they were too unscientific, and exerted too pernicious an influence on TV. Beginning in the late fifties, a three-man technical committee headed by Dr. William G. Madow evaluated the seven companies and their methods and provided its findings in 1963 to the Congressional House Committee on Interstate and Foreign Commerce, headed by Oren Harris. The heads of all seven ratings firms were called to account for their methods and reports.

At the hearings, compared to many of the services, who revealed gross inadequacies and in some cases outright fraud, Arbitron was lauded by the committee for doing what it purported to do. Other services did not fare as well, as many services were either disbanded or were forced to undergo major revisions (Buzzard, 1990).

In fact, the committee uncovered a Nielsen master plan to monopolize the national ratings field (Buzzard, 1990). Instrumental to this plan was patent litigation as a strategy to lock out potential competitors. In part, Nielsen had successfully used this strategy to drive out ARB from the national ratings field a few years earlier. A second tactic employed by Nielsen was its considerable economic muscle. For many years, Nielsen ratings divisions were but one arm of its larger marketing services. This meant it could make use of its better capitalization to drive smaller firms from the market.

In particular, the hearings revealed serious inadequacies in those services who measured radio. The transition of radio listening from mass medium to a personal activity necessitated a new approach to measurement. The invention of the transistor meant radio was no longer bound to the living room set but was now mobile and portable. Now radio's largest audience was its out-of-home one as people listened in such places as at work, in the car, on the beach, locations not recorded by the previous methods. Also, its content had now become primarily music and news programmed so similarly that many viewers were no longer aware of the station to which they were listening. The emergence of television meant that radio was left with less money and lower ratings, required bigger samples, and faced formidable technological and economic barriers in adjusting to these new measurement conditions. The major rating services, including Hooper's and Nielsen's, used methods that understated the radio audience.

So troubling were the new hurdles in measuring radio that Nielsen dropped its Radio Index in 1964 shortly after the hearings. Nielsen's method had resulted in a strong effect on radio audiences and sales because its Audimeter failed to measure the out-of-home audience in offices and cars. That same year, Arbitron was asked by RKO to measure radio in Detroit using diaries designed to measure both the at-home and away-from-home audience. Thus it was that, as Nielsen left in 1964, the ARB first entered the radio rating business. Nielsen had successfully straddled the rise of television, but the same cannot be said for radio measurement. By 1964, it had withdrawn from the national radio ratings measurement and, by 1965, from local radio measurement, leaving Pulse unchallenged. According to A.C. Nielsen, Jr.:

> We could not measure the portables. Furthermore, the highway system that the United States built enabled the movement to the suburbs and allowed automobiles and automobile listening to grow. We did develop an Audimeter to be put in an automobile as a result of criticism for the shortcomings for our service. My father developed a proposal to improve the system and planned to use a diary for out-of home listening and install these systems in cars. But they [his customers] wouldn't pay for the added costs....That's when we quit.
>
> (Nielsen interview, 2001)

After the Harris hearings in 1963, Nielsen concentrated on measuring national TV audiences while Arbitron (now without the original founders) developed a virtual monopoly in local radio, for which the diary was at that time the only economical method of determining ratings. Nielsen soon joined the competition to measure local TV markets, and these two services divided the field until Arbitron withdrew in 1993 to focus exclusively on radio measurement. Innovations in product design, a less expensive method, and a unique sales and pricing strategy proved to be the successful elements of the ARB's local market strategy.

Demographic Measurement and the Personal Diary

Hired back as a consultant in the mid-sixties by Control Data on product design and marketing shortly after his exit, Seiler also heard and paid attention to a new problem that the radio industry was grumbling about. He was now able to convince the ratings industry to abandon the old sets-in-use base in favor of a per-listener basis, an idea that he had first proposed in 1947 but which had fallen on deaf ears at that time—but no longer. The sets-in-use base failed to identify who and how many were listening but merely how many sets were on (Seiler, 1947). In place of the household diary, Seiler recommended the personal diary, a diary designed for each individual in the household to carry with him or her throughout the day.

The new diaries were unique in that they were now sent to each member of a selected family. Each member recorded his or her viewing separately rather than asking a single family member to record for the entire family, as had the former household diary. They were also distinctive in that they emphasized cumulative (cume) audiences rather than the former average program audiences. Cume audiences indicated a station's number of different weekly viewers, much like circulation figures for magazines and newspapers. The result was that the ARB decided not just to measure television but now had a viable method to measure radio. The personal radio-only diary allowed many radio audiences to show up for the first time since the mass defection to television. Radio now had a measurable audience, and the ARB grew to monopolize radio measurement.

Unlike other ratings pioneers, James W. Seiler did not become synonymous with the company he founded. While Crossley exclusively ran the CAB, A. C. Nielsen Sr. and Jr. ran A. C. Nielsen Inc. for more than thirty years before selling it to Dun and Bradstreet, and Hooper exclusively ran his Hooperatings until his death. Arbitron continued successfully without Seiler, even though it was Seiler and his management crew and their creative leaps in local market measurement that led to industry standards, such as geographic and demographic targeting.

Arbitron after Seiler

By 1992, Control Data had split into two companies—Control Data Systems Inc. and Ceridian Corporation, with Ceridian becoming Arbitron's parent company. In 2001, Ceridian Corp. announced it would split off Arbitron into a publicly traded company. As Arbitron prepared to become a publicly traded company, it held a near-monopolistic leadership position in radio ratings.

Competitors in Local TV: Nielsen

Throughout the eighties and nineties, the Arbitron local TV service faced increasing loss of revenue as stations discontinued the common practice of using both Nielsen and Arbitron rating services. Increasing cancellations were estimated to cost Arbitron and Nielsen between $12 and $15 million annually in lost revenue. Arbitron also faced criticism over its measurement of cable TV (*Broadcasting*, 1991).

Arbitron's loss of subscribers to its TV and cable reports was so significant that, in 1993, Arbitron announced it would terminate its broadcast and cable TV ratings services. A company spokesperson noted that competition from Nielsen resulted in fewer contracts and declining price per contract. Arbitron had lost money for several years in the television ratings part of its business. It would cut more than 700 positions from its workforce, leaving the company with about 550 employees. The company planned to continue developing information tools for TV and cable stations to work with advertisers, and it planned to continue development of its people meter for radio and TV (*Broadcasting & Cable*, 1993; *Electronic Media*, 1993; *Television Digest*, 1993; *Communications Daily*, 1993; *Billboard*, 1993).

Competitors in Radio: Birch Radio and Accuratings

Besides Nielsen, Arbitron had faced other competitors. Throughout the eighties and early nineties, Birch Research Corporation, established in 1978, was the primary competitor to Arbitron in the radio ratings business and grew to cover 230 radio markets. Following a merger with VNU, Birch bowed out in 1992. To fill the void, Accuratings was launched in 1992 but also had left the field by 1998. Both companies used telephone methods. These two competitors are detailed further in Chapter 5.

New Products: ScanAmerica and MediaWatch

Arbitron made an unsuccessful attempt to introduce a single-source measurement service, known as ScanAmerica, using a people meter method, in the late eighties and early nineties, detailed further in Chapter 3, "Establishing the Analog Currency for Network TV Audiences: The People Meter Initiative" (Moshavi, 1992a). It planned a second single-source venture in partnership with VNU, using the portable people meter known as Apollo, which also proved unsuccessful.

In addition, by 1990, Arbitron introduced a new electronic monitoring system called MediaWatch, targeted to advertisers who wanted to monitor their commercials and those of their competition. MediaWatch enabled more accurate identification and classification of TV ads on a full-time basis in most of Arbitron's seventy-five markets. With the addition of Lifetime and TNT cable networks to its MediaWatch service, Arbitron was monitoring about 80 percent of all cable TV advertising, including CNN, ESPN, Family Channel, MTV, USA Networks, and WTBS.

In May 1994, Arbitron joined with GE Capital and investment banker Veronis, Suhler to make a multimillion-dollar equity investment in ADcom Information Services. ADcom used a technology that combined pay-per-view with passive measurements. It maintained household panels to provide local cable operators with demographic and consumer behavior data.

Controversy over Sample Size

> If you have a bowl of soup in which all the ingredients are thoroughly mixed, you do not have to eat the entire bowlful to know how the soup tastes. One spoonful will give you accurately the flavor of an entire vat of soup. The ingredients, of course, must be completely mixed though all of the soup.
>
> James Seiler (McArthur, 1953)

During the 1990s, as radio grew, sample size would become a controversial issue for Arbitron's radio ratings. The company was advised by the Arbitron Radio Advisory Council to increase its sample size by 33 percent over a three-year period (*Broadcasting & Cable*, 1994). It also wanted the company to reduce the reporting service from four books to three books a year (*Billboard*, 1991b). Furthermore, the National Association of Broadcasters announced it would hold a summit in November 1992 to discuss problems with Arbitron's rating system for radio. The chief complaint seemed to be that audience samples were too small, due largely to low response rates from some audience segments. Arbitron had consistently rejected increasing the sample size as being too expensive. Instead, it wanted to lengthen the current three-month reporting periods. Ultimately, the radio and advertising subscribers voted to continue the four 12-week audience surveys. However, the company vowed to continue to try to find ways to increase the sample size and, thus, the reliability of its surveys.

At the end of 1991, radio stations continued to apply pressure to Arbitron to improve its radio ratings system. They wanted Arbitron to broaden the sample size, improve diary reporting, and make the system more economical. Weak reporting was especially prevalent among Hispanics and young males. Major issues involved ways to improve reporting among eighteen- to twenty-four-year-old males. Arbitron's policy at the time was to exclude group quarters, such as college dormitories and the military, from its samples.

In 1995, ARB's sample size was increased 40 percent to achieve a 70-percent increase over 1993 levels. As part of the plan, radio stations would be charged an additional four percent and, beginning with its spring 1995 radio survey, Arbitron began calling college and military residences that were equipped with private phones in an effort to better measure the traditionally hard-to-measure eighteen-to-thirty-four-year-old male group. More than 400,000 such numbers were added to the sample base in 51 markets (*Billboard*, 1995).

Arbitron moreover revised a plan that included the concept of an eighteen-week rolling average to increase sample sizes, an idea not well received by radio stations, and announced it would increase sample sizes by 30 percent (*Billboard*, 1993). Arbitron was plagued with data collection errors that same year, when books from nine markets had to be reissued. To address this problem, the company created a new position, director of data collection, and rehired Pierre Bouvard as general manager. Arbitron began using a computer imaging system for diary storage and retrieval that fall, developed jointly by Arbitron and IBM, to capture exact images of every diary page and sorted it on CD-ROMs for retrieval during processing and review.

By 1999, low response rates had again become a crisis of sorts for the diary method of tracking radio and television audiences. As a result, both Arbitron and Nielsen were under pressure to develop alternatives to the diary method. Arbitron's average response rate on its radio listener surveys was 35.9 percent, compared to 39.1 percent in 1998. The lowest response rate in any single market dropped to 26.3 percent. Among the steps Arbitron took to boost response rates was to offer higher cash payments, make more telephone calls to survey participants, and repackage the diaries (Bachman, 2000).

Measuring Internet Radio Audiences

By the end of 1999, the company had released its first monthly report on Internet radio usage. By 2000, the monthly reports covered nearly 400 channels on the Internet. Arbitron would form an alliance with Lariat Software in mid-2000 to use its MediaReports software to collect data directly from servers to report the number of unique listeners to an audio channel on the Internet (Saxe, 1999; Torpey-Kemph, 2000).

Portable People Meter

In December 1992, Arbitron announced it would test a new passive measurement system using a device called the *portable people meter*. The device would pick up inaudible sound signals encoded in radio and television programs to record viewing and listening.

Pretesting Co. already had a patent on a wristwatch device that used an inaudible code and filed a patent infringement suit against Arbitron, centering on its portable people meter, which Pretesting claimed violated its portable sound technology patents. Because of the lawsuit, Arbitron had only developed a working prototype until the mid-nineties. Arbitron's launching of the portable people meter as a replacement for the diary is explored in Chapter 5.

3

ESTABLISHING THE ANALOG CURRENCY FOR NETWORK TV AUDIENCES

The People Meter Initiative

Introduction

During the 1980s, U.S. advertisers and marketers continued to center their efforts on consumerism seeking increasing degrees of precision targeting. In an era of product deluge, saturated markets, loss of consumer buying power, and zero-growth population, marketers fight for their slice of a mature economic pie. To do this, advertisers need to further identify market segments and "rifle" desired products to designated segments with maximum efficiency and effectiveness.

This same efficiency sought in the world of marketing and advertising was also sought in television measurement. Earlier rating methods were designed to zero in on the household unit—the nuclear family—that had been identified as the target for most merchandise. Household ratings, however, had become inadequate to meet the needs of this new marketing area. As a result, advertisers were looking for methods to obtain more-individual demographic and geographic information about viewers and local markets.

Furthering this economic thrust toward segmentation of audiences and marketplaces was the technological impetus caused by the Federal Communications Commission's deregulatory policies in the 1970s and 1980s; through a series of decisions, the broadcast marketplace was opened to a number of competitors. Whereas, before, the industry consisted of the three broadcast networks and a handful of independents, now competition in the form of cable TV, home satellite dishes, video recorders (the first threat to linear programming and network controlled scheduling), and even remote controls with their ability to zap commercials were transforming the industry. The result was a decline in profits at the networks. Each network was taken over by a new, larger corporate owner or manager. ABC and

NBC were acquired in mergers: ABC by Capital Cities and NBC by General Electric. At CBS, Lawrence Tisch assumed managing control.

The new corporate management diversified into cable ownership and program production, and each company instituted major cost-cutting measures. A penny-pinching attitude toward program production resulted in a shift toward weekly series programming and away from the elaborate and expensive mini-series and movie formats that characterized the 1970s. More predicable drama series such as Dynasty (which some felt reflected the zeitgeist of the Reagan era) and situation comedies such as the Cosby Show lined network schedules. In particular, the three networks sought more up-scale programs that targeted affluent heads of households eighteen to thirty-four (Danner *et al.*, 1985). The danger in the networks' undifferentiated or mass marketing strategy—targeting commonalties rather than differences—was the threat of competitors who sold specialized products to smaller market segments and, thus, better satisfied each segment.

In response, networks subtlety shifted away from their traditional mass audiences, known as *lowest common denominator programming*, toward smaller, more targeted audiences, known as *narrowcasting*, as network share of the audience declined from 93 percent in 1976 to 74 percent in 1984 (Danner *et al.*, 1985). They ordered fewer program episodes and cancelled programming more easily. The three networks still remained profitable, however, because of profits from their locally operating stations and the return on investment resulting from syndication of these programs later in local, non-primetime markets.

Despite the growing segmentation of TV audiences and the shifts in marketing to reach these audiences better, however, the sole remaining network TV ratings service, A. C. Nielsen, Inc., was slow to respond to the changing marketplace. For thirty years, Nielsen had enjoyed a virtual monopoly in the network TV ratings field, a monopoly secured by its patents on the household Audimeter. Without competition, Nielsen made little effort to come up with new methods or to refine the older household meter. This was about to change, however, with the attempted entry of four potential competitors into the national ratings marketplace. Each company offered technologically differentiated methods to measure fragmented audiences to provide advertisers with more accurate details about their consumers.

The Nielsen Business Strategy

Nielsen had been effective in maintaining its monopoly as a result of a series of strategies that effectively warded off competitors and their attempts to enter the ratings market. One such strategy was not only securing exclusive rights, or patent protection, for its electronic meter method but locking up patents on any conceivable future device that might give competitors a foothold in the market. The Nielsen Company used this to its advantage with the American Research Bureau's planned instantaneous service, known as Arbitron, in draining money from the company

TABLE 3.1 Overview of Network Ratings Marketplace Peoplemeter Competition, 1995 to 1999

Ratings Services	Date of Entry and Exit	Investment (in millions)*
Audits of Great Britain	1985–1987	$84
A. C. Nielsen, Inc.	1987–present	$50
Percy	1988–1988	$25
Arbitron-Burke	1991–1992	$125
SMART	1994–1999	$40

*AGB tells networks, *Broadcasting*, 1989; People who… *View*, 1989; Peoplemeters raise.
Source: TV/Radio Age, 1988; Layfayette, 1999.

through both a costly patent litigation process and its consequences, which forced the company to pay royalties fees to Nielsen for use of its meter (*Harris Commission*, 1963; Buzzard, 1990).

A second tactic was its considerable economic muscle. Nielsen's monopoly was a propitious climate for technological innovation, because as a large-scale and diversified corporation, it could better support and execute ambitious research and development (R&D) projects than smaller ones, in part because of economies of scale (Schumpeter, 1942).

The Nielsen ratings division was but one arm of its larger marketing services. This meant that it could make use of its better capitalization to drive weaker, smaller firms from the market. As a result, Nielsen operated like a sleeping giant. Rather than taking a leadership role in innovation, Nielsen, in general, followed the business policy of letting smaller firms suffer the expense of risky innovations and new developments. Then the company entered the marketplace with its own product after quick R&D efforts produced a knock-off of rivals' products and methods or checked to see whether it might have a patent on some part of the innovation and therefore could pursue patent litigation. Because of its diversification into other marketing areas, Nielsen was better able to bankroll the products through the crucial later functions of development, entrepreneurship, investment, and successful diffusion.

Nielsen's product—the electronic meter method—was in a later product life stage by now and, because it had become a cash cow, further improvements were not necessary. Without competition to stimulate new product development, Nielsen's R&D energy shifted from innovation to perfection of their existing processes (Table 3.1).

The period 1984 to 1999 was one in which various competitors brought different versions of a new measurement device, known as the Peoplemeter, to the marketplace. These new meters collected both demographic and channel information. Therefore, they were purported to provide more reliable demographic data than Nielsen's hand-written diaries use in conjunction with its household meter because viewers now pushed buttons on a remote control-like device while watching to record their age and gender rather than recording viewing later using diaries. Each potential viewer in the household was assigned a button to push that was correlated to various age and gender demographics now desired by advertisers. The Peoplemeter used telephone lines that did not require special wiring adding to their appeal.

Audits of Great Britain and Its Peoplemeter

The first competitor that came armed with this striking new piece of technology was Audits of Great Britain (AGB). AGB promised to be a formidable competitor to Nielsen because it was the largest measurement service in Europe, already operating in fourteen countries, and therefore offered both experience and credibility. Moreover, it claimed to be able to do the job for half of what Nielsen was charging for its service while increasing accuracy by doubling the sample size. Therefore, unlike many smaller competitors, AGB also had financial muscle and the operating expertise to become a real threat to Nielsen.

AGB was not entirely unknown to Nielsen. In the 1950s, the Nielsen company had entered into a partnership with the leading market research firm in England headed by Bedford Atwood. Their joint laboratory, established in Bergenstead, developed the first Peoplemeter. According to Arthur C. Nielsen, Jr., three of the employees of the joint company—Messrs. Audley, Gapper, and Brown—were terminated when they asked Atwood for a raise (Nielsen, 2001). Several years later, when the time came to bid the contract to measure TV in the United Kingdom, Audley, Gapper, and Brown formed their own company and succeed in obtaining the bid over the combined Atwood/Nielsen Company. They changed the name of their company to Audits of Great Britain, or AGB, which was the first letter of the names of Audley, Gapper, and Brown (Nielsen, 2001).

Although the Peoplemeter principle had been successfully demonstrated, it was far from ready for commercial use. In attempting to enter the national ratings marketplace in the United States, AGB encountered a number of unforeseen barriers. One problem was what some see as its arrogance in misjudging the U.S. market, one that diverged radically from its European base. Whereas AGB's meter had been sufficient to supply standardized data in Europe because syndication was virtually unknown and cable underdeveloped and not competitive, the sheer number of programs to keep track up in the United States was staggering. This included factors such as station clearance, because affiliates added to the measurement confusion by preempting network programming. Nielsen had resolved the clearance problem through its automated measurement of lineups technology—an electronic coding system that identified and recorded programs broadcast by a local station, thus increasing its ability to deliver station line-up information from sixteen-and-a-half to thirty-four hours (*Broadcasting*, 1986). AGB's problems were further complicated by the fact that each potential customer—agencies, syndicators, cable, and broadcast stations—wanted its own twist to the information provided.

Ironically, in the early 1980s, AGB had considered but decided against a joint venture with Arbitron, who better understood U.S. business models and already had working relationships with most of the major clients (Trachenberg, 1988). In particular, cable and VCR measurement offered AGB unique competitive advantages but required understanding their uniquely U.S. conditions. A primitive move toward developing metered (household) measurement for cable in the United States had occurred in 1980 when Turner Broadcasting asked Nielsen to provide national (household) meter measurement for its satellite-distributed WTCG, now superstation WTBS (Sieber, 1988). For some time, to get national measurement, cable networks had been forced to accept the existing hybrid method that merged household meter data with diary data to provide demographic information. This two-sample method had evolved from the earlier household meter system originally designed to measure the broad audiences of the Big Three networks rather than the narrow audiences of cable channels. As a result, the Peoplemeter offered a unique methodological advantage for cable companies with its emphasis on demographics rather than the former household measure of viewing.

Its unique VCR ratings methodology also offered AGB another significant product differentiation and sales opportunity. Since 1978, when the videocassette became popular in the U.S. market, Nielsen had merged VCR ratings with standard live ratings to produce one set of national ratings. To do this, the company asked two questions: What percentage of recordings is subsequently played back? What is the demographic composition of viewership during playback? The Nielsen system assumed that every home that records a program eventually played it back and that the demographic composition was the same as it was when viewed live. These two assumptions are known as demographic ascription (Sims, 1988).

AGB believed, however, that demographic ascription was not valid and had identified a unique VCR ratings method in its campaign to enter the market. AGB's Peoplemeter was designed to place a code on the tape when a recording was made and, on playback, to recognize the recording. It provided information about who watched the program and when, rather than who recorded it. AGB planned to provide national ratings estimates that included only live TV viewing and to supply electronic, projectable, and representative VCR ratings by demographic groups (*Electronic Media*, 1988a, 1988b). Because AGB failed to enlist sufficient subscribers, this project never came to full fruition.

AGB tested its Peoplemeter technology in Boston for two years, 1985 to 1987. However, because its start-up period was so slow, Nielsen was able to rebound by testing and installing its version of the Peoplemeter with a speed that astonished everyone, growing from 450 to 2,000 households between 1985 and 1987 (Trachenberg, 1988). On September 13, 1987, Nielsen discontinued its household meter survey, and ironically, given its own history of litigating patents, used a virtual copy of the

AGB meter to begin a new network measurement service. This meter took a single sample rather than the two samples formerly necessary to provide demographic data. Thereby, Nielsen eliminated AGB's technological advantage and left it without sufficient product differentiation to compete against such an established name.

In underestimating the technological barriers, AGB found itself with limited access to the distribution channels necessary for entry into the marketplace. AGB had measured European television but did not have the technology necessary to catch cable signals before they hit the converter or have the cable companies' cooperation as the entrenched Nielsen did. Impeded by significant barriers including lack of managerial familiarity with the U.S. market, underdeveloped distribution channels, insufficient marketing, and a subsequent inability to achieve name recognition status, AGB failed to enter the marketplace. According to Arthur C. Nielsen, Jr.:

> They set up their system in Boston but never got it to run properly. They learned that measuring the TV audience in the United States is very difficult. Few people realize how complicated the job is…. People wishing to enter the business mistakenly believe that if they have a meter they can measure what a home is viewing, they can render a service. Having a working meter, however, is only part of the problem. There are other obstacles to overcome such as hiring and training a field force, persuading thousands of people to permit the Company to attach their equipment to their TV sets which requires a lot of wires. Furthermore, the problem become really horrendous when you begin to contemplate that there are hundreds and hundreds of stations and cable companies broadcasting 24 hours a day. One must determine what programs are carried at what time on all of these stations and then match them up with what the meter say the listener/viewer is turned to. Furthermore, program broadcasts are often changed within a given day; for example, a ballgame runs over cutting into the regular schedule, or there's an important news-breaking story, the President goes on the air pre-empting the regular schedule.
>
> (2001)

AGB suspended its service after its merger with Mediamark Research Inc., which operated a consumer database to supply information about media use and product purchases. Thus, Mediamark Research Inc. had the opportunity to merge TV ratings and product usage data into a single-source information system but elected not to. Although AGB lost $17 million testing its Peoplemeter in Boston and $67 million during its first year of operations, its legacy—the Peoplemeter technology—was here to stay because of Nielsen's $50 million investment (*Broadcasting*, 1989). The Peoplemeter, as a technology, achieved diffusion, because it became the industry standard. Both AGB and Percy demonstrated that invention alone is not sufficient. As Sir Bernard Audley, chair of AGB Research, said: "We had a better mousetrap, but we got out vital parts caught in it" (*Electronic Media*, 1988c).

By the fall of 1988, both broadcast and cable networks had switched from household to Nielsen Peoplemeters. Just as with broadcast stations, cable companies now got their household and demographic data from the same source, allowing cable networks to break away from the methodological disadvantages of an earlier system designed for network advertising and television.

R. D. Percy and Its "Voxbox"

In April 1988, R. D. Percy announced yet another national Peoplemeter service, which offered significant product differentiation: Percy's Peoplemeter service measured commercial, not program, audiences. Percy's meter contained a passive infrared device that verified how many viewers were in a room at any given time, thus registering viewers who did not have to push buttons, or passive viewers. Percy's ratings showed what advertisers had feared: commercials are watched, on average, 17 percent less than the programs on which they air because of channel switching and leaving the room (*Electronic Media*, 1988a, 1988b). Although CBS, NBC, Fox, and several advertisers and agencies signed up for the "Percy's "voxbox," as it was known, the idea of an electronic peeper in the living room was controversial and invoked privacy issues. (*Electronic Media*, 1988a, 1988b). Many also felt that Percy's work needed further validation to eliminate animals from being registered and to allow households that participated to move past the behavior-altering first period. The Voxbox also raised questions about prevalidating homes that did not respond during sampling, or nonresponse, as the more sophisticated the in-home technology, the more likely homes agreeing to have such equipment there would not be representative (*The Media Report*, 1988). Percy's Voxbox never made it past the entrepreneurial function as its developer failed to get out of New York. The capital investment proved insufficient, and Percy did not succeed in moving from technical attempts to work out the problems to actual application of the process.

Many felt that the Percy legacy might influence whether the meter was to take on an active (introducing human bias) or passive form and whether to measure programs or commercials. Some felt that Percy's aim was ultimately higher in removing the use of the program audience as the surrogate for the real commodity— the commercial audience. Nielsen responded to Percy by beginning work on its own version of a passive meter, which used heat sensors to register body size and promised to help remove humor errors in recording. This work was done as a joint venture with David Sarnoff Research Center (*View*, 1989; *INTV Journal*, 1989). The day of the passive meter was postponed, however, when staffing working on it was severely reduced so Nielsen could turn its full attention to rushing a new type of meter, known as the Active/Passive (AP) Meter, to market to effectively counter a new competitor, SMART (discussed later in this chapter).

Not achieving the number of distribution channels necessary to move from a local to a national ratings endeavor, neither AGB nor Percy was able to enter the market. By late summer 1988, both new Nielsen competitors, AGB and Percy, had withdrawn. Neither Percy's $25 million nor AGB's $67 million investment proved sufficient (*View*, 1989; *INTV Journal*, 1989). Michael Poehner, president and CEO of AGB, said that AGB's marketing efforts fell far short of Nielsen and that CBS was its lone network subscriber, but AGB needed multiple-year commitments from NBC and ABC to survive.

ABC's Alan Wurtzell said it would have welcomed a competitor but the two services were not strikingly different and that AGB had not replaced Nielsen as the principle service used by advertisers (*Broadcasting*, 1989). David Poltrack of CBS noted that AGB needed to acquire a higher profile; he cited both its failure to get support from the two other networks and the reluctance of the press to use AGB numbers (*Broadcasting*, 1989).

Arbitron's ScanAmerica Service

As AGB and Percy left the marketplace in the fall of 1988, Arbitron, together with Burke, Inc., announced plans to challenge Nielsen with another national Peoplemeter service, ScanAmerica, claiming it would offer further product differentiation. Arbitron was determined to break up the Nielsen Media Research monopoly on measuring network TV audiences. The company felt that its Peoplemeter was superior to Nielsen's in that it displayed a prompt for viewer data entry on the screen instead of on the unit's set-top box. The on-screen display, Arbitron said, would increase the likelihood that viewers would enter the data (*Communications Daily*, 1991). The ScanAmerica technology provided advertisers with single-source data by merging two streams of information: Peoplemeter ratings and a record of purchases from the small wand consumers used to scan the UPC Code of products. The service would require participants to scan the bar codes on purchased products with a wand. Critics argued that ScanAmerica was too ambitious, that it would be too difficult to collect both household product purchase information and national TV ratings, and that Arbitron placed too much of a burden on a single sample, leading to the potential for unacceptable bias. After testing and fine-tuning its ScanAmerica service in Denver for three years, Arbitron was prepared to install ScanAmerica in 1,000 households in Atlanta, Chicago, Dallas, Los Angeles, and New York in the Spring of 1991.

Peoplemeters provided a method to address changes in television viewership as it become increasingly fragmented between broadcast networks, independents, syndication, and cable television. Arbitron felt it would succeed where others had failed because of its competitive pricing, significant product differentiation, and unique access to distribution channels, which had proved a major stumbling block for AGB and Percy, and targeting of advertisers who were concerned about getting the most value from their advertiser dollars.

Even though ScanAmerica was copyrighted, making its direct duplication impossible, Nielsen quickly implemented plans for its own version, ScanTrak, which combined product-purchasing data with household meter data using two separate samples. Nielsen responded, as it has to most significant innovations, by imitation. Both services offered product purchases information by scanning UPC codes on store items, and measurement of TV viewing.

Nielsen's plan was to have Scan Trak gather both purchase data and viewing data on it main computer every sixty seconds. At the heart of the Nielsen system was a new research project called Electronic Research for Insights into Marketing, which tested commercials in 2,500 homes using household meters. This household meter-based system sent the test commercials to a set one day in advance, stored the commercial, and then inserted it into whatever program was being watched. The viewer, according to Nielsen, was unaware that the substitution occurred. Nielsen used low-power microwave and was able to test the commercial in cable and non-cable homes. The sample was random and custom-designed to individual clients' specifications based on purchasing behavior, demographics, number of stores shopped, and cable versus non-cable households. A step-up from reliance on respondents recruited at shopping centers, this new system was test-marketed in Springfield, MO and Sioux Falls, SD.

The Arbitron-Burke ScanAmerica system differed from its competitor in several ways. Arbitron's TV viewing panel was equipped with Peoplemeters rather than household meters. Nielsen had decided not to combine marketing and media information into ratings information and continued to use two separate panels, making Arbitron the only single-source service. Arbitron sampled 1,000 households in five markets and planned to increase its sample to 2,000 households by 1993; it also created a new consumer—the advertiser. Forty percent of its revenue was to come from advertisers (minor customers for Nielsen), 25 percent from agencies, and 65 percent from broadcast and cable networks (*TV/Radio Age*, 1984a, 1984b, 1988). Both systems asked the consumer to record shopping information by passing a wand over UPC Codes to provide a continuous record of purchasing data. Both shopping and viewing data were sent to a central computer.

As the 1980s drew to a close, this less-lauded, but no less significant, battle was taking place because Arbitron had tied TV viewing to product purchases, thereby creating a single-source system and opening up new vistas to marketers. "Pantry surveys" and studies of product usage had a long history and continued to do so; what was new in this case was that electronic measurement provided more accurate real-time purchase information. ScanAmerica offered the prospect of comparing product sales to households exposed to commercials to those not exposed to them to determine advertising effectiveness. These new selective-targeting methods further refined the now-standard demographic groups to what Arbitron called "buyergraphics"— the percent of product users—that gave advertisers more value for their money.

Arbitron launched its ScanAmerica network ratings service on November 4, 1991 (*Communications Daily*, 1991). After only ten months of operation, however, by fall 1992, Arbitron discontinued its network ratings because it had failed to sign enough clients to support the expensive experiment, even though launched with three clients (Cap/ABC, Fox, and NBC) and having added six advertisers.

Arbitron did not have the support that was needed to make it financially viable. According to Arbitron president, A. J. (Rick) Aurichio,

> Our potential customers have in effect told us that while they are genuinely interested in the link between network TV viewing and product purchase behavior, the value they place on that measurement isn't high enough to make ScanAmerica a financially viable network service.
>
> (*Communications Daily*, 1992, p. 4)

Nevertheless, Arbitron continued ScanAmerica in local television (*Communications Daily*, 1992).

Even though Arbitron discontinued its network service, it continued ScanAmerica at the local level. In local TV measurement, the fight between Nielsen and Arbitron soon turned into a winner-takes-all battle. The choice boiled down to whether stations would use Arbitron's ScanAmerica people meter system, which asked those on its panel to record product purchase data in addition to TV viewing, or Nielsen's household meters, which recorded which station the household was tuned to. By the fall 1993, after forty-three years of competing with Nielsen in measuring local TV stations audiences, Arbitron decided to leave the field of TV ratings altogether. (See Chapter 2 for further background on this decision.)

Arbitron cited a number of factors in its decision to withdraw. Local stations claimed to be unable to afford the cost of both Arbitron and Nielsen, which resulted in a declining number of contracts and revenue per contract. Although there were no clear differences in their services, Nielsen and Arbitron had waged a price war. Nielsen signed 634 commercial TV stations, 359 exclusively compared to Arbitron's 455 clients, with only 180 exclusive ones. Nielsen had thirty-one metered markets, and Arbitron had fewer than twenty (*Communications Daily*, 1993). Others in the industry pointed out that because of the loss of station contracts, the soft economy, its parent company Ceridian's own losses, and the decline of Arbitron's share of metered markets, Arbitron's pullout did not come as a shock (Layfayette, 1993). Arbitron's decision to pull out of TV ratings meant Nielsen was once again a monopoly—this time not just in network TV but in local TV ratings.

Arbitron had hoped to be one of three firms that provided single source data that tracked consumer behavior to determine the influence of advertising exposure among individual consumers or groups of consumers. A. C. Nielsen and Information Resources Inc. were the other two. All of the systems were scanner-based, generating a database at the store level to determine the effectiveness of marketing promotions. Arbitron planned to expand its ScanAmerica service from its initial test in Denver to provide local coverage for the top twenty-five markets by 1995. In October 1990, Arbitron dissolved its supermarket tracking unit, Sales Area Marketing Information

(SAMI), which tracked supermarket sales data through warehouse withdrawals, and entered into a cross-licensing arrangement with Information Resources Inc. (IRI) of Chicago. Now, Arbitron would use IRI's data, which was gathered through the use of scanners at retail checkout counters. IRI also got access to Arbitron's broadcast tracking data. In November 1994, Arbitron acquired a 50-percent interest in Scarborough Research Corporation from VNU Business Information Services. In exchange, VNU received a 50-percent interest in Competitive Media Reporting, a subsidiary of Ceridian Corporation. Scarborough conducted qualitative research on the habits and media usage of consumers in fifty-eight markets. It was expected that a joint venture between Arbitron and Scarborough would bring new research techniques to Arbitron's radio ratings service.

At the time, Arbitron, like many other broadcast industry-related services, was undergoing financial difficulties. Arbitron announced company-wide layoffs in early 1991, eliminating fifty-two positions. Although Arbitron committed $125 million to develop ScanAmerica, its failure was to lead to Arbitron's withdrawal from the local TV measurement market in 1993. After four years of research and ten months of operation, Arbitron dropped its ScanAmerica service for lack of a viable subscriber base. The move left Nielsen as the only company measuring national network TV audiences.

President and CEO Anthony "Rick" Aurichio was replaced by Stephen Morris. Morris was formerly president and CEO of Arbitron media company, that tracked broadcast commercials, and head of the Maxwell House division of General Foods. As president and CEO of Arbitron, Morris would report to Lawrence Perlman, chairman, president, and CEO of Ceridian Corporation, the successor to Control Data. Aurichio's sudden departure was clouded by concurrent setbacks at Arbitron, including the end of ScanAmerica. In addition, several radio station groups, including Hearst, Westinghouse, and Post-Newsweek, had cut back on Arbitron service.

The SMART People Meter

One further attempt to enter the network ratings marketplace using people meter technology was undertaken by a former Nielsen employee, Gale Metzger, who began his own company called Statistical Research Inc. (SRI), in New Jersey. The System for Measuring and Reporting Television (SMART) was a research project commissioned by the three networks, the National Association of Broadcasting, and the joint industry Committee on National Audience Measurement. Just as Arbitron conceded in 1994, SMART entered the field because of growing industry frustration with Nielsen. The principal backers of SMART were the broadcast networks who contended at the time that Nielsen figures were not accurately measuring broadcasting and were favoring cable TV. As the number of channels proliferated, competition for viewers led to a smaller share of ratings as audiences became fragmented. With the target audience getting smaller, sample sizes were smaller and less reliable, leading to considerable industry dissatisfaction. According to Metzger, "Without competition, there's a tendency to stay with the same old methods" (*Broadcasting & Cable*, 1996). Veteran observers speculated that the networks were using the SMART project as a bargaining chip to force Nielsen to upgrade service, just as the threat from AGB had spurred the innovation and diffusion of the Peoplemeter.

With the era of digital television almost here, the TV industry needed a metering technology that would be adaptable to the interactive nature and addressability of TV of the future. The advent of digital TV created a new distribution system capable of bringing high definition and increased program choices into the home and accelerating the convergence of programming with information services. As the medium metamorphosed both in its delivery systems (over-the-air, cable, wireless, DBS, home video, backyard satellite, video-on-demand, and computer) and TV's overall structure, audience measurement methods needed to be prepared for a day when any of 500 programs could be delivered on a local channel because viewers would be able to select from a smorgasbord of programming. The key to digital delivery was to identify programs directly off the screen instead of from the transmission source.

The key piece of technology for SMART was a system based on a barcode-like universal TV product code that would be embedded in the video portion of the program. Nielsen's people meter monitored TVs, VCRs, and cable from the transmission source rather than the site of reception. Researchers later matched data with specific programs to determine ratings. To determine who was watching, each family member was assigned a symbol that was registered in a set-top box via remote control; the data was stored and downloaded through a phone line to Nielsen's collection center. By comparison, the SMART revolution hinged on the industry's cooperation in developing a universal coding system at the point of transmission but to be read at the point of reception. Data was to be sent via a household wire to a storage device in the home and transmitted through a phone line to SRI. SMART's hardware did not require special wiring and dismantling of the TVs for installation, making recruiting easier; it seemed to offer a unique advantage over the Nielsen measurement system.

A joint venture between broadcaster, cable network, advertisers, and agencies, SMART received seed money of $40 million from investors. For test marketing, SMART selected 500 homes in an area near Philadelphia, PA. Following a pattern that was emerging as typical, the broadcast networks and six large advertisers signed letters of intent to launch SMART. By 1999, as the first stage in its national rollout of service, SRI had selected the sample. In May 1999, however, the project faltered after five years of development. At that time, the broadcast networks balked at the hefty funding needed to get the service running. SMART did not enter the market but was stalled. Although the four major networks had put up tens of millions of dollars over five years as seed money to subsidize SMART development, SRI estimated that it needed $100 million to launch a national service, half of which they asked the networks to contribute as an upfront investment and the other half to be raised by capital markets. In addition, the networks were asked to agree to long-term contracts. The plan was to recoup upfront payments by later discounts on SMART rates.

Ultimately, the business plan proved unworkable, because it relied too heavily upon financial support from the major networks. The networks urged SRI to seek independent investors to eliminate the perception that they would influence the SMART process. Some in the cable industry were concerned that SMART was not an open process due to the secrecy of test data, and suspicious that the project was an effort to boost network shares (*Broadcasting & Cable*, 1997). As a result, SMART did not receive the support necessary from the various business entities necessary for its success.

The networks needed to continue to subscribe to Nielsen's reports. Despite increased complaints against Nielsen, the Big Four TV networks refused to put up $12 million each, essentially carrying the whole freight (Katz, 1999). According to Alan Wurtzel, president of research and media development at NBC, "I think we underestimated the business side of the thing. The SMART model required an economic commitment from four players that was extraordinary, and in these difficult financial times, it wasn't possible." David Poltrack, executive vice president of research and planning at CBS, did not see SMART as a viable option by 2002, when CBS's contract with Nielsen contract will expire. He was concerned that the SMART system would be obsolete by 2005 because of the convergence of digital technology and computer. "It was a good research deal, but a bad business deal," according to Poltrack. The industry was concerned that by 2005, the technology for both SMART and Nielsen would be obsolete and would be replaced by some form of two-way interactive measurement methodology, a change that has not yet occurred (McClellan, 1998). The SMART ratings system was contingent on acceptance by the advertising community (the buyers) but, financially, was primarily dependent on the broadcasting community (the sellers).

It is worth noting that Nielsen developed its own version of a digital people meter after a short period of test marketing in the 1990s, known as the Active/Passive (AP) meter. Nielsen's new system provided ratings estimates for programs running simultaneously on the same channel or frequency. The AP meter reads program codes directly off the set rather than at the transmission source. It also has the ability to identify the source of programs and commercials without opening up the TV set in sample homes, the technology to identify how the TV set was being used (broadcast, cable, VCR, satellite, video game, computer, etc.), and a fail-safe backup system capable of identifying programs transmitted without ID codes, which ensured a program would be rated. Nielsen partnered with Lucent Technology, who was to develop digital TV encoding and decoding products for use in the consumer electronics marketplace (www. nielsenmedia.com/news/). The plan was to use it in conjunction with the current people meter so clients could continue to receive audience composition information.

SMART was now in the unhappy position of being perceived as a "me-too technology." Broadcasters insisted that they preferred a rival with a very different technique rather than one that replicated the current system (*Advertising Age*, 1999). When it decided to focus on the AP meter, Nielsen made a choice to cut back on its plans to invent a truly passive meter. It chose to let someone else create and develop image-recognition technology and then enter the market. According to Barry Cook, Nielsen Media Research vice president of research,

> The choice was should we try to lead the world in the development of a difficult engineering and software problem—image recognition technology? Or let the world do it because they were going to do it anyway and then we come in a later point when the technology is ready to be applied.
>
> (*Advertising Age*, 1999)

In doing so, Nielsen had already made a conscious business decision to set its sights on a new advertising medium—the Internet—and a new competitor—Media Metrix (now known as Jupiter Media Metrix—the then-dominant rating service for the Internet, rather than place its energy exclusively on measuring the traditional TV world. As David Poltrack, vice president of research at CBS notes,

> With a mature product, Nielsen will most likely used a maintenance strategy concerning that product. The incentive for fixing the current system is low when future growth lies in measuring the interactive world of the future. Convergence is the pathway that links Nielsen's core business with the opportunity of interactivity.
>
> (*Advertising Age*, 1999)

As Nielsen Media Research was spun off in July 1, 1998 by its parent Cognizant, a key concern of industry was its new stand-alone position. Nielsen was saddled with $300 million in debt, making it difficult to update its meter technology and worrying industry that increased rates were a distinct possibility. Just at the dawn of the twenty-first century, Dutch VNU NV, which published consumer magazines such as *Billboard* and *Hollywood Reporter*, purchased Nielsen Media Research to become the biggest provider of U.S. TV ratings. This merger allowed Nielsen to broaden its efforts to measure the Internet, to expand into international markets, and to insulate itself from potential competitors.

Conclusion

The final irony of the people meter wars was that no one really liked this metering system. Arbitron and Nielsen planned dramatically different courses of actions, and some felt Arbitron charted a course that led to its demise in the

TV rating fields. Arbitron took the more aggressive strategy by implementing people meters at the local level, forcing acceptance by local stations whether the equipment was affordable or not, a strategy later employed by Nielsen (see Chapter 4: "Establishing the Digital Currency for Local TV Audiences: The Local People Meter Initiative"). Nielsen converted to people meters in major markets and continued with household meters in smaller markets because it believed the increased costs due to the technology and larger sample sizes were prohibitively expensive. Overall, people meters resulted in lower viewing levels, because they reintroduced the need for viewers to actively participate in the ratings process, and sharply lowered kids and teens ratings—the audience segments least likely to participate. Most industry sentiment supported passive scanners that did not require viewer registration.

As the beginning of the twenty-first century, Nielsen was alone in measuring TV ratings despite attempts by four rivals to compete. Many felt that without competition, Nielsen's incentive for innovation had been eliminated. It was competition that spurred the development of critical changes in methods, including the people meter, increases in sample size, the AP meter, and even the research on a truly passive meter. It was clear that new competitors were critical to methodological advances.

PART II
Digital

4

ESTABLISHING THE DIGITAL CURRENCY FOR LOCAL TV AUDIENCES

The Local People Meter Initiative

Introduction

Throughout the years, Nielsen had faced down and bested a number of ratings rivals who attempted to enter the TV ratings marketplace. The switch to digital TV and its new measurement challenges promised more major battles in store.

Since the 1990s, the advertising and media industries had depended on TV market measurement provided by the Nielsen Company alone. In the 1980s, both Arbitron's and Nielsen's parent companies had attempted a single-source ratings initiative, tying TV viewing to product purchasing, the Mecca of many advertisers and marketers, but both ventures failed. (See Chapter 3, "Establishing the Analog Currency for Network TV Audiences: The People Meter Initiative.") Subsequently, Arbitron left the field of local TV measurement entirely in 1992, while Nielsen persevered.

The new digital era held the potential of these former rivals joining forces in Arbitron's new technology, known as portable people technology, as each continued with its monopoly status in its specialty areas: for Nielsen, TV, and for Arbitron, radio. They were even considering partnering in yet another single-source measurement initiative known as Apollo. Moreover, Arbitron and Nielsen were both vying to develop a meter to measure outdoor marketing using a global positioning system device until Arbitron abandoned the project. However, faced with increasing agency and advertiser dissatisfaction with the outmoded diary measurement still in use at the local level in TV and radio, a showdown of sorts was underway on how best to measure the local TV and cable markets (addressed in this chapter) and the national and local radio markets (addressed in Chapter 5, "Establishing the Digital Currency for Local Radio Audiences: The Portable People Meter Initiative").

Besides a national market for radio and TV measured by a sample of network or national viewers or listeners, each local market was measured separately through samples drawn from each of the local designated market areas (DMAs). The DMAs were Nielsen's version of a market geography originated by Arbitron as Areas of Dominant Influence or ADIs that allowed all TV and radio stations to be divided into exclusive, non-overlapping marketing areas even though, in truth, signals continued to overlap. This had facilitated measurement beyond the former metro areas and took away the guesswork necessary previously. After Arbitron's withdrawal from measuring the local TV marketplace, Nielsen monopolized both the national and local television markets.

Since 1987, Nielsen Media Research (NMR) had employed the national people meter (NPM) for its nation-wide measurements in the United States. Nielsen had converted to the people meter when a British rival, Audits of Great Britain, introduced this method in an unsuccessful attempt to compete with Nielsen, which, at that time, used only the household meter estimates with a smaller sample of 1,200 national viewers. (See Chapter 3, "Establishing the Analog Currency for Network TV Audiences: The People Meter Initiative.")

The NPM provided data for the seven broadcast networks, fifty cable networks, and hundreds of national syndicators and consisted of a national sample of 5,000 households until Nielsen national sample initiative sought to triple the size by 2011. The conversion to the NPM eliminated the need for the diary altogether at the national level as the people meter provided demographic ratings by having viewers push a button on a device that resembled a remote control but contained buttons indicating age and gender. However, the people meter did reintroduce what had previously been considered the third rail of Nielsen's business model—the active viewer. Unlike the earlier passive meters on which Nielsen had based his electronic method, the viewer was now required to participate, thus opening the door to methodological errors avoided by the earlier meters.

By 2008, all of the major television networks had witnessed significant pricing rollbacks, as the average price of a primetime network TV commercial fell to $122,133 (down 15 percent), and ratings saw an overall drop of 13 percent across all networks. While CBS experienced the steepest decline of 22 percent, NBC was down 13 percent; ABC, 10 percent; and Fox, six percent. The prime-time price deflation was caused by two key factors—the economy and the networks' declining share of TV audience viewing (Mandese, 2009a). As a result of declining revenue, the broadcast networks increased the number of commercials in primetime in 2008 by 3.5 percent (Goetzl, 2009a). Interestingly, it never dawned on those in the commercial industry that the medium was oversaturated. This oversaturation had led the consumer down the road to commercial-skipping DVRs and alternative media, such as the Internet. Though the economic model of advertising seemed to be cracking, the broadcast industry seemed united in its denial and resistance, as it attempted to plug each hole individually in the commercial dyke.

Users of Nielsen's local TV audience data (still based on the passive household meter merged or fused with diary information) voiced many additional concerns: the lack of good analytical software to evaluate ratings, reach, and frequency and to target audience composition; Nielsen's decision to report local people meter data by quarter-hour rather than minute by minute, which interfered with seeing the actual commercial audience; the continued use of broadcast survey areas, known as the DMA, as the basic local market geography despite the fact that neither cable operators nor advertisers conformed to the broadcasting-created boundaries; and the lack of measurement data for interconnects, informal cable companies who joined together to achieve reach and frequency for advertisers.

In this increasingly complex digital environment, ratings services were forced to address new technological demands. How would rating companies address the increasing viewing of TV programming or the listening of radio stations on the Internet? How would programming that was recorded and played back later be addressed? Could the current sample-based methods, designed for mass audiences, reliably report on universes of fragmented channels in an era of a reluctant sample base where cooperation rates had been undergoing significant decline? How would they address the phenomenon of zero cell, the problem of sample participants whose diary and set tuning measurement did not match (explained in more detail later in this chapter)?

A New Digital Environment and Its Demands

Major changes were essential to address this new environment. For Nielsen, a push to improve sample quality, called the expanded local and national sample performance initiative, was crucial. Further, technological changes (such as the Active/Passive (AP) meter discussed in the previous chapter); a merger with NetRatings to gain a software meter to measure the Internet; methodological changes (such as the introduction of the local people meter); and new data delivery hardware and software to help users sort out the dramatic increase in volumes of data were all strategies implemented in an effort to stay current.

Though it had been forced to change its method to the people meter at the national level in 1986, Nielsen had continued with its more conventional diary method at the local level due largely to concerns about the impact of increased costs on stations and networks and, in part, due to complacence. The broadcast ratings market was a mature market. Without pressure from some outside force, there was little incentive to change. In larger and medium-size local markets, Nielsen used a set meter but one fused with diary information and, in smaller markets, which could not afford the expense of a meter, it employed the diary only. Each local television market still used the same geography established in the sixties and the idea then was that advertisers could match their advertising by purchasing area. So if the major outlets for product were in the "metro area," the advertiser could purchase ratings by metro area. The area of dominant influence or designated marketing area measured counties and assigned the counties to those stations where they accounted for the largest share of the viewing. The total survey area or Nielsen survey area measured viewing wherever it occurred and provided a measured of spill-in or spill-out of viewing between markets and counties as signals were not restricted to discrete areas.

However, as the digital era emerged, the increasing use and influence of the Internet was forcing older more opaque TV platforms to transform toward models of more accountability. One such area was the push by cable companies for what they called *zone addressability*. This was to be achieved by a new model emerging that gathered data from 60 million set top cable TV boxes in consumers' homes, allowing advertising to target by zone rather than by the older market area designed for broadcast. (See Chapter 7, "Exploring New Digital Currencies for TV, Cable, and Internet Audiences: Digital Cable and STB Data Initiative.") In this brave new world, marketers and advertisers felt that the older business models were dragging behind the technology.

Another area that was also dragging behind was the fusing of Nielsen's diary and the household meter used in many local markets. Therefore, Nielsen determined to employ the NPM at the local level but here known as the local people meter (LPM for short), as part of an ambitious campaign to cover a total of 56 local markets or approximately 70 percent of U.S. households by 2011. The first part of its plan was to install people meters in the top ten markets (covering 32 percent of the population and 46 percent of the advertising dollars) before adding additional markets (Ramos, 2009).

The diary system, designed for an earlier era of the Big Three networks (no cable, and certainly no digital technology), gave what many felt were distorted results. Stations still set their advertising rates during the sweep months of February, May, July, and November when diaries were mailed to randomly selected families who then indicated what and when they were watching. Local broadcasters artificially boosted their ratings through these easily exploited "Sweeps" months. Worse yet, with the diary system, viewers had been known to wait until the end of the week to jot down what they watched, making the diary entries less than perfect—a point that even Nielsen conceded. Some felt that this led to over-reporting where participants remembered viewing more easily; and for larger channels and more heavily used day parts, such as prime time, this belief that was later confirmed by test marketing of the LPM.

The LPM offered significant advantages over the diary. It could provide continuous demographic measurement rather than the monthly reports of the diary system, it improved analytical abilities by providing more detail, it reduced sampling error by eliminating the need for a paper record, it eliminated reliance on recall as the viewer was prompted on screen to push required buttons, it used larger samples by incorporating national and local sample data, it provided faster overnight delivery, improving only the monthly diary data, and it eliminated the zero cell problem delivery of merging two types of measurement systems: the diary and the meter.

LPM samples combined with larger sample sizes purported to eliminate what researchers called the zero cell problem. This occurred when a set meter measuring household tuning from one sample differed from a diary measuring viewing from a different group of people, resulting in data that did not match. Nielsen assumed zero viewing or tuning if it did not match. As a consequence, ratings estimates were not issued for a quarter-hour period unless both the set and diary register agreed. The market gave no value to a zero rating. As much as 33 percent of quarter-hours during the average broadcast day (7 PM to 1 AM) could be counted as zero cell viewing; for cable networks, even higher (Nielsen 101, 2006). This could amount to significant loss of the sample audience and its representativeness.

Given the importance of these numbers for tracking segmentation of different audiences, the LPM implementation had the industry watching its development very closely. Some saw this as a necessary upgrading of a badly neglected sector whereas others were concerned about whether the LPM sample was representative of minorities, and still others were concerned about the possible shifts that it could bring in the TV network and station share of the market when compared to cable television.

Furthermore, many in the industry began to have significant issues with the accuracy of meter/diary fusion as TV morphed into cable and satellite TV, adding a multitude of channels. The concept of fusion (factoring the diary to the higher viewing levels of the meter) had been developed in recognition of the weaknesses of the diary whereas the household meter was considered more reliable because it did not require active participation. Nielsen had switched from providing household data alone, which characterized the desired mass audiences sought by advertisers in the thirties, forties, and fifties to demographic targeting in the sixties. Since the 1960s, Nielsen had used estimates determined by the fusion of its household set meter with diary methodology in local markets to track TV viewership for 70 percent of its larger and medium-size markets.. The shift to demographic targeting provided data on segmented viewing, as more and more products were designed for audience segments. This had an enormous influence not only on advertising but on programming, as programs were now designed to reach what some have called the "commodity audience," the audience segments most desired by advertisers. (See Introduction for an overview of the commodity audience.) To provide this information, Nielsen had created panels of diary keepers who recorded their viewing for one week over a four-week period. Four weeks of diaries were mailed to Nielsen headquarters where they were factored to the level of the household meter in an attempt to compensate for underreporting errors from diary keepers. However, though the diaries did provide the ever-important demographic information needed by advertisers and the increasingly important out-of-home viewing (as it could report viewing wherever it occurred), there was continued industry dissatisfaction. Sample size and response rate fluctuated, certain demographic and ethnic groups were under- or over-reported, viewing was exaggerated in certain day parts and in "brand name" network programming, cable programming tended to be underreported, and some felt a great deal of viewing was not reported at all.

Nielsen decided to adjust its method by replacing the diary but decided to employ the sample principle of fusion to the new LPM sample using set-top box data rather than diary data. (Nielsen Connection Web site, n.d.) The basic idea was to start with the electronically gathered set-top box data, now available as a result of digital television, collected for fifty-six markets, and apply these national levels to local data (viewers per household) information derived from the LPM. (See Chapter 7, "Exploring New Digital Currencies for TV, Cable, and Internet Audiences: Digital Cable and STB Data Initiative.") Set-top box data could provide a replacement for the diary and provide demographic data through the people meter.

Inclusion of LPM Data in NPM Sample

Nielsen also planned to merge its national data from its NPM sample with data from its local LPM panels, leading to economies of scale in data collection costs and an increase in its national panel size from 5,000 to 10,000 by 2006, and 200,000 by 2011 (James, 2007). Given that now few programs achieve a rating higher than two or three percent of the total audience, Nielsen's goal was to be able to provide more granular information on diverse television viewing through its larger national television sample, and other investments in research and technology. Therefore, growing the national sample was seen as crucial as growing local samples as the plan was to counteract known sample bias for smaller less well-known channels and to overcome a decline in cooperation rates. Furthermore, as a result of growing audience fragmentation, Nielsen admitted that it 5,000 household people meter sample was no longer adequate. Expansion was essential to deal not only with fragmentation but with differences in the way in which audiences now watched TV. For example, between 2008 and 2009, time-shifting viewing increased as digital video recorders grew to 30.6 percent of all households (by 2011, 39 percent of all households), while Web-shifting, watching TV programming on computers, had increased 50 percent, and mobile-shifting increased 52 percent with mobile TV seeing strong gains as more programs were downloaded from TV to portable devices and viewing out of the home increased (Levin, 2007; Shields, 2009). Furthermore, advertisers' increasing demand for granularity meant that to achieve commercial minute ratings and digital video playback measurement, larger samples were essential.

The need for a larger sample size was the impetus behind what Nielsen called its LPM/Expanded NPM initiative. This initiative offered significant advantages to TV and cable networks. It offered local and national data combined up front and reduced reliance on sweeps as stations could now receive daily data. It provided greater network leverage for affiliates in offering more comprehensive data for escalating programming rights fees. In anticipation of the LPM roll-out, Nielsen decided to include the costs of the LPM roll-out in each network contract for its NPM service rather than breaking out the costs separately. For example, according to its contract, at this writing, GE (the parent company of NBC) supported the roll-out of the local people meter in any market where they have one or more network owned and operated stations.

Test Marketing the Local People Meter

Between May 2001 and April 2002, Boston, the sixth-ranked market in the United States, with more than 2 million TV households, became the first local market to test run the LPM. During the test run, Nielsen prepared to install the LPM service in nine additional markets, varying the size of the sample by market, over the next three years, depending on customer support

According to retired Nielsen CEO, John Dimling, "We are proposing a People Meter service in Boston to serve as a demonstration market for the industry. Customers will be able to evaluate the service concurrently with the existing metered and diary services" (*Business Wire*, 1999). "The times they are a changing," said Nielsen spokesman Jack Loftus:

> For many years, station executives and the buyers and sellers of TV time have been clamoring for more complete and immediate data about whom exactly is watching what. With LPMs, Nielsen is about to give them their most devout wish and possibly their worst nightmare.
>
> (Maynard, 2005)

Loftus was correct in warning advertisers and agencies about nightmares. With the introduction of the LPM, they faced a massive increase in the volume of the data. A key concern for buyers was, now that they had five times the data as a result of this massive surge, they now needed analytical software capable of analyzing it effectively.

After two years, during which it conducted its trial test in Boston, results showed what to some was concerning while to others quite alarming. The people meter data showed major changes in the ratio of audiences between broadcast and cable, in the distribution of audiences by day parts, and in the reporting of younger demographics. Though Primetime (8 to 11 PM EST) and Access (7:00 to 8:00 PM EST) showed declines in ratings levels, weekends, daytime, and late fringe (11:00 to 11:30 PM EST) showed marked increases. Smaller cable stations' performance improved at the expense of larger, mainly broadcast stations. When Nielsen introduced the LPM in the New York market, for example, the audience for the Simpsons on Fox turned out to be 30 percent smaller whereas Comedy Central's audience increased by 225 percent (Gertner, 2005). The bottom line was that the LPM was wreaking havoc by changing the valuation of programming between cable and broadcast.

Because respondents needed only to push a button rather than remembering what they watched and recording it on paper, the people meter method tended to pick up short-term viewing and viewing to less regularly watched stations than a diary. As a result, cable stations gained audience whereas larger broadcast stations with bigger and more habitual audiences fared better under the diary. This shift meant an opportunity for local cable to gross a significantly larger share of the advertising budget. It also meant a surge in the organization of disparate local cable networks into city-based interconnects for greater ease of selling and more opportunity. Jonathan Sims, vice president of research at Comcast Spotlight, said a comparison of Nielsen meter-diary measurements and LPMs showed marked discrepancies (Solman, 2004). In February 2002, for instance, LPMs showed that cable ratings could rise as much as ten points, whereas broadcast ratings could fall by twenty-three points (Solman, 2004). Thus, though cable multiple system operators (MSOs) and networks stood to gain significant audience increases, the broadcast networks and stations declined, sometimes significantly.

Overall, households and demographic levels for broadcast TV stations and networks indicated declines in gross rating points and reach. As ratings declined, some stations began to offer guarantees, a common practice in network TV but heretofore rare at the local level. Planners were also left with the problem of how to allocate their budgets between markets using different measurement systems, but some felt that the new data was harder to argue against, as it eliminated the human element of manual diary entry.

Nielsen was not deterred by industry concerns or even by failing as yet to retain accreditation by industry watchdog, the Media Ratings Council (MRC). "The Nielsen Media Research People Meter service is a state-of-the-art methodology with a proven record of performance," said John A. Dimling, president and chief executive officer of Nielsen Media Research.

> Based on a single research sample, this electronic service provides clients with year-round, local demographic data with a speed and continuity that is not available from other audience collection tools. The reality of today's fragmented, highly competitive media environment—compounded by the emergence of digital television—is creating a demand for much faster, more accurate delivery of year-round, local demographic information—and that is just what our people meter service can deliver," said Dimling. Once the LPMs were deployed in the 56 markets, about 70% of U.S. households would be measured by the devices, which track various kinds of TV viewing including broadcast and cable television, mobile-video devices, video games, digital-video recorders, video-on-demand and other time-shifting.
>
> (*Business Wire*, 1999)

As a result, between 2002 and 2006, Nielsen rolled out LPMs to a random sampling of homes in big-city markets, such as Boston, Washington, New York, Los Angeles, Chicago, San Francisco, Philadelphia, Detroit, Dallas, and Atlanta, despite having failed to receive official accreditation by the MRC, although it should be noted that MRC accreditation was voluntary as it had been created as an industry oversight committee to avoid federal intervention. In local markets that accepted the LPMs, the new service replaced existing set-tuning meters and paper diaries.

Thus it came to be that by 2008, over the objection of its television station customers, Nielsen unilaterally planned to replace its traditional Meter-Diary data collection system with a technology known as LPMs. Though the firm had planned to introduce LPMs in all the fifty-six markets that currently use set-top meters, Nielsen decided to take a "pause" in 2011 in the face of a declining economic climate.

Nielsen also was considering ways to replace diaries in smaller markets where the economics were not sufficient to justify 24/7 metered marketing, including a battery-operated meter that would serve as a kind of electronic diary, measuring one week's worth of viewing. Another possibility was the use of set-top box data as a supplement to the Nielsen panels in second tier markets.

In May 2009, Sunbeam TV Corp, owners of Miami Fox TV station, having lost a significant share of its audience and thus value, due to the shift to LPMs, filed suit in a federal court charging the Nielsen Company with violating federal and Florida antitrust laws and with unfair trade practices and breaching its contract with Sunbeam (United States District Court Southern District of Florida, 2009; Mandese, 2009c). However, Sunbeam was not successful in its attempt to halt the advance of Nielsen's new local measurement system. By 2011, a federal judge dismissed these charges, stating that though Nielsen may be anti-competitive and there was evidence of exclusionary contracting practices, Sunbeam had failed to establish the existence of a willing and able competitor as required by antitrust law. Sunbeam, according to the judge, had failed to provide a better way to compile TV ratings than with the PPM or that such ratings would benefit Sunbeam (Garvin, 2011).

Some considered the suit ironic, coming as it did years after Nielsen dealt with and addressed the need of an aggressive lobbying and media campaign brought against it by News Corp-backed "Don't Count Us Out." The suit was the second one filed against Nielsen over charges that its local people meters inaccurately reflected minority viewers. Nielsen had previously won a Univision lawsuit. However, perhaps Sunbeam had hoped to gain some traction as a result of the erinMedia lawsuit against Nielsen, which been settled out of court. In 2005, TV ratings start-up erinMedia, a small start-up ratings company that planned to enter the digital set-top box data field, filed a federal antitrust suit against Nielsen on the grounds that it used anti-competitive and predatory business practices, especially the use of "staggered" contracts with its client to thwart competition (Bachman, 2007c). ErinMedia ceased operations in December 2008 after its settlement (Hinman, 2008). However, there was a key difference between these two suits: in the Sunbeam lawsuit, Nielsen was sued by a customer rather than a competitor (Mandese, 2009c).

Beside a changing methodology, Nielsen was also grappling with advertiser demand for more data on the actual commercial, rather than program, ratings and on how playback devices such as digital video recorders affected commercial audience size. However, at the end of the day, the new currency that resulted was a product of negotiations between the Big Four networks and the major media buying agencies. A key concern for networks was the potential losses they might suffer from switching advertising dollars from program ratings to commercials ratings. The assumption was that the rating for an average commercial minute would be lower than the former program average. Moreover, another concern for media buyers was how to be certain that commercials recorded by digital video recorders for later playback would be included in the ratings data. The traditional program rating did not include playback as part of its average of commercials watched. The compromise was Nielsen C3 ratings.

C3 Ratings

In 2007, Nielsen introduced the first standardized data on the average commercial minute or commercial ratings as the official currency of TV advertising. These new ratings were known as C3 ratings because they combined commercial ratings with three days of digital video recorder or DVR playback ratings. The buyers and the sellers had agreed to use a combination of the average commercial minute ratings and live-plus-three-day ratings with the belief that the gains from the three-day ratings would offset any losses from using the commercial ratings instead of the program ratings. The C3 ratings required the integration of a TV ratings panel with TV commercial data monitored by its Monitor-Plus system. This new system required broadcast networks and TV syndication companies and cable networks to supply Nielsen with their commercial log data. By 2009, Nielsen introduced a system that enabled its clients to automatically log when and where their commercials ran to help Nielsen comply with an audit and accreditation process conducted by the MRC (Mandese, 2009e).

As it turned out, there was relatively no audience loss between program ratings and average commercial-minute ratings. "The difference between live and live-plus 3 day ratings is roughly flat for primetime," said John Spiropoulos, vice president and group research director at MediaVest. "Commercial ratings retained between 95 percent and 97 percent on broadcast network but were anywhere from three to five percentage points lower on cable networks" (*Media Buyer Planner*, 2007). As for live-plus-three-day viewing, it turns out that 99 percent of viewers watch a prime-time program within three days of the original broadcast, which boosts the networks' ratings over live-only data (*Media Buyer Planner*, 2007). In other words, the differences between the commercial and the program ratings were offset by the inclusion of the three-day DVR data.

Nielsen Media Research's new commercial ratings system was significant because the industry-based advertising made purchases for the first time based on commercial ratings. However, buyers eventually rejected the local live-plus-three days of DVR playback. Though used at the network level for a couple of years to buy commercial time, C3 ratings were not available locally due to the prohibitive expense of monitoring 10,000 or more local cable systems. Sales and buying executives requested

TABLE 4.1 DVR penetration

	February 2007	February 2010	February 2011
Households	13.5%	35.7%	39.7%
Total Viewers	15.0%	38.5%	42.2%

Feb 2007: 01/29/2007–02/25/2007; Feb 2010: 02/01/2010– 02/28/2010; Feb 2011: 01/31/2011–02/27/2011
Source: Nielsen Media Research as reported by Seidman (2011).

instead that Nielsen report live plus same-day ratings, which they argued were closer to commercial ratings. Nielsen planned to eliminate the live-only program ratings but would continue to deliver live-plus-same-day ratings, live program-plus-three days of DVR playback, and live program-plus-seven days of DVR playback although there was some significant backlash to the idea of eliminating the live ratings because the actual live commercial rating base would be obscured with playback data. Nielsen planned to produce a converged rating that melded together the live rating and the Internet program rating (Friedman, 2009).

Some saw Nielsen's new types of commercials ratings as a response to TiVo's announcing its first-of-a-kind commercial ratings, a service for local markets. The local TiVo service planned to use second-by-second set-top box data and convert this into C3 data without providing specific viewer demographics. The result was Tivo's Pure Program Ratings, which were derived using the number of TiVo subscribers viewing a program, live or time-shifted, excluded the commercials, to arrive at the total potential audience for the commercials during a given program. This new metric, offered as part of a service called TiVo's Stop||Watch (TM), separated the program ratings from the commercials ratings, making it possible to determine the percentage of viewers lost during a program's commercial breaks, and offered differentiation from Nielsen's current industry method of measuring a program's viewership rating without separating the content from the commercials that aired during it (Bloomberg.com, 2009). Tivo's ratings challenge is explored in Chapter 7, "Exploring New Digital Currencies for TV, Cable, and Internet Audiences: Digital Cable and STB Data Initiative" (Table 4.1).

The industry was still concerned about how DVRs would impact viewing behavior as they became more widely adopted. After all, the industry realized that commercial skipping was a key reason behind DVR usage. However, as program ratings did not incorporate DVR viewing, but commercial ratings did, the ads ended up garnering a higher overall rating than the show. Alan Wurtzel, head of research at NBC, showed that 40 to 50 percent of network prime time viewing in DVR homes is time-shifted (McClellan, 2007). This raised significant questions as to whether the percentage of time-shifting activity would increase, decrease, or remain about the same as DVRs spread to a larger audience, and what the impact would be on commercial viewing (McClellan, 2007). By 2011, DVR penetration had increased from 35.7 percent of TV households with DVRs in February 2010 to 39.7 percent in February 2011 according to Nielsen data via Turner's research department. The percentage of viewers reached in those DVR homes rose from 38.5 percent in February 2010 to 42.2 percent in 2011 (Seidman, 2011).

By standards defined earlier by Alan Wurtzel, head of research at NBC, DVR penetration could no longer be considered emerging but rather had moved into the mainstream. "I define mainstream as around 40 percent," said Wurtzel (McClellan, 2007).

> The early adopters tend to be more extreme in their behavior. On the one hand, as DVR penetration increases, so will usage and its impact on ratings. On the other hand, we are likely to see more moderate usage as new people come to it who do not see it as the most incredible invention since penicillin.
> (McClellan, 2007)

The projection of DVR growth was important because it affected the share estimates that buyers and sellers placed on shows to calculate upfront negotiations.

The LPM Controversy

Through its local people initiative, Nielsen planned to convert the 210 local TV markets in the United States, that it measured using either diary or diaries fused with meters, to set-top meters that were essentially identical to meters used at the national level since the late eighties. As Philip Napoli suggests, resistance to Nielsen's objectives emanated primarily from local broadcast TV stations (as opposed to advertisers or cable companies). The focal points of resistance were the sudden dramatic shift in methodology taking place and its disruption of established practices, the costs associated with the shift, and local station executives' ability to cope with the enormous data flow provided by the service (Napoli, 2010). In particular, the LPM tests suggested a dramatic shift in the previously held beliefs about the commodity audience. Under the LPM system, broadcast stations experienced significant decreases, and cable stations experienced significant increases, altering the competitive dynamics of the local market in such a way that local cable would now be a viable competitor for the local advertising dollars, upsetting the broadcasting apple cart.

For many, the LPM was still far from the gold standard, as it still required viewer activity. Furthermore, alone it could not report on out-of-home viewing in an era where portable devices proliferated. Many in the industry were mystified that in a period of fragmented audiences who demanded mobility, immediacy, and control over their media consumption, Nielsen would choose to continue with its traditional delivery model albeit applying it at the local market level. With broadcast and cable networks and stations contending with time-shifting and place-shifting, the Nielsen LPM still seemed all too home-centric and failed to address the digital redesign of traditional business models of media audience delivery. The NPM and the LPM were considered a twentieth-century solution to television audience measurement due to serious limitations in measuring "technically difficult" homes and in light of the significant changes introduced by the new digital era. Furthermore, the decision to use an active method over a passive one raised red flags. For example, a recent report from the BBM, Canada, a partner of Nielsen Media Research, found that people were not pushing buttons when compared to a more passive method, such as the more passive portable people meter (PPM) (Pellegrini and Purdye, 2004). The PPM and its emergence as the standard for radio are discussed in Chapter 5.

Even since the company first had introduced the LPMs in 2004, their arrival as a method to measure the local TV markets was mired in controversy. Nielsen's monopoly voice appeared to cause the greatest industry concerns when the result led to undesirable or controversial outcomes. The LPM came under intense criticism from dozens of members of Congress, community leaders, and broadcasters. In particular, the challenge to Nielsen's LPM method came from two directions: concerns about minority representation in sampling and, thus, programming and concerns about Nielsen's being the single voice, given that as a monopolist, there were no second opinions. For a discussion of the policy issues, especially competition, diversity, and First Amendment status of audience ratings raised by the LPM and the PPM, see Napoli's article (Napoli, 2010).

Nielsen faced the growing wrath of minority advocacy groups that resulted when Boston and New York test markets indicated that LPM measurement resulted in declining ratings points for minority programs and questioned whether Nielsen's selected panel audiences for this new system accurately reflected the population of the given city, especially minority audiences.

The first into the fray on this front was News Corp., owner of the Fox television network and a number of local stations including WTTG and WDCA, who complained that the new method undercounted minority viewers in cities. As Napoli notes, problems for Nielsen began after a meeting between Nielsen president and CEO Susan Whiting, News Corp. deputy COO Lachlan Murdoch (who also serves as CEO of the Fox Station Group), and News Corp. president Peter Chernin in early March of 2004 to discuss test results from the new LPM system. According to Napoli, Whiting noted at this meeting, Murdoch threatened to discredit Nielsen if Whiting did not delay the LPM roll-out (though this account is denied by News Corp., which claims to have asked only for a delay until methodological questions about minority viewers could be addressed). Subsequently on March 22, Murdoch released a statement condemning LPM results for undercounting minorities. "Nielsen is not investing properly in people on the ground to go out in minority communities and make sure that viewers are comfortable with the technology, [that] they understand it and how to implement it," says Josh Lahey, a spokesman for Don't Count Us Out, a group funded by News Corp. (Maynard, 2005). The Don't Count Us Out Coalition also emphasized the results of a February 2004 study conducted by the market research firm Rincon & Associates (and funded by ABC and CBS) that detailed a variety of methodological flaws in Nielsen's system of measuring Latino audiences in four television markets (Los Angeles, Miami, New York, and San Antonio). (Nielsen posted its own critique of the study on their Web site at www.nielsenmediaresearch. com.) Of particular concern was that the people meter, in reintroducing the need for viewers to actively participate, resulted in sharply lower kids and teens ratings, and Latino homes had higher concentrations of youths than non-Latino homes (Napoli, n.d.). Further, a Nielsen test of its newly installed electronic "people meters" in New York homes reported a sharp decrease in viewership for television shows that featured Latino and African American minorities. Because the diary system had never yielded such a drastic swing, the critics contended that the new technique must somehow be unreliable. Nielsen argued that reliability was exactly what the company had in mind when it decided to roll out the meters in local markets such as New York City. "This is 24-hour-a-day, seven-day-a-week, electronic measurement," said Anne Elliot, Nielsen's vice president of marketing communications. "It's totally passive. It's installed on every television set, every VCR, every video game set. So we know that when the TV's on, we can identify what's going on." Therefore, any differences were to be expected because the LPM was more accurate than the traditional written diaries (*Wired*, 2004). To call the LPM passive was to overlook the fact that the method still required viewer participation to push the button. So, many minorities groups remained skeptical.

A second shot across the bow came from the National Hispanic Media Council who noted that the results were an issue of civil rights for the entire entertainment industry (Littleton, 2004). Other groups, such as the Hispanic Federation and 100 Black Men, launched an aggressive campaign to delay the LPM in the New York market. This coalition was also joined by NAB, Congressman Hilda Solis, Senator Hillary Clinton, Conrad Burns, and Julian Bond, chair of the NAACP, and later to be joined by New York political leaders of minority organizations opposing the LPM. At a Senate Hearing in July 15, 2004, a call for new industry oversight was heard (Napoli, n.d.). However, as Napoli notes, perhaps the greater threat was the decision of the industry watchdog group, the Media Ratings Council, to withhold its accreditation because of the concerns about sampling (Napoli, n.d.). The growing uproar resulted in Nielsen's decision to delay its LPM launch in New York City.

In June, Miami-based Hispanic media company Univision, the only broadcast network not signed with Nielsen for Local People Meters, reported they would not sign until Nielsen improved the composition of the Latino household in the sample. Univision filed a lawsuit claiming the samples Nielsen uses for LPM are "fundamentally flawed" because they undercounted minority viewers, particularly young Hispanic Americans and large Hispanic families, as well as households that primarily speak Spanish (*Video Age International*, 2004). The giant Spanish-language broadcaster eventually dropped its lawsuit against Nielsen in favor of Nielsen's agreement to increase the number of Spanish-speaking households in the sample population used to set ratings for local stations. Nielsen then dropped its related litigation.

To better satisfy its clients and public opinion, Nielsen undertook research on its live currency LPM sample by calling households on the phone while they were watching TV and asking the person who answered the phone about their viewing. At the same time, it was conducting a different test on its live sample to measure their Internet usage along with TV viewing. Though Nielsen had gotten the blessings of the Media Ratings Council, conducting research on a live sample was controversial in raising the specter that calling its own panel members could influence how people in the sample watch TV. Nielsen's findings indicated that the people meter undercounted viewing by about eight percent, with the more people in the home the more likely they underreport viewing. The groups most undercounted were Hispanics and households with more than four persons (Mandese, 2009b). At the same time, it was conducting a different test on a live sample to measure their Internet usage along with their TV viewing. As Philip Napoli notes,

> These stakeholders' central argument was that the undercounting of minority viewers' characteristics of the LPM system will impact the availability of minority targeted programming and, hence, the diversity of content available on television. The minority call-to-arms add a racially charged subtext to Nielsen's attempt to introduce the new technology.
>
> (Napoli, 2008)

In fact, though the people meter raised concerns about the diversity of the new method and its impact on advertising and programmers, Napoli concluded that it posed more of a threat to broadcast stations and their audience base than to a viewpoint and content diversity. To quote Napoli,

> Thus, it appears that the diversity principle has been enmeshed in the local people meter issue primarily to camouflage broadcasters' concerns about more accurate accounting of audience erosion to cable at the local level as a result of the switch to LPM Measurement. By linking the introduction of the local people meter to the diversity issue, and by exploiting the concerns of the minority community (who likely are less versed in the intricacies of audience measurement than many of the other stakeholders involved in the process), the broadcast industry (led primarily by Fox and Univision) has managed to make the LPM introduction a media policy issue (i.e., a threat to diversity) when, in fact, it really is more of an issue of a shift in the competitive dynamics between local broadcast television and local cable.
>
> (Napoli, 2008)

In June 2004, the Senate Communication Subcommittee announced that it would hold hearings regarding the Nielsen LPM. Among those who requested congressional hearings included broadcasters CBS, Tribune, Fox, the American

Association of Advertising Agencies (AAAA), and the National Broadcasting Association. They called on Nielsen Media Research (NMR) to fix systematic problems of undercounting minority viewers. Among their concerns was NMR's failure to acquire accreditation by the MRC. A proposed bill, the so-called FAIR Ratings Act, introduced by Sen. Conrad Burns, R-Mont, gave industry watchdog the MRC the power to enforce research standards. The MRC had concluded that the way that Nielsen planned to weight its ratings by households as opposed to the characteristics of individuals residing in those households was flawed not just for Hispanics but for any of the demographics characteristics for which it weighted. Complainants called for release of an audit by Ernst and Young of the NYC LPM that led to the MRC's decision to withhold accreditation.

The Nielsen Monopoly

Another industry concern was Nielsen's *de facto* monopoly wherein a key strategy was to acquire or merge with competitors in order to forestall competition. Example of this behavior seemed all too frequent. For example, some in industry questioned whether Nielsen's two planned joint projects with its competitor Arbitron were a Trojan horse strategy both to divert and delay its competitor so that it could implement its LPM strategy. Beside a possible joint venture together into the PPM method discussed in Chapter 5, Nielsen and Arbitron were jointly considering a project that combined Nielsen and Arbitron's data collection. This joint venture, called Apollo, planned to use the Arbitron PPM combined with Nielsen's home scan technology for measuring consumer purchase to establish a single-source marketing panel. This three-year venture ended after test marketing Apollo in January 2006. The companies had signed up seven advertisers but cited insufficient client commitments to make the project sustainable in their press release citing the decision to conclude the project (*Advertising Age*, 2006). Originally, Arbitron had considered partnering with Informational Research Inc., Nielsen's competitor in product tracking.

Others were concerned when the joint venture between Arbitron and Nielsen in Scarborough, a single-source media-marketing database, was changed in favor of VNU, Nielsen's parent company at that time, controlling 50.5 percent and Arbitron 49.5 percent. This indicated three possible antitrust concerns for the industry: the PPM, the Apollo, and Scarborough. The industry urged the Department of Justice or FTC to launch an official investigation into the noncompetitive nature of these joint ventures between Nielsen and Arbitron.

Furthermore, in 2004, WPP, the world's second-largest communications services group, and its subsidiary, the AGB Group, and VNU, Nielsen Media Research's parent company, agreed to a joint television audience measurement venture in ten countries. This joint venture in nineteen European countries severely limited competition for television audience measurement in those countries. In March

2005, the AGB Group and NMR International announced their joint venture would offer television ratings under the AGB NMR brand name. The transaction merged all the AGB Group companies with the wholly owned TV ratings service of NMR, excluding the United States.

Other Nielsen business practices that were considered monopolistic included predatory pricing and double dipping on the roll of the LPM/NTI enhanced sample. Local markets' station rates had virtually quadrupled over seven years when there was no competition from Arbitron. In 2003, the AAAA lodged a formal complaint against Nielsen as some members of the AAAA and the Association of National Advertisers (ANA) were concerned that Nielsen had gone from sampling spinning to outright lying (*Media Post*, 2004). Some felt that it was using the LMP roll-out to prop up its outdated local television service and decaying national television service while double-charging clients who received both services. Some industry players felt that its monopoly practices had led to sloth, lack of progress, and failure to deliver quality or services on time and at fair prices to industry (MRC) specifications. Some described the MRC as a toothless tiger as the MRC collected its audit fees from the very measurement services that were to be audited rather than through a more objective approach such as a levy on advertising spending.

As a monopoly, Nielsen could raise or change rates without fear. During the LPM roll-out, marketplace station rates went from 20 to 30 percent in local LPM markets the first year. NMR was charging buyers of the LPM market report additional costs for larger samples and improved technology, but it also increased the costs for its national ratings sample that resulted from the inclusion of the LPM sample with the national sample. Buyers of both services paid additional costs twice for the same LPM sample. This practice of double dipping would not have been possible, many felt, if the marketplace had been competitive. Some felt that the LPM should be suspended, denying Nielsen accreditation for its national television index, and accused Nielsen's sample of being contaminated by the nonacredited elements as the enhanced national rating sample increase was delivered parallel to the LMP roll-out.

Beginning in 2003, Nielsen had also required that a third-party processor pay a service charge to entitle them to load Nielsen data and effectively become direct clients, although this process simply involved loading the Nielsen data on behalf of their clients who were licensees. This was called the *monopoly tax*, and some felt it violated a principle of unencumbered access to licensed data by clients. This policy added around $3 million to $4 million per year to Nielsen's bottom line without additional changes to their data or its delivery. Third-party processors included such companies as Telemar, STRATA, and SQAD; TNS and Datatect, acting on behalf of their clients, complained to the FCC and the AAAA about the additional fees, though no action was taken. Subsequently, this monopoly tax, as some called it, was passed on to their client by the third party processes.

Also at issue regarding Nielsen's *de facto* monopoly was that none of the players could negotiate termination, penalty, or rebate clauses. They could not negotiate quality requirements for surveys nor could they negotiate data access for third-party clients or delivery minimums for samples. Furthermore, most contracts relieved Nielsen of any MRC accreditation requirements.

Another key issue for industry was that the majority of revenue for the Nielsen company was based on the use of multi-year (eight-year) contracts, called master service agreements, which generated around $800 million with price escalators of around six percent annually and staggered renewals. The strategy of staggering contracts had begun around 1990. So networks were, in effect, locked into contracts that expired at different times, making competitive entry into the marketplace for rivals extremely difficult. The major companies using these types of contracts did not pay the same amount nor were the estimates based on similar time periods, making comparable pricing impossible.

What Will Be the New Core Model?

Besides the traditional passive model, two principle models appeared to be emerging in the field of ratings: the hyper-targeted and the transactional models. As channels and media proliferated, buyers and sellers were interested in presenting messages to smaller and smaller subsets of former mass audience, or more targeted programming, known as *hyper-targeting*. Industry players clamored for granularity and breadth of information to provide oversight into decision making. In addition, they wanted information on the program commercial, and they wanted the information tracked and counted no matter whether it was played on television, recorded and played back later, or played on the Internet or other mobile media. Thus, the move to C3 ratings was an important attempt to address the hyper-targeting needs of advertisers in this new era.

Transactional results were a results-oriented model that emerged when consumers purchased on-line or requested information for future purchases. This was certainly possible on the Internet and would be possible eventually in other media formats. Nielsen realized it would need to maintain its core business but also attempt to navigate the transition of its core assets into other essential business models in the future dynamic environment.

With this in mind, Nielsen had expanded its core business into such areas as copyright infringement. In 2009, Nielsen announced plans to join with Digmarc in a joint venture to monitor the consumption of video content wherever it shows up. The move came as big studios and TV content producers looked at on-line as a new source of revenue but also as potential areas of copyright infringement. Digmarc owned patents that enabled content providers to digitally "watermark" their programming to ensure that its usage could be detected regardless of platform. The move combined Nielsen's video consumption analysis across TV, Internet, and Mobile with Digmarc's patent portfolio (Mandese, 2009d).

TV Everywhere Initiative and the Coalition for Innovated Media Management

While Nielsen moved ahead with its LPM, the industry was not satisfied. A key issue not addressed by the LPM was that of digital distribution—as TV audiences shifted from their TV sets and cable subscriptions to viewing on-line. In failing to address this vital shift, the LPM was indeed limited.

In June, 2009, Comcast and Time Warner launched "TV Everywhere" as cable companies banded together to pressure for a new process to measure on-line viewing (Goetzl, 2009b). The TV Everywhere model was designed to give Comcast and Time Warner's paying subscribers access to Internet content, and block-out nonsubscribers. The thought was that those people who pay for the content should be able to watch all of it on both their TVs and computers. Cable companies were especially alarmed that cable programming, such as Comedy Central, FX, and the Sci-Fi channel, could be viewed on the Internet by all, subscribers and non subscribers and, worst of all, for free. After seeing the Internet barbarian at the gate, TV Everywhere tackled this problem by placing content behind the closed walls of an authentication system at Fancast.com., which only permitted access to cable subscribers. This was to be their last refuge to protect the last remaining business model in the industry—cable TV—not yet destroyed by the wrath of digital audiences. The industry impetus for the video-on-demand TV Everywhere model was a way of preventing viewers/users unlimited access to programming and was now being considered by many players in TV as their programming moved to the Internet. The question remained about whether the TV and cable industry was closing the proverbial gate (or erecting the proverbial wall) after the cows were already out. These changing industry models are addressed in more detail in the conclusion.

Conclusion

TV and cable networks were particularly frustrated by Nielsen's declining ratings as viewers increasingly time-shifted and watched content online. Much of potential viewership was no longer accounted for by single TV ratings. The industry still believed that ratings measurement needed to evolve. Rather than a blizzard of numbers representing every fraction of the audience, at some point there needed to be a new agreed-upon standard that took multiple platforms into account. The evolution also needed to take place on the reporting side, too. The preliminary overnight ratings were becoming an increasingly narrow way to look at the popularity of a show, though they still gave a reasonable idea of how a show performed compared to competitors and whether a series was getting more or less popular as time went on.

In 2009, the *Financial Times* reported that NBC Universal, Time Warner, News Corp., Viacom, CBS, Discovery, and Walt Disney formed a consortium, known as the

Coalition for Innovative Media Measurement (CIMM), which planned to launch its own ratings system that combined linear and digital viewing (Rosenthal, 2009). The consortium put out a call for proposals to offer a new merged TV-Internet service.

In response to the consortium, Nielsen announced its "three-screen" measurement strategy. It would begin testing Internet viewing and fuse the result with its national TV ratings to yield a single C3 rating for the on-air and online viewing of a show.

Changes in the Network–Affiliate Relationship

Another major change loomed as local TV stations, which had dominated the TV business for more than half a century and whose web of stations delivered programming from the networks and inspired the term *network*, began to undergo marked decline. Because the stations had licenses to broadcast TV signals, the networks had needed them to distribute their content. In turn, local stations had became the vehicles for the greatest mass marketing advertising blitz in history. In the 1960s and 1970s, local TV stations had profit margins of more than 50 percent, and networks competed to sign up local stations as "affiliates," paying them huge fees to show their programming. The handful of TV stations owned by the networks in New York and Los Angeles drew enough revenue to fund the business of making prime-time shows, running news divisions, and sports events.

Then came cable, and the balance of power between the stations and broadcast networks shifted. Stations were so crucial to the network in the 1980s that networks had agreed not to syndicate older episodes of series while the local stations were airing new episodes. However, by 1993, the profitable system in which TV stations controlled the market crumbled. NBC affiliates saw the program "Wings" sold by the studio in reruns to cable network USA while first runs were still available at the local TV stations. By the 1980s, TV networks began launching cable networks of their own. ABC bought a dominant share in ESPN, NBC launched CNBC, and Fox began the FX network and Fox News. The clout of local stations with the network began to erode. Each year, local TV stations were a smaller part of the TV ecosystem as their advertising revenue declined. Network compensation fees declined to almost nothing and, in some cases, stations paid networks for certain programs, such as sporting events.

However, with viewership in decline and ad revenue down, many stations faced the prospect of being cut from the delivery picture. TV executives at major networks began discussing taking their programming straight to cable, an option previously unthinkable. There they could take in subscriber fees even if advertising slumped. CBS and NBC executives warned investors that the entire broadcast TV model must change or, as Jeff Zucker, former chief executive of GE's NBC Universal said, "otherwise it will be like the newspaper business or the car business" (Schechner and Dana, 2009). Cable operators were also fearful that if the same on-air content appeared on-line, people might opt to drop pricey cable subscriptions, a prophecy that proved to be quite true.

Local stations began scaling back their original programming, cutting down on weekend news shows and trimming staff, with ad revenue falling as much as 20 percent to 30 percent, according to Bernstein Research (Schechner and Dana, 2009). Walt Disney Company faced a 60-percent decline in its broadcast revenue, which included ABC and ten ABC-owned stations, while News Corp., which owned Dow Jones and the *Wall Street Journal* and seventeen Fox stations, was undergoing major cost cutting due to a 30 percent decline in ad revenue (Schechner and Dana, 2009). Many station owners began to cut budgets for the syndicated series that filled the station air outside of prime time, such as *Oprah* or reruns of *Seinfeld*. Many local newscasts ceased operations, cut staff severely, or pooled operations.

For their part, stations were struggling to find new revenue streams. The endgame for stations could occur when network affiliation agreements came up for renewal. Some networks had already signed more lucrative deals with cable networks, and stations owned by the network, known as O&Os, are now up for sale, as earnings plunge. In some markets, local stations have tapped a new revenue stream, which may provide money, albeit in the short run, by charging cable operators to carry the station's signals. Federal law requires cable and satellite owners to get the consent of TV stations to carry their signal and gives stations the right to withhold them. However, one drawback to this new model was that the networks were telling their local affiliates that they were expecting a piece of the pie, a percentage of the retransmission fees. In fact, cable operators have offered to pay the networks the fees directly and cut out the local stations altogether, which networks feel may happen in five to ten years.

Some stations were testing out technology to send their signals to mobile devices to increase their audiences for advertising. Others were considering expanding their news coverage as it was, for many, the only source of original content. Some group-owned stations were forming new collaborations. Chicago-based Weigel Broadcasting was collaborating with Metro Goldwyn Mayer to create a content provider called *This TV* to deliver old movies from the MGM library. Nextstar, which owned fifty-one stations, launched a local community Web site.

Overall, as the industry morphed into whatever new business models were to develop, the advertising industry actually did not mind targeting more specific audiences as the more specific the audience, the more confident they could be about reaching them. For niche-branded products, fragmentation was a blessing.

As a result, advertisers placed pressure on ratings companies to provide (as they call it) "more granular information" for increasingly fragmented audience segments. This, in turn, has called into question the validity of sampling when programs and channels received a sliver of the audience. As the numbers of channels grew, the number of sets increased, and the number of devices that carry TV multiplied, sampling became more difficult. The more the markets fragmented, the bigger the sample was needed to be representative. The larger the sample, the more difficult it was to maintain it in a door-to-door labor-intensive manner. Nielsen had put prodigious efforts and millions of dollars into maintaining a representative sample of American viewers. Field reps knocked on hundreds of doors, and if they agreed, monitored the household by maintaining day-to-day oversight for several years to ensure they complied with the rules and pushed the button correctly. For a business based on sampling, Nielsen was at a crossroads, with its business model evaporating overnight. Some saw Nielsen as a relic of a simpler time, an era of three networks. However, after a couple of years of gnashing of teeth, heated *Sturm und Drang* among networks and broadcasters, due to lower ratings, and backlashes by minorities advocates that led to Congressional hearings, Nielsen tweaked its LPM service and the industry seemed to adjust.

5

ESTABLISHING THE DIGITAL CURRENCY FOR LOCAL RADIO AUDIENCES

The Portable People Meter Initiative

The Diary Crisis in Radio

Whenever a medium changes metrics, these changes affect everything from programming to buying and selling. The TV business had gone through two measurement changes: one for network and one for local services, both leading to the people meter methodology. Despite an early outcry, the industry accepted Nielsen's local people meter (LPM) initiative even though some significant outliers still clamored for additional changes. This same struggle was taking place in the radio business with Arbitron. The big push for a new metric was driven in radio, as it had been in television, by agencies and advertisers. They eagerly signed on for Arbitron's new metric, the portable people meter (PPM), while the radio networks and stations balked at signing contracts with a 60 percent increase and lower ratings to boot (Bachman, 2006).

In 2002, the FCC approved radio's transition to digital broadcasting, although the equipment to receive digital signals would not be available until 2003. In addition to better sound, digital radio broadcasts allowed for more data to be displayed on a receiver's readout, creating more opportunities for advertisers.

With the advent of digital broadcasting, digital broadcast satellite, the Internet, and other new technology, the task of measuring electronic media audiences had become increasingly complex. To be prepared for the new digital era, Arbitron had been developing and testing a meter system, known as the portable people meter (PPM), capable of detecting exposure to any audio medium both in-home and out-of-home using a single panel of respondents.

The methodology behind local radio market measurement, similar to local television, had not changed for forty years. For years, radio ratings had rested on paper diaries completed by listeners. Similar to local television measurement, the radio markets still used diaries, a method first introduced in 1949.

However, increasingly, radio advertisers wanted a broader picture of the media usage for individual consumers and a measure of advertising's impact. The current norm of producing separate ratings for each of the electronic media was becoming inadequate as the lines between media began to blur. With the advent of wireless technologies, the home-based attachment was severed and media consumption locations became virtually everywhere. Advertisers now desired a more complete picture of the consumer's total media profile, not just a single slice in time of only one dimension. They wanted additional demographic data, minute-by-minute ratings, and commercial ratings for advertising rather than programming. From an analytical point of view, the older method of the diary put more of a burden on the respondents. Moreover, with the diary, both the radio and local TV markets had to wait months to find out demographics ratings: Arbitron's standard radio diaries had to be mailed back to Arbitron and then processed to generate quarterly ratings. By comparison, network TV has had overnight ratings for years. Diaries could not capture lapses in memory and broadcast hype, not to mention cooperation rates, which had been going south for several years. Some listeners also did a great deal of station hopping, a reality that could not be captured by the diary. Completely accurate listeners' diaries were atypical. The industry sought an idiot-proof device.

In 1999, low response rates had became a crisis of sorts for the diary method of tracking radio and television audiences. As a result, both Arbitron and Nielsen were under pressure to develop alternatives to the diary method. By 2000, Arbitron's average response rate on its radio listener surveys was 35.9 percent, compared to 39.1 percent in 1998. The lowest response rate in any single market dropped to 26.3 percent. Arbitron had begun to take steps to boost response rates such as offering higher cash payments, making more telephone calls to survey participants, and repackaging the diaries, but buyers were still disgruntled. They were particularly upset when, at the start of 2000, Arbitron had to delay the release of its fall 1999 ratings report by twenty-one days. The company explained that the delay was due to its new diary-processing system and issues related to Y2K compliance (Bachman, 2000).

Arbitron, though the leading purveyor of radio ratings since 1965, was not without its competitors but, by the nineties, the field was narrowed considerably. Throughout the 1980s and into the early 1990s, Birch Research Corporation was its primary competitor in the radio ratings business. The two services were largely differentiated by their methodologies. Whereas Arbitron relied on people to recall what they had listened to over a seven-day period in a written diary, Birch utilized phone interviews to gather its data (*Broadcasting*, 1987). Respondents were asked to recall their radio listening over the prior twenty-four hours. Because the phone methodology often yielded higher listening estimates for stations that targeted younger listeners, Birch became the favored ratings service in the eyes of Top 40 and rock stations. Birch's clients were primarily advertising agencies, advertisers, and smaller market radio stations, but it was planning to go after contracts with major market radio stations as well. Birch undercut Arbitron's pricing by about half and was also battling for acceptance of its methodology. Birch also utilized its phone interviews to gather detailed qualitative information through a service it called *Scarborough*.

However, in 1987, Birch merged with VNU's (Nielsen's parent at the time) Scarborough Research Inc., and shortly thereafter, in 1991, Birch Radio, Inc. ceased operations. The demise of Birch left Arbitron as the sole company (Stark, 1992; Bunzel and Flint, 1991; Ozemhoya, 1990; Petrozzello, 1996).

In 1992, after the demise of the Birch ratings, Strategic Radio Research launched a service designed to fill the void called *AccuRatings*. Like Birch, AccuRatings utilized weekly telephone interview methodology and also provided more detailed demographic information than Arbitron. Unlike Birch, which queried people's listening habits over the previous day, AccuRatings asked people to name the station they thought of as their "most listened to."

Also unique to AccuRatings was the fact that, in their initial surveys, no trending data were listed in their reports. Instead, respondents were asked what station they listened to most six months ago. The resulting figure was listed as the "recalled former share." This was to give an idea of a station's rise or decline based upon listener's perceptions rather than simply comparing past raw data. AccuRatings later abandoned the recalled former share methodology and simply trended their data from survey to survey.

AccuRatings became "AccuTrack" in 1997 and, a year later, Strategic Radio Research put an end to its market-wide surveys in favor of focusing on research projects for individual radio stations (Moshavi, 1992b; Stark, 1994).

Thus, by the end of the nineties, Arbitron's major competitors had left the field: Thomas Birch and AccuRatings had both dropped out of local radio measurement, and Arbitron purchased RADAR, the network radio measurement service (Bunzel and Flint, 1991; Stark, 1992; Bachman, 1991). As a result, Arbitron became the single seller of radio ratings holding a monopolistic leadership position in radio ratings.

In July 2001, after nearly thirty years as a subsidiary of Control Data/Ceridian Corporation, parent company Ceridian Corporation announced it would spin off Arbitron (*PR Newswire*, 2001). It was speculated that once it became a public company, another media firm, possibly the Dutch-based VNU, which had acquired Nielsen one year after Nielsen went public, would acquire Arbitron. (Instead VNU, itself, was acquired by a group of six private equity investors in 2006, including the American Kohlberg Kravis Roberts & Co.; Thomas H. Lee Partners; Blackstone Group; Carlyle Group; Hellman & Friedman; and Dutch equity firm AlpInvest Partners.) Taylor Nelson Sofres of the United Kingdom was mentioned as another possible buyer. However, some felt federal regulators would oppose any further consolidation. As of this writing, Arbitron remains an independent publically traded company.

To say that electronic media were undergoing a rapid change is a gross understatement, declared Arbitron's report on its PPM field test in Manchester, England in 1999.

> Thanks to digital technology, the entire notion of "mass media" was becoming obsolete as consumers grazed through a smorgasbord of radio, TV, cable and Internet services tailored to their individual needs and tastes. Advances in technology had made it possible to read published stories on personal digital assistants, such as BlackBerrys, listen to the radio over the Internet, and pause live TV. Despite these major changes, advertisers continued to rely on a diary/set meter fusion combination in local TV markets and a personal diary as in the radio market.
>
> (Lewis, 2001)

Because of all of these factors, Arbitron began to see the handwriting on the wall.

Thus, during the early 1990s, Arbitron developed and patented the PPM to address the problem of an increasingly outdated and ineffective diary measurement system. The PPM was founded on a bedrock belief in the measurement business that passive measurement was more accurate than one that required listener/viewer action. The assumption was that the less that the audience was required to do and the more automatic the information collected, the more reliable it was. Besides technological problems, Arbitron also was to face major problems in getting the people meter accepted in the marketplace.

Development of the PPM

The PPM was based on scientific research into human hearing processes called *psycho-acoustic masking* that was conducted in the late 1980s and early 1990s. These studies dealt with the idea that when the human ear was exposed to certain pairs of sounds, it reacted to only one of the audio signals. Arbitron researchers decided to use the masked, inaudible sound as their code. "We came up with a method that would take advantage of the limitations of the human ear," according to Arbitron engineer and director of technology, Ron Kolessar. Around the same time, the cell phone industry came up with a form of circuitry to create a new digital signal processor, allowing Arbitron to put the audio-making theory into practice. According to Kolessar, "because of that advance that cell phone industry made, we could use their technology without having to pay for custom circuitry" (Everett, 2001).

Kolessar decided to go farther in the direction of passive metering than Nielsen's people meter. He would develop a technology that did not require button pushing. Until then, electronic measurement technology had focused on monitoring the set. Kolessar realized that he needed to monitor the person. The transformation of his idea took thirteen years and $80 million (Everett, 2001).

Kolessar used psycho-acoustic masking as a system for imbedding an inaudible "identification code" or signal in the audio portion of programming using an encoder located at a broadcast station or some other origination point. Once embedded into the audio, the identification code remained intact even after the signal was compressed for digital satellite, cable distribution, or Internet streaming. The trick was how to make the masked code's frequency not too low or too high so as to be undetectable to the human ear but able to be received by a portable monitoring device. The device would pick up inaudible codes etched into radio or TV soundtracks and record viewing and listening habits. The system would work for anything with audio, including radio, TV, or streaming video.

Participants wore a pager-sized device that detected the identification codes and logged the codes and the times they were received. The only way to foil the PPM was to press the mute button because it relied on audio signals. The data, gathered from multiple docking stations in the home, were sent via standard household wiring to a hub, a terminal device that aggregated data and transmitted them to Arbitron via a standard telephone line. Arbitron planned to roll out an updated meter, dubbed PPM360, in 2011, which eliminated the need for panelists to dock their PPM each night to transmit the data back to Arbitron over a land line. The new wireless units did not require docking or a landline to transmit the data to Columbia, MD (Stine, 2010). Because it offered passive measurement and continuous data in all venues, advertisers considered it to be the holy grail of measurement. It offered universal measurement by offering fifty-two weeks a year. According to Steve Morris, then CEO of Arbitron, the code was the only plausible way to follow a piece of content and see whether it reaches an individual (Gertner, 2005).

However, Arbitron needed to get radio and TV stations around the country to agree to run their broadcast through a patented Arbitron encoding device, including over-the-air, cable, and satellite programming. Because stations were not paid for encoding their programming, they had to be convinced that encoding broadcasts would lead to better audience measurement and increased advertising revenue.

Advertising had become so ubiquitous that Morris believed eventually everything would be coded, a somewhat scary thought to unsuspecting future audiences but Mecca to the advertising industry. However, by 1996, Arbitron had developed only a working prototype of the PPM because of a patent pending against it. Pretesting, Co., a company that already had patented a wrist device that used an audible code, claimed that Arbitron violated its portable sound-technology patents. However, in that year, Arbitron won a patent infringement lawsuit initiated by the testing and could now move from the drawing board to the implementation (Petrozzello, 1996)

In the United States, the success of the PPM depended not only on the local broadcasters' and cablecasters' willingness to encode their programming but on finding a sample of consumers who would be willing to plug the device nightly into docking stations to register their multimedia usage and recharge their meter or, as technology evolved to wireless, at least agree to carrying it throughout the day. Two potential sticking points were getting users to bring the device into their living rooms and a low response rate from its sample. Though the PPM allowed the capturing of portable viewing, it still relied on a representative sample to wear it (Gertner, 2005).

To cover all its bases, Arbitron even developed a special attachment to track uuencoded media, such as iPods, iTunes, and global positioning systems, so the company could determine when a person walked by a billboard or visited a store— shades of *Minority Reports*. Also, in the works as part of the PPM was radio frequency identification to track a reader's interaction with newspaper and magazines through embedding a tiny chip in a page, the size of a pencil dot. The PPM could also measure when someone stopped reading an article (Gertner, 2005).

Arbitron had also been on an aggressive buying spree to diversify its business beyond the radio ratings marketplace. It planned to develop an Internet streaming media ratings service but failed to do so. It had acquired Marketing Resource Plus from Nielsen parent VNU in March 2004 (Mandese, 2004).

Arbitron also planned to expand outside the United States. At the end of 1997, Arbitron took the first step by acquiring Continental Research, located in London, England. In doing so, Arbitron planned to bid on the official U.K. radio ratings contract when it came up in 1998. Though unsuccessful in its bid, it still planned to develop a presence in the United Kingdom. In a related acquisition, Arbitron also purchased the overseas TV and cable software products of Tapscan Inc., a software developer based in Birmingham, AL. By 2009, Arbitron had successfully expanded the PPM system to Canada and in many parts of Europe. By 2011, Arbitron had licensed the PPM to Kantar Media for services in Canada, Norway, Denmark, Iceland, and Kazakhstan.

Arbitron hoped to have its fingers in a number of pies as it attempted to position itself in a new digital era. It planned to develop an innovative outdoor media ratings service using global positioning technology but did not succeed due to a rival plan by Nielsen.

Two Competitors Consider an Alliance Using the People Meter

A key strategy for Arbitron in the PPM venture was to partner, in an unlikely alliance, with old rival Nielsen Company. Steve Morris, CEO of Arbitron, made the tactical decision to divide up the potential ratings field for the PPM with Nielsen rather than take a run at its mighty foe. Nielsen would use the PPM meter to measure television ratings while Arbitron used it for radio measurement. Morris had originally considered challenging Nielsen but decided not to:

We looked at this and saw that there's a long history of taking runs at the incumbent, but there's no halfway here. If we go after Nielsen, it would be war, and at the end of the day there would be one person standing. And believe me, there are skeletons littering the trails.

(Gertner, 2005)

While accepting a potential option to join in commercial deployment of PPM, Nielsen had deferred its final decision, instead taking a wait-and-see attitude. As David Poltrack, head of CBS research, noted, the two companies seemed to have put aside their parochial differences for the PPM project and to have forged a united front despite their historic rivalry because of the potential of looking at all electronic media on the same platform (Gertner, 2005).

In 2000, Nielsen Media Research and Arbitron Co. announced that they would cooperate on a test run of Arbitron's new PPM. Nielsen planned to lend its TV survey expertise and panel recruitment experience to a test in the Wilmington, DE market using a sample of 300 people. At the test's completion, Nielsen would decide whether to exercise its option to join Arbitron in a future deployment of the PPM in the United States. That would mean that Arbitron and Nielsen, the two major ratings companies that provide the currency for TV and radio spending ($37 billion in TV and $17 million in radio), would use one method and maintain their current monopoly positions.

However, many in the industry were puzzled by the cooperative PPM agreement between Nielsen and Arbitron. Nielsen provided no clarity on how the PPM would fit into its business plans and, given the Nielsen propensity to vanquish all competitors, it seemed unlikely that the former rivals would divide up the PPM measurement field. Nielsen would have to overcome its long history of defending its role as the currency of TV measurement. The decision seemed likely to be made by one person—John Dimling of Nielsen. Even a joint venture caused some to comment. However, in spite of history, Arbitron's strategy was one of embracing Nielsen.

Nielsen and Arbitron as Potential Partners in Project Apollo

A second joint venture employing the PPM between Arbitron and Nielsen's parent company, VNU, resurrected a second dream of advertisers—the dream of a single-source measurement or linking project purchasing and viewing/listening. Advertising realized that people were fast-forwarding or clicking through commercials, so they considered the next evolution in measurement to be not just improved ratings but measuring advertising impact. This possibility was resurrected under the project name Apollo. However, in 2007, VNU and Arbitron jointly announced that they were closing the doors on Project Apollo.

Test Marketing the PPM

In 1998, Arbitron launched a successful pilot study of the PPM in Manchester, England and, in 1999, it launched a follow-up study involving about twenty radio and TV channels and a representative sample of nearly 300 people ages six and older for a two-year period, spending more than $22 million in three years developing the PPM. Arbitron chose Manchester to pursue a possible national ratings contract with England and due to the relative simplicity of the Manchester market (Everett, 2001). According to Bob Patchen, Arbitron vice president of research, standards, and practices, Arbitron hoped that the Manchester test would answer three basic questions: Would broadcasters agree to be encoded? Would the technology work properly? And would the public cooperate? (Everett, 2001). To their pleasant surprise, all the commercial radio, TV, and cable stations approached agreed to be encoded, with the exception of the BBC radio networks. The encoders did work effectively. And last, the public cooperated well. A key part of the test concerned detecting whether the meters were in motion so that Arbitron could determine whether it was being carried or stashed away in a drawer. Arbitron was also able to collect motion data successfully from the Manchester test.

However, there still were concerns about its adaptation to the American market. "In Manchester, we needed to encode 20 radio and TV stations combined. In a U.S. market of comparable size, we would have had to place 50 to 100 encoders," stated Patchen. Arbitron began a test in the U.S. market with the realization that the U.S. market was more complicated due to the greater presence of cable. To adapt the PPM to the market, Arbitron focused on two concerns: incorporating a data-sorting system to handle the more complex media marketplace and acclimatizing consumers to handle the system because cultural differences were also a concern. As Arbitron's Patchen put it: "Brits, after all, have a queue culture. There're cooperative, they'll stand in line for anything. Americans, on the other hand, will shoot somebody for cutting them off on the freeway. Kind of a different mindset" (Everett, 2001). "If Arbitron were able to work out the various adaptations to the American market, the PPM had the potential to make multimedia buying more comprehensive and scientific," said Linda Dupree, Arbitron vice president of advertiser/agency services. "Buyers have always looked at individual media silos," she said. "For the first time the PPM can bring everything together" (Everett, 2001). In other words, a key advantage was that the industry media could follow consumers as they flow between TV, radio, and the Internet.

In 2001, Arbitron announced it would test its PPM in Wilmington, DE and, if all went well, it would install the PPM in Philadelphia and Houston. Cable networks and broadcasters hoped that the PPM would find the "lost" viewing that was characteristic of other measurement devices, or so they believed. They hoped to learn various lessons, such as more about the behavioral aspects of panelists, how to encourage them to participate and be reliable through the day, and the true values of the PPM service in terms of improved targeting (Everett, 2001). A reward that Arbitron was considering to encourage panel cooperation was earning points like airline miles. Cooperation then could be converted into monetary incentives such as a possible $10 to $20 per month.

The 2002 Wilmington test results, however, were controversial. According to the people meter findings, encoded TV stations were 41 percent higher using the PPM system, and encoded cable networks were 118 percent higher than the diary/meter measurement. Viewing on the PPM clearly surpassed Nielsen's current local diary and LPM measurement. However, the numbers were not so positive for radio. There was little change except in the lucrative morning drive that declined 10 percent. PPM measurement showed more people listening to radio daily but for shorter periods; it also indicated that, though less listening occurred in morning drive time, more listening occurred on weekends and late night. This left radio executives fearful that the PPM would leave radio with less of the advertising pie (Everett, 2001).

By 2002, after two years of testing, Nielsen Media Research, still reluctant to join forces, decided it needed more time and renegotiated their two-year-old agreement, delaying Arbitron's plan to roll out a joint venture on the PPM until 2003. The renegotiated agreement required a new research test that Nielsen wanted performed before it committed to partnering on a full roll out of the new TV and radio audience measurement system. Nielsen wanted further tests on response rates and tests to differentiate in-home and out-of-home viewing. The response rate, the ability to sign up specific households for a sample, had declined as much as 5-10 percent during the test period. (It had received only a 10-percent response rate in Philadelphia where it had been tested since 2000.) Nielsen also wanted the PPM tested in a metered home, to differentiate between out-of-home and in-home viewing (Bachman, 2002).

However, some industry commentators speculated that Nielsen was buying time and slowing down development until it could deploy one of its own technologies, the LPM. Some questioned Nielsen's decision to delay commercial deployment after it had provided significant financial support for the PPM test. They realized that the PPM put a big question mark on Nielsen's plan to replace its diary/meter fusion methods with LPMs in local markets. Though LPMs were superior to the diary method, some felt that they would quickly become obsolete. Tony Jarvis, senior vice president of research and director of strategic insights for Mediacom, said, "Nielsen could be playing along until it can roll out one of its own technologies." Alan Wurtzel, president of research and media development for NBC, said, "It's a mistake if Nielsen is trying to slow down PPM introduction in order to put local people meters out there" (Bachman, 2002).

In 2003, Arbitron and Nielsen Media Research completed testing the PPM in Philadelphia, and Arbitron planned to forge ahead with another test market: Houston. This same year, Nielsen Media Research was completing its test for its LPMs in Boston. For the Houston test, Arbitron planned to use recruitment methods and techniques developed together by Nielsen and Arbitron to raise response rates to as high as 41 percent. However, the Philadelphia PPM ratings test produced a major upset in the radio broadcasting marketplace. Morning drive time fell between 15 percent and 20 percent. Its low response rates remained troubling (Klaassen, 2005).

Some sensed a storm brewing between Nielsen's LPM and Arbitron's PPM. On the face of it, the PPM seemed closer to the holy grail of research because it was passive, single-source, and mobile. The LPM, by comparison, was a remote-like device meant to do away with the error-prone handwritten diaries, but hardly a technology of the future. Competition may have made a better service but, in reality, the difficulty and cost of facing an entrenched system and the industry's unwillingness to support two systems had prevented serious competition.

By 2003, Arbitron was ready to commercialize the PPM after completing its test in Philadelphia but was stopped dead in its tracks when the radio industry insisted on new rounds of test, further research, an economic impact study, and a second test market. The results of the Philadelphia test created additional industry concerns. Of the media measured by the PPM, radio received the least positive news. Except for a decline of 15 percent to 20 percent in morning drive, radio changed little. By comparison, encoded TV and cable ratings were up 41 percent and 118 percent, respectively (Trigoboff, 2003). The PPM was believed to skew viewing toward entertainment programming, but still, with its inclusion of out-of-home viewing and listening, it promised to boost sports content significantly.

Though Houston was planned to be the second test market, Arbitron's people meter service had not yet been accredited by the Media Ratings Council nor did the PPM enjoy the broad base of broadcaster and agency support it received in Philadelphia. Still, Arbitron forged ahead to Houston. If successful by 2006, Arbitron anticipated that Houston would be the first currency PPM market. In Houston, Arbitron planned to use recruitment methods and techniques developed by both Nielsen and Arbitron to raise response rates to 41 percent with current TV measurement systems. It also planned to include estimates for live versus time-shifted viewing and quantitative measures of the out-of-home audience.

Despite the delays, radio advertisers and agencies were ready to bring radio measurement into the twenty-first century by scrapping the diary and deploying the PPM, but the main costs of this new system largely were to be borne by the networks and stations. Arbitron began meetings with networks and stations to discuss costs that were likely to be 40 percent to 65 percent higher in an industry whose revenue had shrunk and was beholden to the shareholders of Wall Street. Alarmed by this increase, radio companies balked.

At the urging of the Radio Station Advisory Council, Arbitron agreed in early March 2006 to wait for accreditation in Houston from the Media Ratings Council before "discontinuing" the diary and making the PPM the currency system. Though the CEOs of some of the largest radio broadcasters were unhappy with the new passive PPM, most had signed multi-year contracts for PPM ratings. However, a growing chorus of complaints led to further complications for Arbitron. This placed Arbitron in further jeopardy as the time it took for the Media Ratings Council to accredit the PPM could be used by a rival, such as Nielsen, to test and implement its methods in the United States.

Revolts, Investigations, and Uprisings

Further complicating the transition away from the diary, Clear Channel, the national's largest radio broadcaster led a charge against the PPM, refusing to renew its contract and putting out an invitation in search of alternative technology. Clear Channel had become the largest radio broadcaster through Congressional relaxation of ownership limits. A key reason for the delay was to force Arbitron to develop a new radio market clustering system that created a means of compiling ratings based on advertisers' actual trading areas rather than the older station geography. Other key industry concerns were the problems in getting participants to carry and dock the PPM, as sample declines affected the validity of the ratings data (a problem hopefully resolved by 2011 with the implementation of the PPM 360, a wireless device). Clear Channel's electronic media measurement evaluation committee put out a request for proposals, opening the door to two potential competitors: Media Audit/Ipsos, which used a smart cell phone–based technology, and MRI/Eurisko's Media Monitor, which used a similar portable meter device. The Clear Channel backlash put Arbitron in a perilous position as Clear Channel accounted for more than 20 percent of its business at the cost of more than $50 million per year, and some feared that as Clear Channel goes, so goes the industry.

However, Clear Channel was not the only problem Arbitron faced. As with the LPM, criticism arose regarding the sampling process, accusing the company of substandard sampling, which led to significant underrepresentation of minority radio audiences. Arbitron had decided to "go live" with its PPM service in Houston, TX and dozens of other individual markets without receiving MRC accreditation. Critics of this decision pointed to the fact that Arbitron's executive bonuses were tied to the commercialization of the service (*Radio Business Report*, 2008; Napoli, 2010).

The result was that the PPM was met with resistance not only from within the radio industry but within public interest and advocacy groups. These included the National Association of Black-Owned Broadcasters, the Spanish Radio Association, the Association of Hispanic Advertising Agencies, the NAACP, and the Minority Media and Telecommunications Council, which demanded that Arbitron delay its roll out. Some minority broadcasters refused to encode their broadcasts with the PPM signal in markets where they accounted for a significant portion of the radio audience, requiring Arbitron to seek court orders to require these broadcasters to encode their broadcasts with the necessary signals for PPM measurement (Bachman, 2009a; Supreme Court of the State of New York, 2010; Napoli, 2010).

As with the LPM, concerns about the potential impact on minority audiences led to governmental involvement with accusations of the abuse of monopoly power and concerns regarding the diversity implications of the new measurement system. In September 2008, the New York City Council issued a resolution calling upon the FCC to open an investigation into the PPM service. At the state level, the attorneys general of New York, New Jersey, Florida, and Maryland filed lawsuits against Arbitron for fraud and civil rights violations that led Arbitron to file its own preemptive lawsuit. The FCC opened an inquiry into whether more formal action was necessary and, in June 2009, the Oversight and Government Reform Committee of the U.S. House of Representatives initiated an investigation (Napoli, 2010). However, by 2010, many of the suits had been withdrawn after Arbitron made changes to its recruitment methodology to address concerns by minority groups.

As with television, radio broadcasters increasingly were being held to tough return-on-investment standards, largely due to the influence of the transparency of the Internet as an advertising medium. Many agencies and advertisers were concerned that Clear Channel's request for proposals had slowed down the necessary change and were perplexed at its resistance. They were critical of broadcasters as they waited for a new technology to get up to speed. Though stations had balked at the costs, advertisers worried about the delay, given the increasing fractionalization of business. Some saw this delay as a sign that business was reticent to change. Radio was no longer a must-buy medium, and some feared that the length of time it took for the industry to find the money necessary for a 65-percent increase would lead advertisers and agencies to pull the plug on radio and find more accountable media (Bachman, 2005).

In March 2006, Nielsen announced it was pulling out of the PPM development partnership. Nielsen CEO president Susan Whiting, issued a statement that the NMR had decided not to exercise its option to partner with Arbitron in using the PPM. Instead, Nielsen announced it would use a "portfolio" approach, a combination of LPMs with DVR data and expand its national sample to include the out-of-home audience. This came as a blow to Arbitron. In a letter to its clients, NMR stated that it believed that television would change more in the next five years than in the previous fifty. Digitalization, time-shifting, Internet video, mobile media, interactive TV, and home networking would all have a profound impact on the way that TV was consumed and therefore on the way it was measured (*Marketing Vox*, 2006). According to Susan Whiting, " Our clients have, in effect, told us to follow the video as it moves to platforms including time-shifted systems, the Internet, cell phones and other mobile devices." Whiting commented that a one-size-fits-all measurement system is not the approach for a currency in television's markets. Nielsen cited the following reasons for its decisions. First, the PPM's exposure-based definition of the audience produced larger and unexplained TV viewership. Second, the PPM would be more expensive than the method it replaced, with the joint venture requiring the TV industry to bear most of the cost and effectively subsidize radio. It would require increasing payments to sample participants and hiring more field representatives to contact households in person, which Whiting said had not been anticipated in the joint venture (Loftus, 2006). Despite having already sunk millions into the Boston demonstration, on March 2006, NMR decided to quit the joint PPM venture with Arbitron, dashing hopes for single-source multi-media data. Arbitron stock slid more than 11 percent at the announcement that Nielsen had determined to "adopt a portfolio strategy, using a variety of methods to measure the at home and out-of-home audience rather than the PPM." Nielsen stated that it believed that the two technologies could coexist.

Arbitron was disappointed but not surprised and, according to Pierre Bouvard, president of sales and marketing, Arbitron would not go head to head with Nielsen in TV ratings. According to Bouvard, "although the PPM may not be the currency, it provides out-of-home and cross-measures of media that no other service provides. We now have two companies with two approaches" (Bachman and Consoli, 2006). In other words, the PPM offered a distinct advantage that Nielsen's current system lacked. David Erst, vice president of futures and technologies for Initiative Inc., remarked that "we need a ratings currency but increasingly this isn't the only type of information we need. There is an increasing reliance on other data. Ratings are like the speedometer, but now we are developing the instrument panel" (Bachman, 2006).

So, after two years of telling the media industry that it needed to partner with Nielsen to deploy its PPM for local radio and TV ratings, Arbitron changed its position and began to outline the bare bones of an alternative strategy for generating revenue without Nielsen.

Advertisers' and agencies' reaction to Nielsen's decision to quit the joint venture was incredulity. Few saw the logic in Nielsen's decision. For its part, Nielsen stated that after five years and millions of dollars, questions remained about using the PPM as the soul of our TV viewing. Though Whiting had cited "unexplained increases in TV viewership" in her rationale for abandoning a project in which it had spent millions, David Poltrack, president of research for CBS, commented,

> What they say is unexplained, I say is missed TV viewing by Nielsen. There are differences in the techniques, and we don't know which is correct. Intuitively, when you look at the different levels in viewing, you can come up with reasons why viewing is higher.

According to Roger Bare, vice president/general manager of KHWB, a Tribune WB affiliate in Houston,

> Nielsen would be wise to make every effort to advance accurate measurement of TV viewing. The most exciting part about this new technology is that it requires so little of the consumers. The biggest asset this test will have is comparing fatigue rates with the Local People Meter. Asking a family to punch in and out every time they change channels or leave a room is a lot to ask.
>
> (Bachman, 2004a)

PPM Accreditation

In March 2007, Philadelphia became the first live PPM market, and the Media Ratings Council announced accreditation of the PPM device for the Houston market. Despite this, Clear Channel still refused to have Arbitron encode its signals, but Arbitron planned to use audio matching—which allowed the PPM to identify uuencoded signals to its service. Media Audit/Ipsos had yet to conduct a field test for its smart cell phone-based service in the United States and stated it would not do so without the financial support of the industry. In the meantime, Arbitron has sued Media Audit/Ipsos for patent infringement and won, leaving Arbitron as the only viable company left standing.

What Changes the PPM Wrought?

All measurement methods are operationalized through first defining exactly what they measure about the media user. Both the diary and the people meter used by Nielsen were active measures of listening and/or viewing. According to Nielsen's National People Meter, the standard definition of the TV audience was when a viewer pushes a button on a remote-like device to indicate both viewing and demographic makeup in a sample drawn to be representative of the United States population. Therefore, this method required active participation by sample members.

In the Top 50 markets, a viewer was someone who entered a station's call letters, channel numbers, or programs in a diary with a start and stop time, integrated with an independent and passive record of set tuning recorded by set meter. By comparison, this measurement of demographic viewing was active, but this active measurement was factored by a passive independent record of household set recording, thereby adjusting for possible problems with sample participation.

The PPM changed the definition of a media consumer from one who actively records to one of passive listening as a measure of exposure. It could even establish whether viewers left during commercial breaks because the code signal was interrupted. Furthermore, the PPM expanded the boundaries of media consumption because it passively registered media inside and outside the home—exposure in bars, airports, health clubs, hotels, hospitals, offices, and the like. Industry believed that at least twenty of this out-of-home viewing were young adults, the most desired of advertisers segments. The PPM not only established a new standard for measuring for radio and TV audiences, it measured ads in movie theaters, DVDs, video games, and MP3 files. This was a real breakthrough in measuring the multi-media audience.

As a result, it was no surprise that this technique produced numbers that were substantially higher than the Nielsen meter/diary or LPMs. It was measuring something very different. Active measures that involve respondents provided better indicators of whether they actually viewed or listened (as opposed to simply standing close by), but passive measures capture a station's share of the audience better because they eliminate respondent error.

Another issue that raters needed to consider was validity. Which operational definition best fits what we think of as viewing/listening? Certainly, the diary adjusted to the levels of the set meter diary was considered to be closer to an idea of viewing and listening than someone standing within range of an audible signal does. Because the PPM's definition of viewing was more inclusive, critics argued that it tended to count, as viewers, more people who do not watch the commercial.

Conversely, the PPM did a far better job than the meter/diary because of known problems with the diary. Diaries response rates were considered lower as they required active participation and were subject to the many errors associated with memory. Diaries were known to overstate broadcast network programs compared to cable programs simply due to memory bias. Because the PPM captured viewing outside the home and from a variety of media sources, all exposures received equal treatment, a huge advantage in a digital era.

Radio advertising had settled into a role as a high-frequency, low-cost-per-thousand add-on to other media. However, the PPM offered a reinterpretation of this old selling adage as testing would hopefully reveal that it also offered reach. In marketing, reach trumped frequency. Frequency (contacting one consumer three times with a message) was not as good as reach (contacting three consumers with one message) because one consumer was less likely to need the product than any of the three would be. Media fragmentation had contributed to making frequency a kind of crabgrass. National advertising dollars largely went to reach for television and used radio as a frequency medium. If radio were seen as a reach medium, the list of stations used by advertisers would increase, and the costs still be lower than television. The PPM's exposure-based definition could only broaden radio's listening audience as diaries relied on recording by discrete program units, which had seen its heyday by the sixties with the switch to news, information, and music formatting.

The radio industry eagerly awaited the PPM technology that they hoped would increase their bottom line. When a Forrester Study concluded that the industry could gain $414 million a year with the adoption of the electronic technology, it seemed to pave the way for the possible deployment out of the PPM (Bachman, 2005).

Competitors in Radio Ratings

Though having decided not to pursue joint deployment of the PPM, by 2008 Nielsen moved aggressively to challenge Arbitron's long-held dominance in the radio measurement business. Sensing an opportunity to reenter radio measurement due to the dissatisfied stations groups such as Clear Channel and Infinity, it announced a new service for radio using diaries, which had listeners use stickers rather than hand-writing their reports. It claimed that its sticker-based diaries delivered more accurate data than Arbitron diaries, which required writing. Nielsen was adding cell phone-only households to its sample to improve data for eighteen- to thirty-four-year-olds and claimed that its survey was more representative of cell phone-only households (Goetzl, 2011). The industry realized that Nielsen not only was planning to rate the fifty-one small markets for Cumulus and Clear Channel but was looking at the bigger markets as well, including the ones now using Arbitron's PPM. Some saw the sticker diary program to be used by Nielsen and Cumulus as another Trojan horse for plans to deploy an electronic device. To no-one's surprise, Nielsen announced development of its own version of the PPM technology, called the *Go Meter*, which had been in development for some time and offered a technological design similar to Arbitron's PPM device. Nielsen was positioned to compete with Arbitron in dozens of midsized markets and planned to introduce an "affinity metric" to indicate which stations viewers liked to allow more differentiation from competitors, moving the audience away from a simple commodity definition. By June 2009, Nielsen had added Cumulus, ESPN Radio, Maverick Media, and Clear Channel to its portfolio. Though Arbitron had moved to PPM in larger markets, smaller and medium-size markets still used the diary. Many stations signed up for a portion of the portfolio as an experiment while still using Arbitron for the remainder.

Thus, some believed Nielsen to be in preparation for an all-out attack on Arbitron's PPM strongholds in the top markets. Nielsen's national roll out of the Go Meter for radio could be subsidized by its TV service, thereby leading to economies of scale by being able to spread the cost across multiple media. Because Nielsen was also exploring streaming video and audio measurement, there seemed to be a number of ways to monetize the deployment of this PPM system. However, by 2010, Nielsen decided to exit its radio business just days after news came that Clear Channel had reached a six-year service agreement with Arbitron to receive PPM ratings. Although Nielsen declined to elaborate on its decision to exit the U.S. radio-ratings business, some media observers suggested that the exit was hardly a coincidence: a company the size of Nielsen, it just made no sense to handle only fifty-one markets (*BMI News*, 2011).

Management Shake-up

By 2009, Arbitron had suffered because its service had been put on hiatus for nine months due to sampling and accreditation concerns. Although it had fourteen PPM markets and planned to add nineteen more in 2009, it had received accreditation in only two thus far. In January 2009, Arbitron announced that Stephen Morris, long-time CEO, had stepped down and would be replaced by Michael Skarzynski. The change had come after a tumultuous and volatile two-year period when Arbitron had battled to gain acceptance for its new PPM. Arbitron, a publicly held research firm, depended on shareholders backing to support its aggressive expansion plans, so the revolt of two of its largest customers, Clearwater and Cumulus, meant a loss of millions. Furthermore, Arbitron had failed to diversify beyond its core radio audience measurement business. Skarzynki was tapped because, though having no experience in radio measurement, he had been responsible for the restructuring and global expansion of a privately held software company, Iptivia (Mandese, 2009d). However, in January 2010, Karzynski resigned as president-CEO when the board determined that he had violated a company policy in a matter unrelated to financial performance, to be replaced by William Kerr, a board member. Skarzynski's resignation was due to providing false testimony about the effectiveness of the PPM system during Congressional hearings (*BMI News*, 2011). Later reports indicated that Skarzynski stated—falsely, according to the company—that he attended a working group in Maryland that dealt with training listeners to use the devices (Hughes and Lublin, 2010). Whoever the CEO, Arbitron was undoubtedly planning for the possible coming battle with Nielsen.

However, by 2010, Arbitron's deal with Clear Channel Radio, worth an estimated $540 million that accounted for 19 percent of Arbitron revenue, together with Nielsen's exit, meant a victory for the PPM. Furthermore in 2009, the MRC announced accreditation of the PPM technology. Launched in 2007, the PPM had replaced the paper diary methodology in forty-three of the top fifty markets and was scheduled for currency in five more by 2010 (Stine, 2010). Despite early stumbles, the PPM seemed to have gained the respect of broadcasting and the advertising community and had become firmly entrenched as the next generation of radio measurement service.

6

ESTABLISHING THE DIGITAL CURRENCY FOR INTERNET AUDIENCES

The Software Meter Initiative

Search for an Internet Ratings Currency

During the 1990s, the economic model employed so successfully by the television networks was transferred to the Internet industry through the development of sites known as *portals*, which, like the TV and cable networks, conglomerated content. A key part of this emerging Internet business model was the rise of a system of audience measurement to identify and track its users. Wall Street investors, banner, pop-up and pop-under advertisers, domains, and Web property owners desired such information in a variety of breakdowns.

The primary methodology that developed during this period—panel-based software data—was rooted in a model provided by the traditional media to give companies and advertisers comparability of data across media. In fact, Doug McFarland, president of Jupiter Media Metrix (JMM), until 2002 the dominant Internet ratings service, criticized Nielsen NetRatings for "shoehorning the Internet into an outdated model" (as quoted in Oppelaar, p. S34). According to McFarland, "We [Jupiter Media Metrix] are in essence, children of the Net. We grew up with the medium. When Nielsen views the world, everything looks like a TV screen" (Oppelaar, 2000; Barlas, 1998).

Though, at first, it appeared that Internet ratings would be shaped to match their sister ratings in radio and TV, similar to what had happened with the development of cable ratings, soon it became clear that the reverse would also be true. The transparency and engagement offered by Internet ratings would also shape radio and TV measurement and thereby put pressure on traditional ratings services to offer the same level of transparency and engagement.

The computer's ability to track a user's every on-line move made it possible to collect far more transparent information about Internet users than has been the norm, with traditional media audiences placing pressure on traditional ratings services to change. Internet ratings providers tracked every link that their thousands of volunteer panelists followed as they surfed the Web, recording how long they spent at a given site and whether they clicked on banner ads, those small rectangular advertisements that appear on all sorts of Web pages and vary considerably in appearance and subject matter, but all shared a basic function: if clicked, Internet browsers went to the advertiser's Web site.

An example of this demand for more transparency for traditional media ratings was the switch in 2005 from program ratings to what were known as C3 ratings, the commercial rating including three days of DVR playback. Advertisers had long clamored for commercial ratings, but the transparency of Internet ratings, together with the growing use of the DVR, provided the push for their fruition. Pioneered by TiVo in 1999, the digital video recorder (DVR) had led a revolution in the TV industry. Although it was not without predecessors, such as the remote control and the videotape recorder, it offered viewers more control including the ability to skip commercials and time shift programming and was therefore considered more of a threat to advertising. The term DVR included stand-alone set-top boxes, such as TiVo, as well as digital boxes provided by major cable companies such as Time Warner. DVRs advanced the traditional VCR because they no longer required a tape. Users were given more flexibility in programming such as recording first run only and recording two programs simultaneously. Since introduced, the device slowly gained in popularity and had become mainstream, reaching four in ten household by 2011 or 38 percent of all U.S. households (Brassine, 2011). Beginning in December 2005, the Nielsen Company adjusted viewership ratings measurement by having diary panel members account for time-shifted viewing and by having their set-top meter track time-shifted viewing. Now Nielsen provided three sets of numbers—the number of people who watch live, the number of people who watch live plus the same day, and the number of people who watch live or within seven days. These ratings are currently reported as C-3 (commercial ratings plus three days of DVR playback) ratings, but Nielsen was considering a move to C-1 (commercial plus 1 day of playback) rating due to pressure by advertisers.

Even the Internet itself was undergoing shifts in business models. During the nineties, the dominant business model had been a trend toward "portalopoly" (Hu, 1998) and an emphasis on mass circulation data. In this view, the Internet was understood as "real estate," what some called the "portopoly" model, similar to the real estate game of *Monopoly*. An early gold rush to acquire property and the desire to see which sites would accumulate the most traffic resulted in pioneer Internet ratings services using visitor circulation or unique visitors, over a thirty-day period, as the basic traffic measurement in the portopoly model to compare possible advertising sites. However, after the dotcom crash at the turn of the century, different business models had emerged such as search advertising, an interest in monetizing social networks, and more targeted return on investment.

Advertisers realized that, unlike TV or radio, the user's engagement and response to advertising were easier to track and follow and soon led to other business models other than simply pulling in high traffic numbers, such as the thirty-day unique visitor. Advertisers began to demand that sites prove that those visitors were not only looking at the ads but acting on them. This meant that more and more advertising was priced on performance-based criteria. Because some sites, such as gaming, news, and chat sites, were known for users who did not interact with ads, advertisers realized that reach and frequency by themselves no longer indicated value and began to search for new models that offered more transparent return on investment (Appelman, 2000).

Initially, the industry distinguished between audience measurement firms who used panel-based propriety methods (the topic of this chapter), and Web analytic firms, who collected census data from actual Web sites. Although this distinction continues, the desire for more transparent data has resulted in services such as Comcore Media Metrix and Nielsen NetRatings, further blurring this distinction as they moved toward a hybrid model.

In addition to audience measurement and Web analytic firms, a few additional firms used traditional audience survey methods, but these were typically done as offshoots of studies of other media, such as magazines and radio. Audience measurement and Web analytics were the yin and yang of on-line metric systems, different and opposing forces. Though my focus is on the former, panel-based audience measurement firms, it is helpful to understand the difference.

Panel-based Audience Measurement Services

As of this writing, the gold standards or benchmarks in the Internet ratings panel-based marketplace are Nielsen NetRatings and comScore Media Metrix. These services use data collected from global panels where thousands of volunteers agree to download tracking software to create online metrics. Because the barriers to entry into this marketplace are still relatively low, smaller companies such as HitWise, Alexa, and Compete have entered the market eschewing panels in favor of tagging Web pages with small pieces of code, called cookies, and Quanticast, which uses both panel and tags. When users visit a site, the servers log them in but, since many users delete their cookies, the larger companies accuse them of inaccuracy (Klaassen, 2007). Few of these smaller services made money, but they charged for consulting services to help increase value of a customer's inventory. Due to these different data collection methods, no shared standards existed across companies. This led to a great deal of friction as standardized metrics were important to help evaluate competition and to determine advertising rates. In other words, similar to media ratings, Internet ratings were used to compare and buy various Web sites. In addition to site performance, internet ratings could be used to determine audience demographics and generalized traffic trends as well as search terms in an era of search advertising.

By comparison, Web analytic data were used for looking inward rather than looking outward. A company or advertisers could use it to help improve site effectiveness, for help in designing a site to attract certain desired demographics, and for understanding what keywords were more effective in driving traffic to a site. For example, though audience measurement data could be used to determine whether a competitor was gaining ground on a site or search term, Web analytic data could be used to determine how best to design a site or search term to be more effective (Phillips, 2007; TV Bureau of Advertising, n.d.).

Panel-based measurements tracked Internet users' habits by developing and recruiting a panel that was representative of the population of Web users. Once a panel had been identified, measurement firms installed software or a software meter on their computers to electronically and passively record usage and automatically transmit the data back to a central office for tabulation. Compared to the expensive hardwiring of TV's set-top boxes, recruited panel members installed (by downloading) monitoring software. This technique allowed audience measurement firms to identify the specific individuals who used the computer and thereby to provide demographic data. For example, Nielsen NetRatings recruited panels using a proprietary methodology—user-prompting software—that combined a random digit dial panel with an online-recruited panel that was weighted by demographic and behavioral weights. Because all sites were measured by the same yardstick, inter-site comparisons could be made for rankings. Knowing the demographic details of users in the sample allowed audience composition calculations. Companies then projected the usage and habits of the U.S. Internet population based on the panel data.

Census or Server-based Web Analytical Audience Measurement

By comparison, Web analytic firms were more numerous and included such firms as Coremetrics, Webtrends, Unica, Visual Sciences, Omniture, and Google. Census- or server-based audience measurement provided measurements directly from a Web site's server, sometimes known as *log file analysis* because it entailed a study of a server's log files. Each time a file was requested of a Web site, the server recorded the request and its actions in a log file. Log files measured the number of hits to a site and page requests and how long visitors remained on a site.

Two methods were used to track log file traffic: by placing a Java script tag on the pages of the Web site to send the traffic activity back to the analytical firm that then produced reports on activity and traffic and by allowing the Web master to upload log files from the Web site into a software program that produced summary reports. The key strength of this method was that it tracked 100 percent of site traffic, or provided what was known as census data, of the activity on any Web site.

While providing a wealth of detail, known in the industry as *more granular data*, a number of problems made log file information misleading. Typically, the industry used Internet protocol addresses (such as www…), cookies, and page-embedded measurement markers to indicate whether a user was logged onto a server, but a problem with this method was a property of the computer known as *caches*. Caches were temporary storage areas for frequently accessed data that were hidden. As a result, log file figures could also be misleading because they included internal traffic that resulted in duplication when the same person visited a site more than once or when the same user accessed the Internet from multiple computers.

An additional problem was that traffic data could be inflated due to a user's cookie deletion. Small text-files, known as *cookies*, were stored on the user's computer to collect data that identified the user. Users frequently deleted cookies, rejecting them as part of their Web browser settings. Because cookies identified unique users, cookie deletion could cause the user to be counted numerous times, as a new cookie was added each time a user visited a site, thus inflating overall traffic.

Determining user geography also was a challenge in that all Internet protocol addresses had to be traced to country of origin and was costly, with as high as 40 percent of traffic unresolved geographically. Another challenge was sorting out robots and spiders, who automatically surfed the Internet to gather information on various sites. Robots could generate significantly higher numbers of log file traffic and were often disguised. Though custom file logs could be made, this information was typically confidential, and therefore comparison across competitors could not be made (Coffey, 2001).

Another critical problem was that Web analytics offered site-centric over audience-centric measures. In other words, they did not allow site owners, advertisers, and agencies to put a face and age, gender, and household income on Internet surfers. The number, age, and gender of surfers' eyeballs on a Web site correlated directly to compensation for Internet real estate, just as ratings did for television. This information was used by the Internet industry to set advertising rates. However, unlike their old media counterpart, Web raters offered their clients data on what advertisements visitors clicked on and what they purchased on each site, a factor leading to increasing advertiser interest in a new currency based on return-on-investment.

The Hybrid Model

Quanticast, a newer arrival in the field of Internet measurement, developed a hybrid model of audience measurement and Web analytics by collecting panel data and page tags and actual site data, when were then merged. This model, which merged a panel's demographic data with data directly from a subscriber's Web site, was one toward which the other major audience measurement services were moving. For example, in 2007, the Nielsen Company, now owned by Valcon Acquisitions, acquired the remaining interest in Web analytical company Buzz Metrics, and Internet rating partner NetRatings. The two services were merged in 2008 to become Nielsen Online. Also in 2008, Nielsen Online announced the first release of VideoCensus, the first syndicated online video measurement service to combine panel and server research methodologies to measure video-on-demand information. The goal was to combine TV ratings with on-line ratings to eventually produce what Nielsen called "Extended Screen" service by 2011. Similarly, comScore Media Metrix had released a service integrating browser-based research and user panels, a service known as Media Metrix 360, a panel-centric hybrid that bridged panel-based and Web site server-based metrics.

Survey-based Measurement

Beside panels and server-based measurement, a third type of measurement was used by companies who used survey-based methods. These were generally companies whose primary measurement efforts were for other media. For example, Media Audits and Scarborough originally measured newspapers and radio but added Internet usage to their surveys. Surveys from a sample of users drew a sample of Internet users and then queried the respondents through standard survey methods, typically based on random digit dialing telephone surveys. The advantage was that detail, such as age, gender, income, and geography could be captured. The problems in this type of method were over-claiming, similar to branding, which occurred for well-known properties, and under-claiming occurred for less well-known sites. Other sites were under-reported due to social desirability, such as adult content, and others with perceived attractiveness reported. Finally, usage estimates were based on recall, thus the list of problems associated with memory when asked whether they had visited a site in the last thirty days. The survey-based method was used primarily as an adjunct to other media surveys, so it is included here as a point of reference.

Because the focus here is on audience measurement, the remainder of this chapter will be centered on the first group—the panel-based companies with proprietary software that are now including more hybrid methods. The key rivals in this market are Nielsen NetRatings and comscore Media Metrix. It was these pioneers who developed a system of metrics to measure the Internet audiences that allowed them to be compared to traditional TV ratings.

The Battle to Measure the Internet

The battle to become the household name in Internet ratings was initially fought between four-year-old Media Metrix and a joint venture of Nielsen Media Research and NetRatings, known as Nielsen NetRatings. Nielsen's Media Research, the foremost TV rater, was slow to enter into the Internet ratings fray. This delay was because of an intense battle it was waging against four potential entrants into its TV people meter market (Buzzard, 2002). Because of its later entry, the door to the market was wide open for pioneer Internet ratings services, such as Media Metrix, Relevant Knowledge, and NetRatings.

Crucial to traditional analysis of technological innovation and its relationship to market structure has been some kind of first-mover advantage. The first firm to complete its research and development successfully received a patent that allowed it to monopolize the relevant product market more or less permanently. However, in the case of Internet ratings, as we shall see, Nielsen was not a first-mover in terms of development of the technology—downloadable software—that monitored surfer activity on the Internet.

Instead, Nielsen found it more profitable to pursue what economists call a "fast- second policy" allowing smaller pioneers a modest inroad before responding aggressively. Rather than taking a leadership role in innovation, Nielsen followed the business policy, in many instances, of letting smaller firms initiate new forms of technology and methods and then entering when its own research and development produced a virtual knock-off of rival products and methods and when it could use its economic muscle to merge with more experienced rivals, enabling it to gain their advantages. As Scherer notes, market-dominating firms tend to be slow in developing new products but "roar back like lions" when smaller rivals challenge them (Scherer, 1992; Buzzard, 2002, 2003). Competition from rivals was the driving force behind many of the technological and methodological changes made: neither Nielsen nor its clients were willing to upset the status quo without an external threat.

Just as in other markets, in the world of Internet measurement, having multiple services made for lower prices and better products, but it also made for conflicting traffic figures. As Eileen Meehan has suggested concerning TV Measurement, having multiple contradictory ratings for any single time slot complicates and disrupts the routine of buying and selling (Meehan, 1990). In fact, this disruption had predisposed networks and advertisers to accept a monopoly. Ralph DeMuccio, research manager at AltaVista, had put it this way: "It's like having 3 watches on that all have a different time. You don't know what the hell time it is" (as quoted in *CCN Disclosure*, 2000). As a result, the driving engine of the TV ratings industry had traditionally been a combination of both monopoly and competition. As economists Scherer and Ross note,

> Much theory and empirical evidence suggests that the most successful market structure for rapid technical progress is a subtle blend of competition and monopoly, with more emphasis on the former than the latter and with the role of monopolistic elements diminishing when rich technological opportunities exist.
>
> (Scherer and Ross, 1990)

Internet Ratings Pioneer: Media Metrix

The oldest pioneer service for Internet ratings was Media Metrix (originally known as PC Meter). Many in the industry felt it was destined to be the industry leader as it accounted for 85 percent of the advertising dollar before the dotcom crash. Jupiter Media Metrix (JMM) was owned and managed by Todd Johnson, president of NPD Group, a marketing service. The origin of what was originally known in 1994 as PC Meter was when Steve Coffey, heading up the advanced research and development team at NPD Group, had the idea of creating a metering device that could measure actual software usage in computers. Previously, purchase data were among the only figures available to estimate software ownership and usage.

A year later, Coffey and his team began installing meters on panelists' computers to monitor and project usage of those computers. This invention would be critical in building what would be one of the Internet's most influential companies and pave the way for the growth of e-commerce and e-marketing. Not only did the meter indicate what software was used, it had the capability to specify the Web pages users visited. JMM patented its meter device that measured actual software usage in computers (material provided to author by JMM, 2000).

With the meter patent in place, the NPD Group launched PC Meter as a separate company in 1995, to be renamed Media Metrix in 1997, to reflect its expanded coverage of digital media. The earliest subscribers of Media Metrix's syndicated reports included leading New York advertising agencies and media companies, who had learned about its products through promotions at industry conferences and trade shows.

Media Metrix pursued a path of technological innovation and aggressive expansion and soon developed new generations of its patented metering methodology. The software technology worked with PC operating systems and Internet browsers to monitor passively *all* user activity, including the World Wide Web, proprietary online and e-mail services, software applications, and hardware ownership and usage in real-time, click-by-click, page-by-page, minute-by-minute. The company offered monthly, weekly, and daily data collection. Moreover, Media Metrix captured in-depth demographics for each sample member, including age, gender, household size and composition, income, education level, geographic location, and more, allowing user behavior to be linked with product demographic characteristics (*Dot.com*, 1998).

In addition to its own innovations and organic growth, a key strategy for Media Metrix's continued leadership was to acquire and partner with other leading companies. In 1998, Media Metrix merged with Relevant Knowledge, the top Internet ratings competitor. Founded by two former executives from Turner Broadcasting, Relevant Knowledge added local market ratings and analysis of fast-breaking events in real time, increasing the speed of delivery for Media Metrix's numbers, which resulted in overnight reports rather than the previously used monthly mail-in diary. The merger ended a war between the two companies that previously criticized each other in the press for both the size and quality of their samples and the timeliness of their data.

In February 1999, Media Metrix forged a strategic research alliance with McKinsey & Company to develop an understanding of on-line consumer behavior and its implications for e-businesses. In October 1999, Media Metrix acquired AdRelevance, an innovator and pioneer in Internet advertising measurement technology. In July 2000, Media Metrix bought Jupiter Communication to become Jupiter Media Metrix (JMM) to add more analysis to its reports and to better position itself to compete with Nielsen Net Ratings (Kerschbaumer, 2002).

To protect its position from competitors using the same or similar software, JMM soon filed infringement suits against key competitors. It was successful in forcing a two-year upstart, PC Data, from the field and had filed two additional suits—against Paris-based NetValue, a company owned by Taylor Nelson Sofres (a European research leader) and against Nielsen NetRatings (Thompson, 1999).

Enter Nielsen

Another major competitor into the field, NetRatings, was a spin-off of Hitachi, Ltd and was the only service to provide lifestyle and consumption information that helped advertisers to target niche groups. However, it was criticized for its method of soliciting panel members from Web banner ads. In November 1998, just two weeks after the Media Metrix–Relevant Knowledge merger, NetRatings teamed with Nielsen Media Research to form Nielsen NetRatings. The merger helped NetRatings overcome its weakness in panel size and selection (originally 3,500 compared to 40,000 for JMM) by offering the benefits of Nielsen's considerable experience in audience panels to the newly combined service. The partnering also offered NetRatings an ability to launch a global service, eRatings, as Nielsen NetRatings had earlier joined with A. C Nielsen to invest $500 million over the next two years to get a service running in thirty-three countries.

With the competition reduced to two main competitors, Jupiter Media Metrix buckled under the financial pressure of the 2001 dotcom crash. In 2000, JMM recorded revenues of $143 million compared to Nielsen NetRatings' $20 million. However, by 2001, the situation had reversed, with Nielsen NetRatings making $335 million to JMM's $20 million (Joyce and Sanders, 2001). When the NASDAQ sell-off hit in early 2000, followed by recession, many of Jupiter's dotcom clients went bust or pulled back. The dotcom meltdown resulted in a loss of 22 percent of its subscriber base, leading to a net loss of $48.2 million in 2001 (*Advertising Report*, 2001). In response, the company underwent major restructuring changes and changes in top management. In an effort to help bail out the troubled company, Todd Johnson loaned JMM a $25 million letter of credit. By late October, JMM struggled to remain afloat, having slashed operating expenses by $40 million and laying off 300 employees (*Advertising Report*, 2001). By 2002, JMM, the leading Internet audience measurement firm, itself unable to raise additional capital and having expanded too far and too fast, became a victim of the Internet bubble burst.

As its revenues dropped, JMM tried to merge with one-time rival Nielsen NetRatings. Nielsen NetRatings agreed to lend JMM $25 million to replace its letter of credit between Jupiter and Todd Johnson. The loan was considered crucial for JMM to last long enough to consummate the merger. Interestingly, JMM and Nielsen NetRatings had both been criticized for reporting widely disparate figures for the number of unique visitors to the same sites. With the merger, this problem would disappear. However, Nielsen NetRatings and JMM were forced to call off their $71.2 million merger agreement after federal trade officials raised concerns about the competitive impact of the merger, which consolidated much of the audience measurement business in the hands of Nielsen NetRatings (Joyce, 2002). Nielsen NetRating's purchase of JMM, and its control of A. C. Nielsen's eRatings and its international Internet ratings business would have streamlined Internet ratings into a single brand and created a *de facto* standard for the Internet. The merger would have effectively made the California-based Nielsen NetRatings the only player in audience measurement.

Though Nielsen NetRatings made overtures to acquire Media Metrix, it was comScore that eventually prevailed. In 2002, JMM sold the on-line audience measurement half of its business to rival comScore network for $1.5 million, bringing the troubled Internet firm a step closer to complete dismantling. The Reston-based comScore had entered the on-line metrics fray in 2001 after developing a marketing partnership with DoubleClick. ComScore, like Media Metrix, measured site traffic but also offered tools to analyze Web surfers' buying and transactional behavior, using a panel of 1.5 million participants (Saunders, 2002; Hansell, 2002). In 2002, comScore Media Metrix released Media Metrix 2.0, a service that integrated its browser-based service with a syndicated panel recently acquired from Media Metrix. The acquisition allowed comScore to integrate Media Metrix's random digital dialing methodology, on which many traditional marketers insisted. Further, comScore changed its method of panel recruitment from paid users, which had limited its panel size (to approximately 60,000), to allowing panels to access the Internet for free in exchange for panel membership, leading to an increase of 1.5 million (*Electronic Information Report*, 2002). ComScore's syndicated audience measurement services were marketed under the comScore Media Metrix brand name and remained a major competitor to Nielsen NetRatings.

ComScore's purchase of JMM marked a final chapter in the history of the New York–based company, which had sold off $27 million of operating units amid a two-year shakeout in the Internet and technology industry. In June 2002, INT Media acquired the remainder of JMM's research business.

ComScore Media Metrix also completed several other strategic acquisitions. In 2004 and 2005, comScore acquired Q2 Brand Intelligence and Survey Site, both leading providers of custom survey research and consulting services to Fortune 1000 companies. In 2008, using proceeds from its successful Internet protocol offering, the now public comScore completed the strategic acquisition of M:Metrics, the leading mobile measurement firm, expanding its portfolio of products and services to encompass the fast-emerging mobile media field in response to

Nielsen's acquisition of Telephia. These purchases prepared the service to measure Internet usages on mobile devices. In 2009, comScore unveiled Media Metrix 360 combining a two million global panel with Web site metrics in an effort to provide unified numbers consistent with server counts used for advertising payment and which some felt represented the web first true measurement currency (*Bloomberg News*, 2009;).

The economic incentives toward monopoly had been strong, encouraged by the advantages offered in reaching optimal size (through economies of scale, diversification, and vertical integration) and by folding the Internet ratings in a single currency rather than two sets of contradictory numbers. However, this time that incentive was foiled by anti-trust concerns.

Patent Wars Come to Web Measurement

However, the future was far from certain. In 2011, Nielsen filed a patent infringement suit against comScore (March 15) accusing it of violating five patents related to measuring and displaying online content, citing more than thirty products that it believed were in violation. Three of the patents mentioned in the lawsuit were granted to Nielsen in 2008 and 2009, whereas the other two were granted in 2000 and 2001 and were previously owned by JMM, which had previously used them to sue Nielsen. Nielsen had settled a suit in 2002 against JMM by paying them $15 million and acquiring the two patents as part of the settlement. Some saw this suit as Nielsen's effort to target almost every product that comScore offered. ComScore filed its own lawsuit about a week later, with similar accusations.

Many in the industry recognized that the dueling patent lawsuits were more than a routine spat over intellectual property. After all, the patent litigation suits had not been filed in a vacuum. For the two rivals, the litigation was rooted in the escalating battle for supremacy for the online audience measurement markets. They were but the latest chapter as the two companies competed for market share. Some industry observers saw this as Nielsen's attempt to best the competition through costly patent litigation rather than through better products or cost (Masnick, 2011). In the ratings business, as in other high-tech businesses, competition seemed not to be limited to innovation and enterprise. Rather, patent litigation had become a bigger part of business strategy for many firms. Patent infringement was a successful means to delay or inflict considerable financial damage on the competitors. This means that all competitors needed to acquire a considerable arsenal of patents in their portfolios. These patents were usually bought from companies that had failed or were about to close shop.

Both Nielsen and comScore employed online panels made up of Internet users who agreed to have their browsing monitored. However, the wildly divergent results brought protests from an industry whose rates were determined by traffic volume but preferred only one set of numbers. Having a competitive landscape had brought substantial improvement in transparency leading to an independent audit by the

Interactive Advertising Bureau and accreditation of their methods. The rivalry had spilled into mobile measurement in 2008, with comScore's $44 million purchase of M:Metrics about a year after Nielsen's purchase of mobile research business Telephia, Inc. Now the rivalry had prompted Nielsen to try a legal tactic to gain control of the marketplace. Nielsen was no stranger to patent litigation, having sued SageMetrics, Sane Solutions, and Visiual Sciences in 2005 and Omniture and Coremetrics in the past (Rick, 2011), but this was comScore's first suit.

As these suits demonstrated, building a great technology or information company required not only good ideas, execution, or good customer service but going on the offense with intellectual property. From social media to online video, a key strategy was to control all present and future patents. Indeed, some felt that the patent system was broken when government bodies opened the door to "business method" patents, which were defined, such as in Nielsen's claim of "owning patents that relating to measuring and display of online content," so broadly that all competition was eliminated by default. In addition, in opening the door to such broad definitions, the Supreme Court had begun such an onslaught of patent applications that the government was both unprepared to keep up with them and equally ill equipped to evaluate. Business and software patents were especially prone to problems of "abstraction" and obviousness. As a result, software patenting had been a major contributor to litigation explosion. Many legal scholars felt that the court had extended the patent system beyond its founding ideals in opening the door to these broad definitions, which ironically forced smaller innovators out of the market by allowing larger ones to adopt a business strategy of competing through patent litigation rather than product innovation and pricing. The average cost to litigate a patent lawsuit was $3 million to $10 million, giving bigger business the advantage over smaller ones (LawyersUSA, 2006).

In a second Supreme Court Decision, the Court further disadvantaged smaller competitors who sought to challenge larger competitors. The Supreme Court decision in EBay Inc. v. MercExchange, L.L.C., 547 U.S. 388 (2006) unanimously determined that an injunction should not be automatically issued based on a finding of patent infringement; smaller entities had less viability in commercializing their inventions with injunctions no longer an option. This placed them at a disadvantage to larger competitors, who with greater resources could copy inventions and elbow smaller players out of the market because an injunction provided the smaller company a chance to commercialize their products.

Internet and Privacy Concerns

Another issue for marketers and advertisers was the Internet privacy concerns raised by bills introduced into both the House and Senate, with the Obama administration and the FTC calling for some means of disclosure and control over how personal information is used on the Internet. The Commerce Department accused Facebook, Google, and other Web companies of not being up-front with customers about what information was collected and shared with advertisers. In the House of Representatives, Rep. Jackie Speier introduced a bill entitled "Do Not Track Me Online Act." A Congressional subcommittee opened hearings on issues around privacy and the Internet, often citing what was deemed the poster child for privacy violations, Google, especially after the WiFi scandal, where Google admitted collecting personal information and data for three years across the globe while its cars traveled through neighborhoods snapping pictures for its Street View program. The cars collected information from people's WiFis in their homes, leading the subcommittee chairmen to suggest that tey ought to drop the "G" from Google and call themselves "Oggle" (*Capitol Confidential*, 2011). Many Internet commerce sites and virally all social networking sites tracked the activity of their users, collecting personal information in the process. Some of the sites had serious security breaches in which users' private information was disclosed, with many users unaware that their personal information was collected and shared with others. Many major browsers were in the process of incorporating a means to block browsers' tracking, but cooperation for some, such as Firefox, depended on the cooperation of the Web site. An Internet privacy bill would require an expansion of FTC powers so that it could enforce any new provision. The Obama administration wanted a "privacy bill of rights" to prevent information being used without explicit permission and a "Do Not Track" policy implemented for Web browsers giving user control of the data online (Rashid, 2011). Any of these policies could have implications for Web-tracking services.

Developing a System of Web Metrics

The Sampling Process

Just as it does with TV viewers, Nielsen NetRatings and comScore Media Metrix recruited samples, called *panels*, of surfers who agreed to provide data on site visits, including when and how often the visits occurred. Although NetRatings (prior to its merger with Nielsen) originally recruited surfers from Web sites, it came under heavy criticism from industry because Web-recruited surfers tended to be heavier users, disproportionately male, and more experienced then typical Web users. After its merger with Nielsen, NetRatings used enumeration studies, a set of procedures for listing all members of a set in some definite sequence, to decide how to project data and how to weight their sample, to make it representative of the overall Internet population. The company also switched, following Nielsen's method, to a technique known as *random digit dialing t*o gather recruits (Oppelaar, 2000). Random digital dialing was based on the premise that because the telephone was the most pervasive technology in the home in the United States, phone numbers could be chosen at random and recruits asked to disclose information about their Internet usage and to load monitoring software on their computer. Both comScore Media Metrix and Nielsen NetRatings have now switched to a combination of panels with census- or server-based data to provide the demographic data and the level of transparency desired by advertisers.

Who Uses Audience Ratings Services?

The first Internet ratings clients included stock analysts and certain business or commercial Web sites. All were hungry for information about the people visiting their sites and eager to set themselves apart from the crowd. Ratings helped analysts value the various Web properties in hot stock markets, and these figures were used for buying and selling. Web sites sought to give advertisers as much information as possible about how many and who were the people viewing or surfing their sites. According to Beth Haggerty (1998), vice president of World Ad Sales at InfoSeek, "Viewership ratings and measurement will have a major impact on how the Internet is perceived as a mainstream media, to how Wall Street values Internet companies, to how our customers measure value of market investments" (quoted in *PR Newswire,* 1998).

The Dominant Business Model on the Internet: the Portal

The central metaphor, mentioned earlier, that illuminated the dominant business model that first operated on the Web was the board game *Monopoly*. Similar to *Monopoly*, Internet businesses, new and established ones, rushed to stake claims to Internet properties to own and rent valuable Internet real estate, a game some analysts call, as mentioned earlier, Portalopoly (Hu, 1998). The game was played like this: Internet companies raced to build sites (know as portals) that served as hubs or gateways to the larger Internet. Just as local TV stations served the needs of their local audiences until networks came along to aggregate content, traffic, and revenue, so portal sites served a similar function.

Portals functioned like the mass circulation magazines or TV networks: they were sites that meta-aggregated content and offered a range of services to be the home page for as many users as possible, thereby attracting more advertising revenue. These sites have evolved to include a laundry list of free services such as e-mail, news, and weather. Portals were viewed as the new shopping malls, town centers, and news hubs all rolled into one (Kawamoto, 1998). Many of today's portals were once known as innocuous search engines but matured into the new media conglomerates of the new millennium. The new media giants included companies such as Google, Yahoo, Excite, Lycos, AOL, Alta Vista, Snap and Infoseek, Facebook, and Twitter.

The Portal Business as One-stop Gateway to the Web

In this landscape, the name of the game was market share. Competition for eyeballs had led to a spate of acquisitions, partnerships, and distribution deals. Companies spent millions in the hope of eventually cashing in before the window of opportunity closed. Portal stocks soared, and companies, in turn, used this stock to acquire new properties.

In an effort to attract new Internet users, portals spent millions of dollars. The goal was to get users to designate a specific company's portal site as *the* "home page" on their browsers. Once that was done, the page was the first one seen on logging in and launching browsers. To keep the surfers longer, portals loaded their sites with customized features and accessories. The longer users stayed, the more features they used, and the more revenue they generated for portals. The future was seen as determined by those who controlled the first screen to be seen on whatever user device of the future was tuned in (i.e., computer, TV, or some combination thereof), whether it be called the home page, portal site, electronic programming guide, system interface or "first boot."

A portal site earned the coveted spot of home page in two ways: getting users to manually plug its address into their home page or by delivering a preprogrammed browser to the users with its sites already designated as the home page. Most preferred the latter strategy, and many made deals with Internet service providers. For example, AT&T signed deals with three portals sites—Lycos, Excite, and Infoseek—to form a "Web-based online service." MCI and Yahoo joined forces to form a "Web-based online service" (i.e., a home page linked to a portal). The traditional TV networks, fearful of being left behind, made major portal investments: ABC in Go.com owned by Disney, CBS in iWon.com, and NBC in NBCi portal.

The portal idea was an expensive business model but seen as a gateway that translated into millions, with lucrative advertising deals and multimillion deals in renting out valuable real estate to commerce partners. As the industry became more concentrated, search engines and others were competing to demonstrate their dominant position to advertisers. Portal site suppliers and community sites were pairing up to create vertically integrated media companies. Yahoo merged with GeoCities, AOL with ICQ/Netscape, InfoSeek with Disney, and AltaVista with Compaq. (The logic was that community sites, e-mail, and the like attracted visitors who tended to be sticky, i.e., stay longer in a site, thus creating advertising opportunities.)

Portals offered a business model similar to network television. They were big advertiser, audience-gathering sites that acted as hubs, feeding traffic to other sites and gathering content from sites for an integrated community, not unlike the networks' role in television. Although TV had become fragmented, with hundreds of channels available, the big four TV networks still were the focus of a lot of viewing. Studies indicate that the same gigantism that afflicted the old media now dominated the new, and the Internet's myth of indestructible diversity was called into question as

TABLE 6.1   Rating Traffic Patterns: The Top 5 Web Properties for December 2001, U.S.

	Property	Unique Audience	Reach %	Time per person
1.	AOL Time Warner	65,522,808	62.72	0:44:54
2.	Yahoo	58,030,507	55.55	1:20:31
3.	MSN	49,551,935	47.43	1:08:28
4.	Microsoft	30,160,176	28.27	0:10:22
5.	Amazon	23,733,016	22.72	0:17:18

Establishing the 30-day unique visitor as the standard
Source: Nielsen NetRatings

more and more properties became controlled by fewer and fewer entities. By 2001, fourteen companies captured the largest share of the user's time, and 50 percent of all time was spent with four companies (Taylor, 2001). These companies now steered visitors to other sites they owned or cross-promoted. Mergers and marriages whittled down the field while the evaporating dotcoms forced weaker sites to close. By 2011, four companies were positioned to define commerce in the twenty-first century: Apple, Google, Facebook, and Amazon. Sometimes known as the "Gang of Four," these major companies had huge "platforms" and dominance in their spaces that are difficult for others to challenge.

Audience measurement firms provided ratings based on dividing Internet real estate into four types of property measurements: Web property rankings (a collection of Web sites owned by one company); Web site rankings (a collection of related Web pages, images, videos, or other digital assets that were addressed with a common domain name or IP address in an Internet protocol-based network); domains (sites that used generic domain names making the name easy to remember and type in and increasing the possibility of repeat customers for services and products, known as Direct Navigation or Type-in Traffic); and unique visitors to each site, the number of different people who visited a site typically reported by week and month, and the amount of time each person spent at a Web site.

Audience measurement metrics in traditional media were designed to help advertisers understand how many people had an opportunity to see an advertisement or commercial. TV offered the average-minute audience as the primary metric for assessing a program's or commercial's potential. Radio was reported in terms of average quarter-hour ratings, providing an estimate of the number of people likely to hear an ad during that period. Magazines were evaluated in terms of a title's "average issue" audience providing an estimate of the number of people with an opportunity to see an ad in the publication.

Each type of measurement provided an estimate of the number of different people with the opportunity to see a single ad placement. Frequency objectives were met by placing ads across multiple TV programs, magazine titles, radio stations or networks, or across a variety of time periods.

The Internet posed a special problem for audience measurement because there was no program or title, and the medium was indifferent to quarter-hour slots. Thirty-day reach, an estimate of the number of different people who have viewed at least one page on a particular Web site over the course of a measured month, was selected as the primary metric by PC Meter in January 1996 with the release of the industry's first metered Internet ratings (Coffey, 2001). Time-specific programming was not applicable to the Internet, rendering the average-minute audience on the Internet unhelpful. The idea of an issue or publication cycle did not exist, as in print. Cable TV provided some guidance when, as a new medium, it faced some of the same challenges as the Internet. Cable networks had also gravitated toward the thirty-day cumulative audience estimates to illustrate the overall potential of their reach. According to Steve Coffey,

> In the early days, we pushed the monthly unique figure because, well, it was the biggest we had. Actually, initially we pushed hits, then page impressions, but they got rather stupidly large, so we went to monthly unique. At the time it was the only way to get figures which compared with newspaper circulations or TV audiences.

> (Coffey, 2001)

In 1996, on-line advertising was not yet developed. The demand for Internet measurement at that time was driven by the need to promote the site to consumers who visited, to internal managements for support, and to capital markets for investment. Total reach seemed suited to be the best metric for this purpose, and it became the quickly adopted standard since 1997.

Each of the major rating companies, JMM and Nielsen NetRatings, established a system of Web metrics based on the thirty-day unique visitor by published ranking of sites and properties monthly by total reach (Coffey, 2001). JMM and Nielsen defined unique visitors as the number of total users who visited the Web site once in a given time period. All unique visitors were unduplicated (counted only once). Unique visitors were a measure of reach, the percentage of the population who visited a Web site or property over a specific time period. If the percentage of unique visitors was multiplied by the number of times an average person visits a Web site during the same period, frequency, estimates of gross, and terms familiar to the traditional world of advertising can be determined.

The Banner Ad

The primary means of advertising during this period was known as *banner advertisements*, a form of display advertising employed by the print media. Web banner ads functioned the same way as traditional advertisements were intended to function: notifying consumers of the product or service and presenting reasons why the consumer should choose the product in question, although Web banners differed in that the results for advertising campaigns could be monitored in real time and targeted to the viewer's interests. The Web banner was displayed when a Web page that referenced the banner was loaded into a Web browser, known as an "impression." When the viewer clicked on the banner, the viewer was directed to the Web site advertised in the banner, known as a "click through." When the advertiser scanned their log files and detected that a Web user had visited the advertiser's site from the content site by clicking on the banner ad, the advertiser sent the content provider some small amount of money. This payback system was based on how much the content provider needed in order to pay for the Internet access to supply the content in the first place.

Banner ads were valued and sold based on the number of impressions they generated. This approach to banner ad sales proved successful and provided the economic foundation for the Web industry from the period of 1994 to 2000 until the market for banner ads "crashed" and there was a radical revaluation of their value.

The types of data delivered by the two key services were not always the same. Nielsen's reports were unique in reporting banner ad click-throughs and their demographics on a weekly and monthly basis. As such, the company established a special category for top Web advertisers and banner ads. Though JMM ranked both the Top 50 Web sites and Web properties, Nielsen ranked only Web properties. Subscribers to Nielsen, as a result, had to make a special request to receive individual-site data. Some felt that the absence of standardized individual-site data potentially posed a critical problem.

Significantly, Internet ratings were similar to the ratings used for television. TV ratings measured how many people tuned into an entire network during a given week or month (the counterpart to the Web property) or how many watched a particular program (the counterpart to the Web site). Web property numbers, like network numbers, indicated how many people a Web media owner was able to reach. For example, in February 2000, the Yahoo network had 45 million people, compared to 32 million for Lycos and 12 million for AltaVista (*Search Engine Reports*, 2000). Web site numbers were comparable to individual TV show ratings. They indicated how popular a Web site was among surfers, just as one might wish to determine how popular a particular show was.

The Search Advertising Model

By 2007, the majority of on-line ad budgets were spent on search advertising, which proved more effective than banner advertising at driving traffic. The ability to place an ad on the screen exactly where someone was searching was compelling. With search engines, advertisers typically bid on keyword phrases relevant to their target market. The undisputed king of search was Google, whose business roared even during the recession because its specialty—selling ads—tied to on-line search requests. This type of advertising tended to be the last thing cut from marketing budgets and the first thing to attract more money in the early stages of a recovery. Google search engine powered an on-line network that grew from $411 million in worldwide ad revenue in 2002 to more than $22 billion annually in 2009 (Liedtke, 2009). Even in 2009, when other businesses were floundering, the company's ad revenue rose seven percent in the third quarter, and Google's executives indicated they are gearing up for even more rapid growth in the months ahead (Liedtke, 2009).Yahoo, which ran the Internet's second-most-widely used search engine, still retained its forte in display advertising, online billboards, and other more visual forms of marketing.

Search requests have proven to be a highly effective way to identify consumers shopping for a specific product or service. Advertisers typically paid for ads only when the links were clicked on. For instance, a Google ad tied to a search request containing the word *shoes* hypothetically costs about $6.80 per click, whereas an ad generated by a request with the term *car parts* costs just $.48 cents per click. Buying ads in major newspapers or on TV could easily cost thousands of dollars with no assurance the investment would deliver customers. As Fernando Bermejo notes,

> instead of taking watching time as a measure of exposure, which is a substitute for audience attention, keyword advertising takes the languages used in searches as a proxy for people's interests, needs or cravings. In this context, the product that media (i.e., search engines) sell to advertisers is not the watching time of specific audiences but words.
>
> (Bermejo, 2009)

Besides the Internet's lower prices, Web-tracking technologies have made it easier to measure whether a search ad campaign is yielding adequate sales to justify the expense. Furthermore, if an ad was not paying off, advertisers typically could pull the plug more quickly than in print and broadcast, which often required financial commitments that last several months. According to Patrick Keane, an analyst at Jupiter Communications, "At one time differentiation was adding features. Now the true search and directory players all provide the same things. Search has become a commodity" (quoted in Hu, 1998).

Other types of advertising were also growing. With broadband, the ability to show full-motion video, after a search ad popped up, had grown. Beyond search advertising, marketers were using the Internet as part of a broader, more interactive campaign. Many TV programs and magazine ads sent traffic to their Web sites. Though social advertising sites, such as Facebook and YouTube, were being considered as an important presence due to their popularity, the performance of advertising was less clear on these types of sites. Major media companies Google and News Corps owned sites such as YouTube and MySpace, respectively, who were still figuring out how to monetize them.

The Performance-based Model of Advertising

The transparency of the Internet for advertising was a new feature that caused a huge ripple throughout the world of advertising. In the online world, advertisements could be linked to action through clicks. In May 1994, Ken McCarthy, an early Internet commercialization pioneer, had introduced the concept of a clickable/trackable ad (zamp wiki, n.d.). He stated that he believed that only a direct response model—in which the return on investment of individual ads was measured—would prove sustainable over the long run for online advertising.

His prophecy appeared to be becoming true with a new on-line advertising model that emerged in the early years of the twenty-first century, which closely resembled the pioneer's 1994 projection. Pay-per-click or cost-per-click was increasingly a model used on Web sites, in which advertisers paid their host only when their ad was clicked. Many content sites commonly charge a fixed price per click rather than using a bidding system.

In contrast to the generalized portal, which sought to drive a high volume of traffic to one site, pay-per-clicks implemented a so-called affiliate model that provided purchase opportunities wherever people were surfing. It did this by offering financial incentives (in the form of a percentage of revenue) to affiliated partner sites. The affiliates provided what was known as " purchase-point click-through" to the merchant. As a pay-for-performance model, if an affiliate failed to generate sales, it represented no cost to the merchant. The affiliate model was inherently well suited to the Web, which explained its popularity.

Online advertising had matured from the early portal model and its measures of unique visitors. Direct response has gained solid footing. In part, this shift could be accounted for because new types of ad-serving technology had changed the landscape by separation of ads from pages. Advertisers now purchased impressions independent of the size of the site, paying more attention to the site's audience composition or editorial fit than to its total reach. Increasingly, the pertinent question was whom the ad reached and with what frequency rather than how many people were exposed to at least one page during the month in which a campaign runs. What mattered increasingly, some argued, was not the scale of the audience but its loyalty and engagement.

As a measure, unique visitors did not indicate audience loyalty. Increasingly, advertisers realized that the value of an advertisement increased the more a visitor was exposed to it. In other words, the value to deliver an ad to the same user multiple times was essential to evaluate a site's ability to attract users and to keep them. A site with a million onetime users may not be as useful as a site with a 100,000 visitors who return ten times. Loyal users were seen as being exposed to more ads and therefore more desirable, as they could be reached repeatedly to achieve frequency objectives. Further, advertisers were also seeking more demographic characteristics of sites to better target loyal users. Some such as Stephen Coffey, a pioneer in Media Metrix, called to put the monthly unique-user figure to rest (Coffey, 2002).

By 2009, after bogging down in the recession, Internet advertising appeared to be regaining momentum as the decade's most disruptive marketing machine. While print and broadcast remained in a slump and triggered massive layoffs and pay cuts, advertisers allocated increasingly more of their budgets to the Web. Internet ads were less expensive, and returns on investments were easier to quantify. "You can draw a straight line from the time when people hear an ad on the radio or television to when they search for that company on the Internet," said David Karnstedt, chief executive of Efficient Frontier, which helped to manage ad campaigns on search engines (Liedtke, 2009). These trends will give Internet advertising 19 percent, or nearly $87 billion, of the worldwide ad market in 2013, up from just 4 percent, or about $18 billion in 2004, according to the predictions of PricewaterhouseCoopers and Wilkofsky Gruen Associates (Liedtke, 2009). That would make the Internet the third-largest marketing medium, next to TV and newspapers, respectively.

Conclusions

How the Internet Affects Other Media Business Models: Convergence

Whether music, movies, journalism, publishing, or TV, the impact of having high-speed, always-on connectivity continued to revolutionize how we interact and entertain ourselves. However, in the wake of these changes, media companies were left struggling to monetize their efforts, all of a sudden discovering that their old business model now looked like a square peg getting hammered into a round hole.

TV viewing habits were just one example of this change. According to recent findings, by 2009 nearly one-fourth of U.S. households now watch TV online (Perez, 2009). New shows are most popular, watched by 43 percent of viewers followed by 35 percent of viewers who watch sitcoms, dramas, and comedies. And 90 percent of the viewings take place at home (Perez, 2009). A key part of this shift was the breakdown of the cable monopoly systems, as viewers saddled with higher escalating and unexplainable fees and poor customer service were leaving in droves as they looked for more affordable models such as the Internet. Cable attempted to prevent the defection through establishing proprietary walls through a number of hardware devices, such as Apple TV, Boxee, Sony Media Player, and the like, which essentially limited access to the Internet base of free programming, and by allowing viewers to access pay-per-view or video-on-demand Web sites only if they were cable subscribers. As a result, there was a huge rush by media companies to establish video on demand as a commercial model as companies forced ratings services to struggle to find a way to effectively monitor and measure on-line TV viewing. Not only were companies uch as Comcast and Time Warner experimenting with on-demand on-line viewing initiatives, the networks now posted their top shows to the Web. Several networks and studios, including NBC Universal, FOX, and ABC, have even banded together to offer Hulu.com, a popular destination for commercial-supported streaming video.

As a result, Nielsen was struggling to begin its "extended screen" reporting to allow ad agencies to count viewers watching video on-line. However, by 2011, only three channels—TNT, TBS, and E—had signed up to code their ads and allow them to be tracked by Nielsen. These shows were not available to everyone but gated behind password-protected broadband services of pay-tv providers. Since 2009, backers of the TV Everywhere Initiative had tried to persuade program providers and distributors to make content available wherever viewing is watched as long as programming was secured behind the password-protected locked gates of the pay-tv providers. However, not all broadcast networks and cable channels had participated. Many still needed to work out an authentication process with distributors to access shows on-line, and still others needed approval of advertisers to stream their spots online before agreeing to participate with Nielsen's "extended screen" ratings. This had left Nielsen unable to measure the on-line viewing of TV programming and to meld it with on-air viewing and constituted a major stumbling block in the TV Everywhere services. Cable was concerned that viewership that shifted from on-air to on-line would impact their ratings and advertising revenue.

Nielsen planned to accelerate the deployment of its TV and PC software that used part of its national people meter sample to measure on-line viewing. In 2006, Nielsen announced it would expand its ratings coverage to include the Internet, mobile phones, and other gadgets, an initiative known as Anytime Anywhere Media Measurement or A2/M2. Nielsen planned to install software on computers owned by sample audiences who now have people meters linked to their TVs to create a single group that combines TV and Web viewing, creating Internet meters.

However, there were many other issues to be addressed with on-line viewing: how these new measures would be aligned with its C3 ratings, how to account for the mobile audience, and whether the online ads would be comparable to those on-air. This was in addition to the question of how to blend the on-line and on-air viewership. Still Nielsen was under pressure to move forward as a result of the formation of the Coalition for Innovative Media Measurement (CIMM), a group composed of 14 TV networks, agencies and advertisers whose goal was to explore new methodologies for audience measurement, in particular for set-top box data and cross-platform media consumptions. Some felt that this industry-backed group was viewed by Nielsen as a challenger and would lead its tracking efforts.

Advertisers and Web property owners continued to grumble about the lack of standardization for online measurements making it difficult to accurately determine audience counts. A brand, whether Hulu.com, a Web video streaming site, or any other online video provider, receives very different measurements from major firms such as comScore, Compete, or Quanticast. This result is that companies pick their highest estimates to draw advertisers.

However, putting shows on-line has its drawbacks, as networks are finding out. Without solid measurement tools, making the shows available on other platforms has, in the short term, hurt the network's bottom line. In a recent issue of *TV Guide* magazine, for example, it was noted that networks are specifically facing problems with re-runs. Whereas before, a second airing of an episode from a popular show could make decent money, networks are now finding fewer viewers tuning in— thanks to on-demand offerings and on-line viewings. According to one unnamed network executive, this presents a huge challenge for the networks: "We're not like cable, which has a second revenue stream from subscribers. We need to amortize these very expensive shows" (Perez, 2009).

Despite on-line's reputation as the most measurable of all media, marketers continue to grapple with how much to invest in the medium because of the sheer abundance of data generated and the myriad ways to measure it. "There are too many ways to look at it," said Steve Wadsworth, president of Walt Disney Internet Group, who delivered the state-of-the-industry address at the Interactive Advertising Bureau's first Audience Measurement Leadership Forum on Thursday. "It's too confusing. We're awash in data. It's not simple, and it's not clear" (Krol, 2007).

In another sign that the world of TV and on-line were converging, the Nielsen company put its top on-line research guru, Manish Bhatia, in charge of development, audience data, and analytic from TV's burgeoning digital data stream. He was responsible for finding new ways of exploiting the data generated by TV's digital set-top boxes (discussed next) and integrating it with traditional TV and on-line measurement. Manish Bhatia, president of global services and U.S. sales at Nielsen Online, called it "a problem of plenty" (Krol, 2007).

Once the Nielsen data go live, it will reveal a plethora of information regarding not just viewing numbers but the demographics of who watches what and when. Advertisers and marketers who want to target niche audiences such as the hip crowd who watches sci-fi shows on-line can then use the information. More ratings information could lead to more networks programming on-line and—who knows—eventually audiences may even be able to purchase on-line-only cable TV subscriptions.

7

EXPLORING NEW DIGITAL CURRENCIES FOR TV, CABLE, AND INTERNET AUDIENCES

Digital Cable and STB Data Initiative

Mainstream versus Clickstream

Since its purchase of Hooperatings in the 1950s and Arbitron's exit of the local TV ratings field in the 1980s, the Nielsen Company had maintained its status of being the dominant player in the CPM/Currency market for national and local television, which it considered its core business. However, at the same time, the company realized that it needed to consider new business models in a digital era. Nielsen was aware that many in the industry did not see it as receptive to newer models or new ways of conducting business. Its older methods, based on samples of audiences who reported viewing by meters or paper-and-pencil diaries, were beginning to seem quaint. Advertisers and agencies were beginning to look past traditional survey-based methods of TV audience measurement to see whether census-based rather than sample-based data of TV tuning behavior might not be a better way of determining TV's advertising effectiveness, now that the digital transition had made this type of data available through a new device, known as digital set-top boxes (STBs).

By 2009, Nielsen also had undergone changes as its parent VNU had been acquired by six private equity firms, a consortium consisting of the Carlyle Group, Kohlberg, Kravis, Roberts, and Co., known as the Valcon Group, and led by former General Electric executive David Calhoun. Calhoun changed the name of the various parts of the company to the Nielsen Company, integrated A. C. Nielsen, Inc. (the marketing segment) with Nielsen Media Research (the TV ratings business), and acquired the portion of Nielsen NetRatings it did not already own.

The industry well knew the problems and pitfalls of sample-based media measurement services with particular reference to television. Many felt that sample-based measurement was rapidly becoming defunct in its ability to reflect what was truly of importance to the advertiser: return on investment (ROI). This view was driven by changes in the broadcast environment, by the inability of research companies to recruit representative samples, and by new technologies allowing viewers to personalize their television experience, whether through time-shifting using digital video recorders, or place-shifting using cell phones and other portable devices.

In many other countries, advertisers and agencies were used to making commercial placement decisions based on measures of commercial audiences. In the United States, advertisers continued until 2007 to make commercial placement decisions based on program audiences with the assumption that if advertisers had actual commercial audience data, it would not change the decisions made.

However, with the advent of the Internet and its more transparent model of reporting, advertisers were increasingly dissatisfied with this opaque method. This had led to Nielsen's introduction of C3 ratings and was behind the push for mining the STBs, which were now in homes and in many forms, partly due to digital video recorders such as TiVo, and partly as a result of the massive industry switch to digital television technology. STBs offered a possible solution for the increasingly problematic surveys or samples.

Early indicators from various measures using digital measurement suggested a change in viewing behavior not seen in decades, and so the industry pressured for more accurate measurement technology to keep pace. Digital STB data were considered superior to mainstream, smaller sample-based measurement in offering broadcasters, agencies, and advertisers a potential measurement technology. It provided measures of set tuning virtually down to the second, for even the most fragmented TV markets, based on what eventually might come close to a census of homes in the market.

The industry was abuzz with studies comparing the value of mainstream data, diaries, and people meters to clickstream data, literally a recording of what a computer user clicked on while Web browsing but now also applied to the second-by-second audience viewing data collected from digital STBs. This new methodology offered new data of significant economic impact to buyers and sellers, particular in providing actual commercial ratings and recording actual viewing. Advertisers were tired of paying for program ratings when programs were increasingly time-shifted and commercials fast-forwarded, leaving them little assurance regarding what they were getting for their investment.

However, as with any change, vested interests dragged their feet, as it was in their interest to keep things as they were and make any change difficult. The slowness of the Nielsen Company to introduce change led to such industry pressure groups as the Coalition for Innovative Media Measurement (CIMM), an industry group whose stated purpose was to develop a more cross-platform measurement using STB data. Unsatisfied with how media audiences were measured in a multi-screen age, fourteen of the nation's largest media companies, agencies, and advertisers launched a multi-year commitment to fund and evaluate a series of research studies focused on STB data and cross-platform TV measurement. Founding members included Time Warner, Disney-ABC TV Group, Interpublic's Mediabrands, News Corp.,Viacom, arcom MediaVest, Proctor and Gamble, Unilever,AT&T,WPP, CBS Paramount Network Entertainment Group, Omnicom Media Group, Discovery Communications, and NBC Universal. Though the group indicated that its intention was not to go head to head with Nielsen, nevertheless the handwriting was on the wall. If Nielsen failed to find new methods to measure the new digital media, they would take matters into their own hands.The group's first charge was to call for proprietary meetings with the five major research firms providing STB data: Nielsen, Rentrack, TiVo, TRA, and Taylor Nelson Sofres (TNS) (Bachman, 2009b). Once a hypothetical exercise, STB data as a measurement tool were quickly becoming a reality as companies struggled for dominance, with their varying methodologies, data footprints, and sources.

An STB was a computerized device that connected to an external source and decoded signals into content that could be presented on a display unit such as a TV. STBs came in many forms and could have a variety of functions (see Table 7.1).The analog generation of cable company's boxes allowed subscribers to view numerous channels and pay-per-view programming but not much else. Many did not provide a backchannel or return path for data and therefore were not interactive. At least 65 million households existed with this type of box, most of which were due to be upgraded to next-generation digital STBs.

A new generation of digital cable STBs enabled a TV set to receive and decode digital TV broadcasts and thereby enabled a TV STB to become a user interface to the Internet.The type of set-top box most widely used was one that received encoded/compressed signals from signal sources, such as a cable or Telco provider's head end, and decoded/decompressed the signals, converting them into analog signals so that an analog TV could understand them. This type of STB accepted commands from the user, often via remote control, and transmitted those commands back to the network operator through a return path.

This new generation of STBs became necessary for TV viewers who wished to use their current analog TV sets to receive digital broadcasts. A typical digital STB contained one microprocessor (or more) for running the operating system and included RAM, an MPEG decoder chip, and chips for audio decoding and processing. More sophisticated STBs, such as TiVo, contained a hard drive for recording and storing TV broadcasts, for downloading software, and for other applications provided by the DTV service providers. An STB was really, in this instance, a specialized computer that could talk to the Internet: that is, it contained a Web browser and the Internet's main program,TCP/IP, thereby connecting the service to which the STB was attached to a telephone line or cable TV company. Most digital STBs had a return path capability for two-way communication so

TABLE 7.1 Set-top boxes may be associated with these major categories

1	Broadcast TV Set-top Boxes (a.k.a. Thin Boxes)	A more primitive set-top box with no back channel (return path). These might come with interface ports, some memory and some processing power.
2	Enhanced TV Set-top Boxes (May be known as: Smart TV Set-top Box, Thick Boxes)	These have a back channel (return path), often through a phone line. These may be capable of Video on Demand, e-commerce, Internet browsing, e-mail communications, chat and more.
3	Advanced Set-top Boxes (a.k.a. Advanced digital Set-top boxes, Smart TV Set-top Box, Thick Boxes, All-in-one Set-top box, Media Center)	A fully integrated set-top box. These have good processors, memory, middleware, software applications and optional hard-drives. They're often used with high-speed (broadband) connections. Features could include high-speed Internet access, Interactive TV, digital video recording & gaming. Instead of this, a "sidecar" (below) might be used in tandem with the set-top box and/or TV. Advanced set-top boxes are more likely to be integrated with DVRs and high-definition TV. See Media Centers.
4	Sidecar (Please note this 2007 update; as advanced set-top boxes now typically are integrated units, the sidecar is not often used)	This type of set-top box provides an additional transport stream of data from the network operator to complement the main stream. With Charter Communications, the BMC-8000 (Broadband Media Center) is/was a sidecar box that works in tandem with the Motorola DCT-2000. A fully integrated unit would not require a sidecar.
5	Hybrid Digital Cable Box	A specialized and often more expensive cable TV set-top box with high end functions. Motorola Broadband's DCP501 home theater system is an example.

Source: Set-top boxes, www.itvdictionary.com; How Digital Set-top boxes Data Work

the devices were designed for interactivity or to make TV more like a computer. By 2010, newer digital STBs, with two-way cable modems, were expected to bring new capabilities to television such as photo-realistic graphics, session-oriented games, and the ability to do file transfers, mail and chat, and video on demand.

STBs' ability to gather data similar to computer viewing data initiated a gold rush by a variety of ratings firms vying to mine the data. It was clear that the future of audience measurement meant measuring exposures across the three screens of TV, mobile devices, and the Internet. This meant going beyond the current Nielsen sampling methods. It also meant competitive entry was now possible for companies with new methods and products. The question seemed to be not whether STB data would be used but who would be the first to standardize it and in what form.

Advantages of Digital STB Data

> Tremendous revenue opportunities exist in driving interactivity between the 60 million digital set-top boxes, 175 million personal computers, and 210 million mobile phones in the US...
>
> Michael Rivkin, CEO, Develop-On-Box,
> parent company of Zodiac Gaming (April 2006)

For companies interested in producing audience ratings, digital STB data offered unique opportunities. STBs were soon to be ubiquitous, reaching huge segments of the population. Their ability to capture viewing through software meters allowed access to unparalleled levels of data. Digital cable was always on, it was high speed, it was bi-directional and it was in real time. Digital set-top boxes (DSTBs) offered a potential measurement technology that sampled census numbers of viewers virtually down to the second for even the most fragmented market.

Clickstream data or CSTB data were increasingly discussed in the media and favored by advertisers, though most advertisers, cable multiple system operators (MSOs), and broadcast entities were now focused on video-on-demand server data, as more TV programming was viewed on the Web. The reasons for industry interest were rooted in channel proliferation and audience fragmentation and were exaggerated by declining response rates, response bias, poor compliance, and technologically challenging broadband and portable viewing devices. As the industry moved forward in the push for CSTB–based television audience measurement, a good part of advertiser focus was on its interactivity and addressability. Mainstream diary and people meter systems, by comparison, were incapable of handling massive fragmentation and were inconsistent with one another in their reporting of viewing.

In the remaining U.S. markets (about 185 of them) where diary data were the sole tool for regular television audience measurement, the existing problem was more than that of just sample size. The diary was an instrument that had worked acceptably well during the period when the average home could receive fewer than a dozen channels and three of those channels commanded a 90 percent share of audience. However, by 2010, the average U.S. home received 120 channels (according to Nielsen), and the diary was hopelessly outclassed by the challenge of measuring that environment effectively. In these 185 or so smaller markets, STB data could regularly gather meter-level data for the first time. An additional reason for interest in STB data was that the sample size in these smaller markets would be more than 5,000 homes per market, about the same sample size per market as the single sample Nielsen used to measure the entire national television audience (although Nielsen had plans to significantly increase the size).

Another advantage of STB data was that such data tended to provide far less nonresponse bias as compared with conventional meter and diary (and in fact all survey) methods. Years ago, before the use of telephone-answering machines became commonplace, during an era when most households contained nonworking housewives and before the advent of telemarketing that created an environment hostile to telephone recruitment for meter and/or diary panels, it was not unusual for media research surveys to achieve response rates in the 60-percent to 80-percent range. In fact, the telephone coincidental method, because of its unique ability at the time to validly assume that 99 percent of households not answering their telephones were currently unoccupied and therefore not watching television, regularly achieved response rates in the 90-percent to 95-percent range. However, this era had long passed, and currently no survey technique regularly achieved response rates much higher than 50 percent, which was considered excellent, whereas in the 1960s, that response rate was considered barely acceptable (Harvey, n.d.). By 2000, Nielsen's meter panels achieved something less than a 25-percent response rate (i.e., in tab or the actual number who participated, as a percent of original predesigned, or selected-to-participate, sample). What this meant was that the types of people whose behavior was supposed to represent 100 percent of the population, in fact, was skewed to less than one-fourth of the population, and this skew involved psychological differences that were likely to impinge upon the accuracy of the behaviors being measured in ways that can only be guessed at. In fact, some considered the bias on nonresponse to have become egregious.

For example, in the one-market Open TV Research study, a study using STB meters and conducted by TV research veteran Bill Harvey, a response rate of 97 percent was achieved, better than even the coincidental telephone methods of the early 1960s. This high response rate was achieved by the following method: (1) Postcards were sent to cable subscribers indicating that STB data were about to be collected in an anonymous manner and offering the option of opting out of such measurement, and (2) only three percent of the subscribers opted out. What this case illustrated was that STB data were valuable in tracking the number of homes exposed to a commercial; if the commercials were interactive, how many of those interacted with the commercial; and if there were an offer, how many homes interacted to take the offer. Then, once the offer was fulfilled, subsequent purchase behavior of the home could be tracked by the advertiser and related back to the cost of the spot. As a result, the STB method could deliver ROI statistics that could be compared with direct mail, Internet, telemarketing, and other precisely trackable marketing methods. Without STB data, of course, television would not be as precisely trackable as these other media; the advertiser could know how many people took the offer via an 800 number for example, but the number who had seen the offer would have to be imputed from sample-based conventional sources, and this had proved to be imprecise and unsatisfactory to many advertisers/agencies (Harvey, n.d.).

STB data promised to be a convenient common source for both audience data and interaction data, becoming ever more relevant as television evolved into a medium more like the Internet every day. The standard meter panel could not be split into finer groups by means of addressability and interactivity without adding to the already-existing strain on sample size and the problematic economics of meter panels. However, the question remained whether the STB data would serve as a complement to other methods or become mainstream.

Addressable Commercials

Furthermore, STB data promised to fulfill another dream of advertisers and agencies: addressable commercials. Because the technology, with its interactive delivery system, could deliver commercials directly to individual homes, STBs further whetted advertisers' appetite for addressable commercials. In the United States, advertisers and agencies had been keenly interested in addressable commercials for many years. Addressable commercials originally were defined to mean targeting individual households aggregated along demographic or buyer-graphic lines, and the same commercial was sent to all households within the same zone. The term also came to apply to the ability to target an individual household. Both the aggregate and the individual household method tended to be in agreement to the extent that the adage "birds of a feather flock together" was true in reality of human beings. To the extent that neighborhoods contained diversity in terms of the characteristics that an advertiser might wish to target (e.g., purchasers of disposable diapers), the zone method would not reproduce the results of individual household targeting. One might easily conclude from these findings that geographic targeting was a poor substitute for individual household targeting. STB data, with the ability to target individual households, offered a unique advantage.

The shift to STB data as a possible currency also had a number of pitfalls including that digital set-top data, though large, failed to represent the entire U.S. population. By 2009, of the total TV households in the United States, about 65 percent received TV from cable, but only 41 percent of households had digital cable and had the necessary STBs (see Table 7.2). Therefore, the data did not represent the entire TV viewing population but only those who received TV signals via a digital set-top

TABLE 7.2 Disadvantages to STB data: data from digital cable and satellite viewers represent at most only about 70% of TV viewership

Digital cable	41%
Satellite	29%
Analog-only cable	19%
Broadcast	11%

Source: Nielsen national sample, Feb. 23 to March 22, 2009

device. The group with STBs was known to be upper-income and better educated than the typical TV users.

Another concern was that because set-tops did not identify individuals or their demographics within their households, some other means of acquiring this type of information would be essential for it to become the currency. Researchers, however, searched for ways of supplementing the digital set-top data with additional survey-based research that could be used to model demographics.

The Cable Communications Privacy Act

Furthering the problem for collecting demographic data for future digital cable STB data collectors were legal restrictions. The Cable Communications Privacy Act of 1984 stated that cable accompanies could not use their subscriber's personal identifiable information without their permission, known as *opt in*. However, they could aggregate data from the universe of their subscribers and generate analysis so long as the data was not personally identifiable. This had served as a major deterrent for cable companies collecting the data themselves. Furthermore, many cable companies were focusing their efforts on a smaller number of potential revenue streams such as video-on-demand data, expanding the market for digital boxes, digital video recorders (DVRs) and tagging applications for commercials rather than creating rival ratings services. Thus, they were more likely to provide the data to third-party services, such as Nielsen, although a few cable companies, such as Charter, Comcast, Time Warner Cable, were exploring and considering its possible uses themselves.

Nevertheless, despite its current limitations, Nielsen realized that, if another company could collect STB data from millions of U.S. cable homes, that company might become a threat to its core business, especially as both cable companies and other third-party providers were seriously considering using STB data. Without efforts in this area, Nielsen Company might become less competitive, possibly leading to its obsolescence due to its lack of granular information, as the industry called this type of clickstream data. For these reasons, Nielsen determined it needed to explore fully the STB data derived from STBs as a possible replacement or supplement for its currency data and as a possible replacement for diary information.

In 2007, Nielsen announced its Any Time Any Where Measurement initiative that included researching whether digital set-top data could be viable for TV measurement in smaller markets. This strategy allowed Nielsen to continue its roll-out of the local people meters at the local level and to conduct tests and cut deals to gain access to digital set-top data with cable MSOs in an effort to keep up with potential rivals who were exploring STB measurement. "With the ability to time-shift video consumption, came the demands for greater accountability and increased data granularity within the commercial broadcast/cable industry," read a statement issued by the Nielsen-funded Council for Research Excellence. "For these reasons, STB data are increasingly being heralded as the future of television audience measurement" (Mandese, 2008).

The period 2000–2011 was one in which Nielsen's strategy was to ally with the major cable MSOs to collect raw data and develop a software that would allow the raw data to be gathered into a meaningful means of reporting. For the first time since its inception, Nielsen was considering using means of gathering raw data other than its former tried and true method of random sampling.

The Cable Industry: New Business Model Needed

As the economy tanked in the early part of the decade, the cable industry faced the same problems as the other media: an entire new business model was needed as investors watched shares of Comcast and Time Warner tumble 30 percent and 40 percent, respectively (Mehta, 2007). Once the only game in town, cable companies such as Comcast and Time Warner Cable were facing competition from phone operators selling television services, and satellite companies bolstering their high-definition programming. In fact, thanks to the recession, more people than ever were deciding to cancel their cable TV subscriptions to save money, realizing that many of their favorite programs were available through alternative methods, including online streams.

Unfortunately, cable was still acting like a monopoly. Ideas for a more Web-centric business model for cable—one that required cable to drastically expand the capacity of their current systems—were floating around. Instead of launching new linear video channels as they did in the 1980s and 1990s, some cable industry insiders believed that instead cable operators needed to partner with online giants, such as eBay and Google, to offer dedicated channels for new media content. This would require cable operators to set aside a big chunk of their network capacity for these channels to enable their possible Internet partners to offer a rich, interactive experience. For this to happen, cable companies would need to spend big sums of money on upgrading their networks for such fare as high-definition channels. In industry veteran Wayne Davis's scenario, cable operators would no longer charge customers subscription fees for the service but instead make money by charging its new media partners for access to customers. Operators could also sell the new media partners long-term leases for capacity on their networks or even forge some sort of financial model based on sharing the advertising revenue these new channels might generate. However, cable operators were still old school and fairly conservative in moving toward different models.

Another big question was just how interested new media players would be. Why would Yahoo, say, spend money on a dedicated channel that reaches just a portion of Internet users (Comcast, the nation's biggest operator, has about 24 million cable subscribers) when it already could reach 100 percent of potential customers as a free Web portal? These were the kinds of dilemmas facing the industry.

Cable Industry and STBs: the Battle Brewing for Control of Your Television Set

The ratings battle for STB data was actually caught up in a much larger battle taking place over the very control of television itself, with both the computer and cable industries beginning to jockey for position in a digital era. The merger of STBs with television required ever-more sophisticated operating systems to run increasingly complex hardware. A number of companies, such as Microsoft and Scientific-Atlantic, were battling to dominate the platform that would control the sophisticated hardware and could provide a platform for third-party programs. Though a formidable competitor, as an outsider Microsoft was not necessarily a shoo-in to dominate the STB field the way it had desktop computers. In addition, smaller specialized companies, such as NCI and Diba, had designs on this market. This was a market that also included the cable companies that were considering their own design.

This was a battle made possible by what was known as OCAP. The Open Cable Application Platform (OCAP) was an operating system layer designed for consumer electronics that had been adopted by the U.S. cable industry. This operating system connected to a cable television system, such as Comcast or Cox, and permitted these companies to remove and replace a suite of open and accepted standards employed internationally but not used in the United States, known as direct video broadcasting technologies and specifications. OCAP programs were intended for interactive services such as ecommerce, online banking, electronic program guides, and DVRs. Unlike operating systems on a personal computer, the cable company controlled what OCAP programs ran on the consumer's machine. OCAP was created as a result of Cablecard 2.0, a set of technologies created by the U.S. cable television industry in response to requirements by the federal government's Telecommunications Act of 1996 that cable companies allow non-cable-company-provided devices to access their networks.

Cable companies have continued to insist on OCAP as part of the Cablecard 2.0 specification, although the proposal was controversial and had not been approved by the FCC. Cable companies stated that two-way communications by third-party devices on their networks would require them to support OCAP. The Consumer Electronics Association and other groups argued that the intention of OCAP was to block features that competed with cable-provided services and that consumers should be entitled to add, delete, and otherwise control programs as on their personal computers. Cable's multiple system operators (MSOs) supported the OCAP effort, believing that if all companies used this middleware, data collection would be greatly enabled throughout the industry. As a result, one possible competitor in STB data were the cable MSOs themselves using the capability of this middleware. The industry was awash in a variety of cable STBs from different generations and manufacturers, so a common stream of data was not yet possible.

As a result, cable companies, such as Comcast, Charter, Time Warner, and Cox, were exploring and considering the possible use of STB data. However, to provide downloadable data, cable data had to be digital. Not all analog boxes had a back stream, or back channels, and, consequently, not all were interactive. Among cable MSOs, even if data were collected, only 10 million STBs had a back channel or 28 percent of all households. With 110 million TV households, this amounted to around 30 million boxes but, of these 30 million, only 10 million, or one-third of all digital boxes had back channel capability.

Satellites could also provide cable STB or clickstream data. More than 10 million subscribers were estimated to be enabled with Navic/DirecTV. Nielsen had conducted a trial using STB data from DirecTV for video on demand.

DSTB Competition

Mining audience data from STB devices that delivered TV content via cable or satellite was not unlike the digital equivalent of the Alaskan gold rush as companies envisioned a promising business that could deliver audience viewing data of unparalleled precision based on millions of households. If companies could only crack the code, they had the potential to produce TV audience data using samples that dwarfed Nielsen's current 18,000 national people meter panel. STB data offered to provide actual, second-by-second viewing habits of millions of television viewers, across the full cable lineup, mapped to demographic data to reveal with unprecedented precision who was tuning into a specific show or commercial. Advertisers ultimately wanted fully addressable advertising, in which a TV spot was essentially matched up with the person viewing it—say, a Disney vacation promo for households with kids younger than 12.

Beside the cable companies themselves, a number of key rivals in the race to offer digital STB data included such companies as erinMedia (now defunct), Taylor Nelson Sofres, Rentrack, TiVo, and TRA. All were looking to supplement—or someday supplant—the Nielsen "currency" using data siphoned out of cable, satellite, and Telco's STBs and DVRs. Big cable operators also were exploring the best ways to crack this code through Canoe Ventures, the advanced advertising company established by the country's six biggest MSOs. However, there was no simple or quick solution. Data formats were inconsistent among different operators, some box models were incapable of capturing and passing back data, and there was the problem of determining who was actually watching.

To gather STB data, cable operators and their research partners needed to navigate multiple technical, business, and privacy issues. For starters, cable operators had to guarantee the privacy of their subscribers' data was protected, not only to comply with federal laws but to avoid negative publicity. Cable operators were highly sensitive to consumers who valued privacy, and many realized they needed to offer basic safeguards to prevent a consumer backlash.

Technically, pooling set-top data from several markets even within one operator was a huge and complicated task in terms of the operational complexity involved in gathering these data. It required significant work from MSOs. Operators needed to find a way to offer standardized data and to maintain consistency across the MSOs. For example, there was not yet a standard way for programmers to provide the actual program start and end times so that it accurately reflected set-top data—a critical issue for live events, such as sports, which frequently extended beyond the prescheduled times. To be sure, even if all these issues were resolved, digital cable and satellite set-tops combined did not represent all TV households. Moreover, it was not always clear who—if anyone—was watching cable TV at any given time. About 10 percent of STBs—6.9 percent of television homes—were never turned off for the entire month of May 2009, according to Nielsen. The ratio was even higher on an average day, when 35.9 percent of homes left an STB on all day long. Some of the biggest names in TV were working on an STB solution (Spangler and Farrell, 2009b).

With the exception of TiVo, which designed, built, and distributed its own boxes, cable system boxes were manufactured by third parties such as Scientific Atlanta and were never designed to collect and process viewing data. Not only were the internal workings of the cable boxes different system to system, but there were multiple generations deployed within each system. The result was a long list of issues that needed to be addressed, not the least of which was figuring out whether the TV set attached to the box is on or off. According to Nielsen, 10 percent of STBs never get turned off over any month-long period; about 30 percent of boxes remain on for 24 hours on any given day. Signal latency was also a tough challenge. Households that had multiple TV sets knew all too well that two sets tuned to the same channel were never in sync. "If the lag is 5, 10 or 15 seconds, that's a lifetime for an ad," said Jack Wakshlag, chief research officer for Turner Broadcasting, which subscribed to TNS's service based on Charter's Los Angeles data (Bachman, 2009b).

Furthermore, as noted earlier, just because the sample was huge did not necessarily mean it was representative or projectable to the universe. Cable systems did not conform to market definitions and could skew toward certain regions or demographic makeup. For example, Charter's Los Angeles system, whose data were being used by all the STB researchers, reflected an ethnic skew not seen in most of the country. Charter was believed to have a particularly unusual concentration of Chinese-speaking viewers not to mention a disproportionately high Latino audience. Even services that purported to be national, such as Rentrak (which pulled data from AT&T), TiVo, or TRA (which used TiVo and two cable systems it declined to identify), were not necessarily producing ratings that were representative. Though TiVo had more clients than any of the other services, researchers agreed the service was limited to an understanding of the viewing behavior of DVR households, a distinct subset of about a third of all U.S. TV homes. Because it measured only

TiVo users, it could not claim to be nationally projectable or a viable candidate for national currency. Though each MSO had a coverage area, there were also areas of enormous gaps.

Perhaps at the top of the list of challenges was finding a way to capture demographics. None of the STB systems could directly measure viewing beyond the household level. "These companies operated by asking subscribers to foot the bill for the research and development. Each had it own strength and weakness." The NBC head of research likened STB data to the first flight of the Wright brothers (Bachman, 2009). At the end of the day, STB service without panel measurement or mathematical modeling to fill in the demographic blanks was simply unimaginable. Even TNS, which has been the most aggressive STB data developer, saw a role for panels, although there was no agreement on how they would be used (Bachman, 2009b).

Though Nielsen had been for many years accepted as the default, as service technology improved, other sources existed in the marketplace to get minute-by-minute (data) and go second by second. Everyone seemed to agree that the people meter sample was too small and was unable to measure smaller, niche networks. With STB data, the industry had the potential to tap vastly larger panels prebuilt and subsidized by viewer subscription dollars. The potential was hard to resist: tons of audience data that was there for the taking at very little marginal cost. For the first time in fifty years, alternatives to conventional TV ratings were possible. "The biggest barrier to entry in TV measurement was gone except for getting access to the STB data," said David Poltrack, chief research officer for CBS.

> There was a chance for an entrepreneur to make a mark and establish a place in the marketplace for the first time. Our goal is to get more accountability. We're working real hard to have a currency based on intent. But CPMs aren't going to go away anytime soon.
>
> (Bachman, 2009b)

ErinMedia

The first company to enter the field of STB data ratings was a small Florida-based company known as erinMedia owned by Frank Maggio, spun out of Cheetah, a company that manufactured and supplied equipment that found and repaired signal leakage for the cable industry. Maggio realized that digital cable set boxes were already connected to the homes of 50 million viewers (McClellan, 2006). Though data could be received downstream, cable could also get transmission back to find out what viewers watched. Cable STB data would allow companies to deconstruct the audience for any show. For example, it could tell that 44,312 household sets were tuned to the first four minute and seven seconds of local news or track

11,812 viewers as they tuned in and out during commercial breaks. It could also determine how many households tuned in and when, acting as a de facto census of actual viewers. Of critical importance was that it could provide small numbers. Future micro-channels would find out who was in its small but specific audience. erinMedia planned to generate its own local reports for advertisers based on MSO footprints. Advertisers wanted information on their coverage area only. Each cable MSO had a different footprint, and viewing was representative only of each system, so this was no easy task.

ErinMedia planned to collect data from cable STBs and to develop a metric system to generate analysis of the data to provide local advertisers with information on viewership. The company's planned technique was to strip STB data of its personally identifiable information and to match that up with zip codes' demographic data provided by Claritas, and through a series of mathematical algorithms generate demographic information in the form of ratings based on STB data. By collecting information on boxes rather than households, its method would comply with the Cable Privacy Act. ErinMedia even had discussed with Nielsen the possibility of providing the raw cable data to Nielsen as a replacement for its diary information in smaller markets.

According to several reports, erinMedia had all but lined up $25 million in funding from a group of agencies, media companies, and advertisers led by Spark Capital to launch its service. (See Brandweek.com Feb 13, 2007.) However, erinMedia withdrew from the market after its potential financing fell through (Bachman, 2007a, 2007b; see also *Business Week*, 2007). On February 12, 2007, Nielsen announced a new service known as Digital Plus that was to be based on STB data from cable system operators, MSOs, and satellite providers to create new insights and services for clients by integrating STB data with other Nielsen information (Bachman, 2007a). However, Digital Plus seemed to provide neither clear business plans nor pricing for any products. No defined product was identified at the announcements although Digital Plus included the idea of integrated STB data with Nielsen panel data. The timing of its Digital Plus service was significant in that it was announced two weeks after Spark Capital, an underwriter to erinMedia, claimed to be putting together a funding round. Frank Maggio, CEO of erinMedia, accused Nielsen of timing its announcement to drive away backers from erinMedia (Learmonth, 2007). According to Katy Bachman, of *Mediaweek*, Nielsen's latest announcement could be seen as the company's answer to would-be competitor erinMedia, which had been developing a TV ratings service based on testing STBs (Bachman, 2007b). The loss of potential funding, together with Nielsen's timing of its Digital Plus announcement, in part led erinMedia to file two antitrust suits against the ratings firm in 2005 (Holahan, 2007). One suit was withdrawn, the other settled out of court, and the company folded in 2007.

The Nielsen Strategy

Nielsen realized that if another company could collect STB data from millions of U.S. cable subscribers, it could pose a serious threat to its core business. Without efforts in this area, it might becomes less competitive, leading to obsolescence due to its lack of granular information, as the industry called clickstream data. For these reasons, it determined to fully explore STB data, especially as a possible replacement for its diary information.

Nielsen's pursuit of STB data was complicated by the fact that at the same time it was pursuing data, it was also attempting to discredit it and emphasize its disadvantages. There was still a need to come up with a convention to address whether the STB was on or off and to indicate how to count whether the box was on but the TV was off. Early studies had found no correlation between STB data watched and what Nielsen sample indicated. The STB could not tell whether a viewer was watching TV, a DVD, VHS, or playing a game.

Nielsen hoped to convince MSOs buyers and sellers that it would be far better to have one currency than multiple ones. Nielsen made agreements with a number of cable companies including Oceanic, Time Warner, TiVo, Gemstar, Comcast, and Charter. About 25 percent of Nielsen's customers were cable companies and MSOs while noncable and broadcast provided the other 75 percent. With open cable standards and standardization on the horizon, MSOs and direct broadcast satellites (DBSs) would have the ability to collect, process, and produce data. If the data gained any degree of acceptance, Nielsen would be faced with combating other standards for TV exchange.

Similar to its Internet strategy, Nielsen entered the STB data late in the game. In 2007, Nielsen announced its Any Time Any Where initiative that included researching whether digital STB data could be viable for TV measurement in smaller markets. This strategy allowed Nielsen to continue its roll-out of the local people meters at the local level and to conduct tests and cut deals to gain access to digital STB data with MSOs in an effort to keep up with potential rivals in this area. As the industry pressed for more accurate information, Nielsen announced at the Council for Research Excellence in 2008 that, "With the ability to time-shift video consumption, came the demands for greater accountability and increased data granularity with the commercial broadcast/cable" industry. Nielsen's challenge was how to create an STB system that did not undermine its core business of sample-based ratings (Mandese, 2008). One way was to use the data as a supplement to its existing flagship ratings service. Nielsen claimed to be embracing STB data as a way to provide additional context. Interestingly, Nielsen had failed to devise new methods even in an era when DVRs, such as TiVo, now around since 1999, were skipping commercials, and broadcasters and advertisers were hungry for more accurate measures of DVR homes, projected to be 30 percent of homes by 2010 (Holahan, 2007). In fact, Nielsen had begun tracking commercial audiences only in 2007 and before then had provided no indication of whether its panel members were tuning in or skipping commercials. By 2008, with an uncertain economy, networks were growing concerned that they were losing advertisers to more easily trackable Internet ads.

In 2008, Nielsen acquired Audience Analytics, which sold software called Audience Watch. This software was used for analyzing and reporting large sets of audience measurement data such as STB data gathered mainly from Charter Communication in Los Angeles. Nielsen also had been quietly working with a broader cross-section of cable and satellite providers under nondisclosure agreements. Nielsen was looking, in particular, for a means of using the STB data in conjunction with its people meter data or as a possible replacement for the diary. According to Manish Bhatia, president of Nielsen's Advanced Digital Plus,

> We think the people meter data panel has a huge, critical role to play in cleaning up and making sense of the STB data. Combing STB data injects fidelity into the panel data; and the panel data makes the STB data more complete.
>
> (Spangler and Farrell, 2009b)

By 2009, Nielsen was facing stiff pressure by the CIMM to provide a single stream of ratings data that included both TV and Internet viewing. Nielsen was planning to roll out a convergence panel of households that were hooked up by Nielsen to measure both their regular TV viewing and on-line media usage, as a subset of its currency TV panel. Nielsen hoped to address the CIMM's pressure by commingling its census level data with a panel of consumers. Some saw this strategy as a means of maintaining its monopoly position by adopting a method that others could not duplicate. In this way, it would both maintain its monopoly over audience measurement via its core TV ratings panels and correlate and commingle data derived from STB census data. In particular, Nielsen was considering using its people meter sample demographics to model demographics for STB data. Nielsen was considering using MSO homes, via the MAC address, the unique serial number on the STB, and identifying homes as being Nielsen homes, then extrapolating the data from them since they had opted in.

Other smaller competitors in the DSTB data market included Navic, a software company that provided back-channel information and interactive applications for MSOs. Headquartered in Waltham, MA, Navic had been operating since 1999 and was acquired by Microsoft in 2008. Navic assisted cable companies in understanding whether their STB boxes were working properly. Navic was experimenting with cross-platform, advertising-centric applications and had long-term relationships with top cable tiers, such as Time Warner, Cox, Charter, Comcast, and Bright House.

Perhaps the biggest effort to build a business of interactive advertising from the aggregation of the STB data was cable's collaborative effort, Canoe Ventures. CEO David Verklin has said Canoe expected to provide viewing metrics, in some shape or form, from some 57 million set-top boxes representing 32 million

U.S. cable households (Spangler and Farrell, 2009b). The first step was to collect data from its member companies, which included six MSOs. By 2010, Canoe planned to provide supplemental audience-measurement data to the industry. In 2011 and beyond, the venture has its eyes on "data integration as foundational for segmentation, targeting and performance metrics." Canoe initially planned to provide STB data with its own addressable and interactive advertising products. Beyond that, there was also the opportunity to supplement the data that were already in the market.

Some considered TNS Media Research to be the sleeping giant in this field as it was the number-two worldwide research firm and active in ratings business outside the U.S. TNS Media Research, a division of global rival Taylor Nelson Sofres, was purchased in 2008 by WPP Kantar Group. It was the most formidable as it was well respected and well established. TNS had three STB panels: one in Honolulu with Time Warner Cable, one with Charter Communications in Los Angeles, and a 250,000 national panel with DirecTV. It had also signed a contract with a number of agencies.

In late 2004, TNS Media Research had become the first research firm to delve deeply into STB data, setting up a trial with Oceanic Time Warner in Hawaii to provide the cable system with a usable data stream it could sell locally. By 2006, TNS offered the industry the first syndicated commercial service based on STB data from Charter Communications in Los Angeles. It had since done partnership deals with every research firm exploring the STB measurement business. "Given the dominance of [Nielsen], we knew trying to compete using a traditional approach would be very difficult," explains George Shababb, president of TNS Media Research (Bachman, 2009b). Shababb said that TNS saw a chance to change the definition of measurement whether it is linking audience data to consumer information, purchase information, or other segmentation breakouts (Bachman, 2009b). TNS Media had launched a service known as DirectView in 2009, based on tuning data from 100,000 DirecTV subscribers including time-shifted viewing across more than 350 channels. It planned to provide granular data and addressable advertising. In 2009, TNS and the TV program guide company Rovi Corp entered into a joint venture to develop interactive and STB measurement systems (Friedman, 2009).

Another player was Rentrak, which saw itself as a complement to Nielsen's existing ratings services but believed that it might offer another currency somewhere down the line. Rentrak, a Portland, OR–based firm, had made its name reporting box office results and DVD sales. Since 2000, Rentrak had accumulated data on box-office receipts from movie theaters and viewing measurement for video on demand. By 2000, its Video on Demand data had captured 100 percent of that market. Analyzing data from more than 70 million set-tops, Rentrak had expanded into measuring the various studios' video-on-demand offerings, had added software to measure linear TV, and was constructing trials to process census-level ratings data. It had entered the linear TV market in 2009, rolling out its product known as TV Essentials. By 2009, the company had deals with three major distributors—AT&T, Charter, and Dish Network—and has access to data from about 10 million STBs, including major cable systems, such as Comcast and Cablevision. In the Charter Los Angeles system, which represented about 300,000 homes, Rentrak was cross-referencing data from linear TV and on-demand platforms, providing information that would help the operator learn how to better promote video-on-demand on linear channels. Dish Network used Rentrak's data internally and to sell their own advertising. Rentrak also saw big opportunities in niche markets, and was targeting unrated networks and local TV stations with the data. It had already landed Mark Cuban's HDNet and The Inspiration Network as customers. In particular, Rentrak had been successful in signing up stations that did not indicate as using Nielsen and who wanted less costly services.

In 2002, TiVo and Nielsen Media Research had developed software that allowed Nielsen to extract viewer information from TiVo's digital DVRs, which essentially were a form of STB. Nielsen had downloaded its software to TiVo devices across the country, but the software remained inactive unless households gave permission for it to be switched on, or opted in. TiVo sold the data collected from 300,000 of its subscribers' DVRs (Shim, 2002). TiVo was the only player that was also a set-top manufacturer. The DVR company claimed to be able to collect far more consistent and reliable data than cable or satellite operators because its own engineers designed the devices from the beginning to be able to report back to central servers. Like Nielsen, TiVo emphasized that its data came from every market and from consumers using every service: analog cable, digital cable, satellite, Telco's and over-the-air broadcasts. However, critics claimed the data were skewed because every household in its sample has a DVR, which was not reflective of the broader television viewership. By 2010, cable operator RCN planned to make TiVo its primary DVR platform, integrating it with its video-on-demand library and broadband content from Amazon Video on Demand. While DirecTV offered a TiVo STB in 2000, RCN would be the first MSO to make TiVo its flagship application (*Media Daily News*, 2009; Spangler and Farrell, 2009a).

In 2009, TiVo introduced the pure program rating, a new metric that separated programming audience from the commercial audience. This allowed advertisers to see for example that the program rating of 17 for an episode of *Grey's Anatomy* compared to a 2.7 commercial rating showing that 14.3 rating points (or 84 percent) of the available viewer were lost to fast-forwarding during ads (Bachman, 2007a).

TRA: Resuming Single-source Measurement

For a long time, advertisers had coveted single-source measures of consumers that linked their media usage with purchase behavior. Most had tried and failed in the marketplace from Arbitron's ScanAmerica in the 1980s to the Project Apollo, a recent joint venture between Arbitron and Nielsen that had folded. Both services had been exorbitantly expensive and required consumers to do a number of tasks to produce the data.

By 2010, another company that hoped to advance the advertising evolution was True Return on Investment Accountability (TRA). TRA used a metric that linked TV ratings to product purchase behavior. TRA was a hybrid among the companies developing audience research services based on STB data. Instead of pursuing a pure ratings application, TRA developed a single-source approach that used STB data as a jumping-off point to integrate it with other databases, initially with product-purchase data from supermarket loyalty cards, allowing advertisers to target programs by the products they purchased. "STB data on its own is interesting but probably not that important. For our consumer-package goods clients, the added benefit of knowing what they viewed and what they bought is very exciting," said Jim Kite, president of Connections Research and Analytics for MediaVest, whose clients included major advertisers such as Proctor and Gamble, Coca-Cola, Mars, Inc., Kraft, Wal-Mart, and Wrigley (Bachman, 2009b). TRA's approach uses STB data technology to provide single-source measures of consumer behavior and hoped to improve on earlier attempts by ScanAmerica and Apollo. "In both cases, the [past attempts] were dependent on paying people money to do too many tasks. The equipment was expensive," explains Bill Harvey, TRA president and co-founder. "We use data that already exists [*sic*]. For us, ratings are the starting point. We're not trying to displace ratings; we're going to co-exist (Bachman, 2009b).

TRA's offering combined STB household data from 2.1 million subscribers with household purchase data from 54 million supermarket loyalty cards to come up with a household panel of 370,000 consumers. "[Traditional] ratings are just a proxy; it gives you the number of eyeballs. But what advertisers are interested in is the call to action," said Mark Lieberman, chairman, CEO and co-founder of TRA. "We live in an age of accountability. Everything needs an ROI component" (Bachman, 2009b).

In 2009, Arbitron still persisted in its pursuit of product-purchasing data, investing $13.5 million in TRA (Friedman, 2009). TRA's main product, Media TRAnalytics, used tune-in data from STBs, household purchase data, and households demographics. Though the TV networks had been skeptical of STB data's role in the negotiation process anytime soon, they took a different view of correlating product-purchase data with TV ratings.

> The attraction of using TRA in the buy-sell process is that…the seller can identify the advertisers for which their programming has the greatest value and sell it with some kind of premium, and the buyer can develop a schedule that delivers more target purchasers,
>
> CBS chief research officer, David Poltrack (Bachman, 2009b)

A Host of Challenges: Changing the Game

Regardless of the challenges, the business implications of a shift or a change in the currency could be staggering. One truism in media market research was that different methodologies produce different ratings and different portraits of audiences. And these differences could mean millions of dollars won or lost if a new methodology were adopted.

Studies by Nielsen comparing estimates from STB data with Nielsen's national people meter panel revealed the winners and losers if there were to be a change in the ratings currency. Cable networks would fare much better in wired digital cable homes, with many networks enjoying a 20 percent audience lift. This potential shift in value between cable and broadcast posed a challenge for industry acceptance. In the end, STB data may be too much of a good thing, stated Alan Wurtzel, of ABC. "The current measurement system we have has its flaws, but we're doing $65 billion worth of business off of it," continues Wurtzel. "To me, a census is not a good thing. It's too much data. When they take your blood, they don't take all of it" (Bachman, 2009b).

However, many of the smaller competitors were able to make inroads in areas that Nielsen had not successfully addressed. In particular, STB data could be used by smaller companies to move beyond the standardized broadcast demographic and geographic categories. Historically, reach had been synonymous with mass, with the belief that bigger is better. However, many saw the current world as one of too much reach, with continued use of such blunt tools as reach, frequency, and gross rating points. Advertisers could better target viewers, through profiles such as "aspirational chefs and "rugged reality watchers" using set-top box data. Delivering premium narrowcast audiences with dollars that might be wasted on the buckshot broadcast approach was seen as an advantage. Another key advantage was the ability for smaller STB companies to match up the client's retail location with more-precise geographic audience rather than the standard designated marketing area (DMA), which overshot the advertiser's target in many instances, providing more granular detail geographically.

In the current marketplace, all these companies looked at STB data in different ways. There were no rules or standardization of product, and it was very competitive. Despite all the challenges, all the potential problems, not to mention the financial investment, all parties still believed that STB data were worth pursuing. Two industry committees were formed to explore options and develop standards. The first was the heretofore mentioned Nielsen-funded Center for Research Excellence, which formed a fifteen-member STB committee in 2005. The Committee for Research Excellence was in the process of reviewing all the services and preparing a white paper. The other was the Collaborative Alliance STB Think Tank, organized by Mitch Oscar, executive vice president of televisual applications at MPG. More than fifty companies represented all of the interests in the alliance, including researchers, suppliers, agencies, media companies, and consultants. The Alliance has asked companies to provide data so it can analyze them and suggest best practices.

Both committees hoped to intervene in and help direct the process before these companies sell their services. Solving those technological and methodological challenges may be the easy part, but the business challenge—getting access to cable systems' data—could be the thorniest. Clearly, the operators will want some compensation in exchange for the data stream they are providing.

The formation of Canoe, a consortium of the six largest cable companies, may help pave the way, giving the research firms a single point of contact for partnerships and business deals. Though addressable applications seem to be the top priority, the other simpler goal was to bring STB data to market. "They've focused on addressability, but I'm optimistic that in the end, cable companies will find it in their own self interest," says CBS's Poltrack. "The fact that no one needs all of them for a viable service will keep access open and affordable." (So, for now, as Katy Bachman notes, the STB gold mine remains relatively untapped, guarded by a gatekeeper that has not given the industry the secret password to unlocking its audience data (Bachman, 2009b).

However, whether a cable consortium chooses a new partner or whether cable companies get together and choose established partners was less important than the net effect of changing the ways that viewers were counted. There have been two precedents. When the music industry switched from survey to actual sales data in 1991, long-standing assumptions were upended. Country and rap were more popular than realized. Similarly, when BookScan replaced the *New York Times* as the source of book reviews, major changes resulted. It remains to be seen whether the same will be true for television.

CONCLUSION

The establishment of any ratings currency and its transformation is, in many ways, a reflection of the changing larger system of marketing and advertisers for which it functions. As the ratings business market opened to new markets, and new competition and ratings services experimented and adopted new methods to measure the digital audiences now characteristic of all the media, the marketplace was also responding to profound changes in the established older business models of the broadcast advertising industry. Digital technology coupled with an economic recession had profoundly changed the nature of value in the industry.

As the industry entered the digital era, the traditional broadcast content creators (the broadcast networks and stations) lost control of the major traditional distribution channels (over-the-air) due to advertising excesses, programming failures only now visible, and scheduling locks that led to consumer revolt. The traditional structure of the program supply chain was based on a distribution bottleneck, which positioned the owners of conduits, such as TV networks and local stations, as the primary sources of value, to reap most of the profits. Their traditional structure of power was now replaced by cable distribution bottlenecks, but who knew for how long as profits migrated increasingly from the distributors, or bottleneck holders, to content owners (see Todreas, 1999).

Nielsen's panel-based people meter ratings method, still in use due to what some believed was its monopoly control of the marketplace, was now implemented in both the national and local TV markets. Nielsen had become the dominant player in the CPM/currency market in an era when television was dominated by the network-station model. Now it was struggling to keep afloat in an era of digital competitors and audiences and clinging to the twin rafts of its panel methodology and patent litigation to ward off competitors. The question was whether it would survive now that digital conversion had shifted television in a new economic direction.

Now the top revenue generator was no longer the single-stream network-station model but the dual-stream- (advertising and subscriber) based model of cable TV whose position had improved tremendously due to both an economic downturn and the resultant decline in advertising revenue and because it was the beneficiary of the digital transition as fewer and fewer over-the-air-based homes existed.

Though cable had begun as a stepsister to the network station model, it now accounted for a dominant share of the revenue; cable (and to smaller degrees, Telcos and satellite companies) controlled the new pipeline stream determining what viewers received and what program suppliers paid. The multi-channel, tiered, cable industry had fragmented the TV audience, separated the packaging from distribution function and, in doing so, introduced a new paradigm for profitability in packaging and a new demand for programming.

A big problem with the now-dominant cable model was that cable franchises had developed as monopolies, with most Americans having only one cable operator to choose in their own neighborhood, thereby calling into question further cable control without regulatory interventions. Because cable had few real competitors due to the heavy infrastructure demands it required, consumers' pocketbooks already were being hammered. Consumer advocate groups were on the warpath after a new FCC survey revealed that, in 2000—the first full year since Congress ended price control on cable TV bills—the average consumer bill had increased 5.9 percent, compared to a 3.7 rate of inflation (Pellegrini, 2001). Satellite television, which lacked cable's need for local infrastructure and was able to enter markets at will, was only now beginning to compete with cable to provide television services throughout the country. However, satellite TV providers had provided their subscribers with even worse hikes. Another source of competition, the deregulation of phone companies and cable companies alike that were supposed to get phone companies into the cable business and cable companies into the phone business, was barely visible as a nation-wide trend. "Clustering," where cable companies achieved greater cost efficiencies and savings through economies of scale through controlling larger regions of subscribers, had failed. Rates in clustered areas were higher than non-clustered (Pellegrini. 2001). Furthermore, attempts to reregulate the cable industry had failed to pass Congress, even by Republican President George Bush, when the Senate, both Republicans and Democrats alike, voted to override Bush's veto on a bill that would have imposed new government control on rates for basic service and equipment where prices had risen three times over the price of inflation (Dewar, 1992). This lack of competition and regulation had allowed cable rates to rise dramatically.

The cable era, in many regards, had served an as important prelude to changes from the previous model in which networks and stations, as distributors, were the key sources of value through its introduction of cable networks as packagers, thereby increasing the compensation for content creators. The packaging of cable programs therefore laid the groundwork for anticipating the future of broadband in its strategic assembling and marketing of programming (Todreas, 1999).

Single-stream networks and broadcast stations saw the handwriting on the wall and made every effort to adapt through either conglomeration or attempts to create dual revenue streams. Even broadcast TV stations, such as News Corp's Fox TV and CBS affiliates, whose signals were transmitted by cable originally free of charge because the broadcast stations used the public airwaves without charge, now clamored to be paid for programming costs just as cable networks were paid, known as *retransmission fees*. As such, Fox TV won a dispute with Time Warner Cable that allowed it to profit per each cable subscriber.

Comcast merged with NBC Universal after receiving FCC approval, giving Comcast control of NBC TV network, its broadcast stations, and cable stations such as MSNBC, USA Network, Bravo, and USA and allowing it to retain part ownership of Hulu. As part of the deal, Comcast agreed to give up management (but not ownership) control of Hulu, an on-line video service originally shared by NBC, News Corps, Disney, and Comcast. Comcast also agreed not to interfere with subscriber Web traffic, the transmission of on-line video to customers, or pressuring programmers and distributors on rules that limited access to Internet content to an open Internet. Critics were concerned that Comcast would unfairly withhold NBC shows from the expanded video on-line market, such as Hulu (Shields and Bliss, 2011).

Although the resulting increased charges for programming would likely be passed on to the consumer, increasing subscriber fees were not without problems for cable multiple system operators (MSOs), the new lords of the pipeline. Most subscribers, already maxed out with cable costs, resented the endless barrage of advertising to which they were subjected, waited for the day when they could unplug cable as the middle person altogether, and became further alienated from attempts by any industry conglomerate to control the pipeline now that they had tasted the freedom of the Internet.

Five media companies dominated the programming shown on cable. Each of these companies was either a national network broadcaster, a cable or satellite operator, or had significant ties to both.

Disney owned the broadcast network ABC, broadcast stations, and cable networks such as ESPN, Lifetime, A&E, History Channel, and SoapNet.

Viacom owned broadcast networks CBS and UPN, local affiliates reaching almost 39 percent of the American television viewing audience, and cable channels including MTV, BET, Comedy Central, Nickelodeon, Showtime, Spike TV, CMT, and VH1.

Time Warner owned the second-largest cable company in the country, the WB broadcast network, and cable channels including CNN, Headline News, HBO, Court TV, TBS, TNT, Oxygen, and Cartoon Network.

News Corp/Liberty Media owned the Fox broadcast network, local affiliates of both Fox and UPN reaching about 39 percent of the American TV viewing audience, national DBS satellite operator DirecTV, and cable channels Fox News, FX, National Geographic, and more than a dozen Fox Regional Sports networks.

Liberty Media was the largest single shareholder of News Corp and owned channels such The Hallmark Channel, Discovery, Animal Planet, QVC, Starz, and TLC.

Comcast was the largest cable operator, with 23 million subscribers, and also owned a significant stake in channels such as TV One, E!, The Golf Channel, Outdoor Life Network, G4techTV, and regional sports networks serving three of the nation's six largest metropolitan areas—Chicago, Baltimore-Washington, and Philadelphia. Comcast had recently purchased a significant stake in MGM, with Sony (hearusnow. org, 2009). According to an article in *Washington Monthly* from television executive Ted Turner, 90 percent of the top fifty cable TV stations are owned by the same parent companies that own the broadcast networks (Turner, 2004).

Wildcard: the Internet

The battle was not just for who would control the pipeline into the home and where it led but for the real estate at the end of the pipe, or vertically integrated companies. While cable companies had become the biggest revenue streams and had wrested control of the home entertainment experience from broadcast TV owners, the war was far from over. There were two main battles being played out as stakeholders jockeyed for control of home networks.

The first battle pitted the personal computers against set-top box providers. In an era where digital content was at the epicenter of more and more devices, the set-top box atop the TV was struggling to be the hub, managing the inflow and outflow of data devices. Cable companies wanted to make sure that their set-top boxes controlled the hub because set-top boxes offered vertical integration as a means of stemming any loss of value from competitors, such as the Internet.

However, another possibility would be that the hub would run through a personal computer (PC). As the PC became the gateway to entertainment services, cable companies and other service providers worried over their loss of control over the home entertainment experience and about customers switching from the triple-play package of voice, video, and data to just data.

To maintain this control, cable companies wanted to install a gateway in the home to act as an über set-top box to allow them to control home networks, while consumers would access content stored on servers at the provider's nodes or central office. They hoped to gain an edge by relying on consumer ignorance about a varying array of digital devices by ensuring all roads led through their cable boxes.

However, cable still presented a big disadvantage in usage based pricing. New wireless standards and faster broadband plus mounting costs had made it easier for many consumers to bypass cable or telecom companies' set-top boxes through the Internet's wireless home network standard (Higgenbotham, 2009).

Large technology vendors, such as Intel, Microsoft, and Cisco, acted as double agents in the battle for control of the television and its standards. While they provided tools to allow providers to control content, they also aimed their wares for consumers, such as Apple TV, the Roku Box, Vudu, Netflix, and Amazon, which also offered on-line video through their set-top boxes, as they vied to control the software in the set-top boxes for interactive TV.

Microsoft won an important battle when a global consortium of electronic companies adopted its interactive platform specifications. However success in defining standards did not ensure success in the marketplace. Microsoft and Intel ran afoul of industry for using market power to force customers to use their proprietary products and standard, while the industry's goals were to ensure a standard that allowed content written for one broadcast set-top box to run on others. Though approved as the standard in 2000, no current manufacturer sold set-top boxes that adopted its platform. Currently, Open TV led the pack as Microsoft's commitment to open standards was questioned.

A second battle was being played out in the booming video on demand field. Video on demand acted as a catalyst, prompting battles over who owned the gateway-enabled set-top box and its revenue possibilities. This battle necessitated a new generation of set-top boxes with two-way functionality, known as the IP-Set Top Box, allowing greater networking and phone services. However, MSOs were willing to invest since they understood that the return on their investment was critical in the face of the current anemia of basic subscribers. The only other revenue potentials were reducing churn and increasing revenues per subscribers (Joyce, 2003).

A key concern for cable companies was not only that they might not keep the larger piece of the pie but that they might be cut out of the pie altogether as programmers headed straight for the Web, skipping traditional distribution channels. Industry leaders foresaw a new era for the network in what David Poltrack, head of CBS Research, called the digital franchise program (Poltrack, 2006). A franchised program used a universal distribution system, selective program devises, and marketing muscle and was seen as a means of transformation of the network TV business. The TV networks as franchise programmers could place their programming on the Internet, cutting out both the over-the-air broadcast stations and the cable/satellite delivery system altogether.

Furthermore, the idea of receiving unbundled cable programming that allowed viewers to select viewing à la carte and thereby do away with the twenty-five shopping, religious and pay-per-view channels seemed all the more attractive, an idea that was circulating in a bill in Congress.

To offset this possibility that viewers might decide to go directly to the Web, cable companies, satellite, phone companies, and big programmers were at work on a model that prevented content from directly going to the Internet, known ironically as TV Everywhere—a cable industry solution to Internet video challenges—that would require Internet users to pay for a cable TV subscription if they wanted to watch popular shows on-line. Spearheaded by Comcast and Time Warner Cable, the TV Everywhere initiative appeared to be built on cable operators (and other distributors) agreeing to work together to pressure content providers to make their content available on the Internet only to viewers who have paid for a cable TV subscription in addition to an Internet connection.

Thus, TV Everywhere tied on-line TV distribution to the existing cable, phone, and satellite distributors' TV subscriptions, thereby ensuring cable MSOs as gatekeepers seeking to control the flow of video on the Web. Comcast planned to launch its On Demand On-line service in 2009; Time Warner Cable Inc. was engaged in a trial. In essence, virtually every major MSO and programming company was preparing TV Everywhere plans. Some saw this initiative as a catalyst for something bigger, a sea change in the way that cable delivered its services. According to industry analyst, Craig Leddy:

> TV Everywhere has moved from the confines of back-office discussions to become the hottest issue in cable. Amid the increased flow of television programming to "over-the-top" Websites, such as Hulu, U.S. cable operators are concerned about free consumer access to the cable programming for which they are paying a license fee. If cable programming is free, the reasoning goes, then consumers will cut the cable cord and the entire TV industry will go the way of the music and newspaper industries—succumbing to Internet competition.
>
> (Leddy, 2009)

With the industry already migrating to "all digital," it was poised to embark on the next major phase: going all-IP. The top MSOs were known to be exploring the prospective advantages and feasibility of IP delivery for all services. Going all-IP could enable cable operators to erase the barriers between its TV and broadband platforms and perhaps more easily feed multiple screens and devices. Furthermore, going all-IP could leave cable's satellite competitors in the dust and keep pace with fiber-rich FiOS from Verizon Communications Inc. and IPTV-based U-verse from AT&T Inc. For some leading technologists, the endgame was a world of unicast delivery of personalized media and services to any device (Leddy, 2009).

Although TV Everywhere was likely to take many twists and turns before cable IP video became a regular part of consumers' media habits, it could well have been the tipping point for a transition to cable's going all-IP. Cable was a long way off from full IPTV delivery of its video channels, and current IPTV technologies still faced some challenges. To move toward this grand IP vision, cable still had to overcome challenges that were inherent in TV Everywhere. Cable operators and programmers had to remain committed to tackling complex issues, including content rights, evolving business models, ensuring positive user experiences, and their own historical record of contentious licensing negotiations. Furthermore, the

FCC's proposed net neutrality rules could affect how operators dealt with content providers. (Leddy, 2009).

However, after having their appetites whetted by the unblocked pipelines of Internet TV, consumer groups sounded the alarm regarding TV Everywhere and argued there was enough evidence of collusion and other harms to warrant a full-scale investigation by the Justice Department or the FCC into the scheme. They called for a probe of the TV Everywhere plan proposed by satellite and phone companies that brought TV shows and movies to computers and other devices but only for those that subscribed to cable TV and high-speed Internet services. The result, the groups said, would allow Comcast, Time Warner Cable, AT&T, Verizon, and DirecTV to unfairly dominate the burgeoning on-line video industry by ensuring video content was locked behind a subscription-based wall and starved out on-line competitors such as Apple, Boxee, Hulu, and Vuze, who needed access to choice shows and movies to attract viewers. Consumer groups called for the antitrust authorities to investigate such an important, potentially illegal and anti-competitive development (Kang, 2010). Rumors were afloat not only that Fox wanted more ads inserted into the Hulu versions of shows such as Glee and Family Guy but that the indications were that free Hulu users would have to be cable subscribers to watch shows the day after they aired, wait eight days for episodes to appear on the service, or be signed up for the paid Hulu Plus service.

Not all industry executives were in agreement with TV Everywhere, as Roger A. Iger of Walt Disney warned that such a gambit would be anti-consumer and anti-technology because such a plan would place cable programming behind a pay wall (Arango, 2009; Ammori, 2010b). Unsurprisingly, the cable industry did not welcome this critique of their plans, arguing that TV Everywhere consisted of *collaboration*, not collusion. While anti-trust authorities encouraged collaboration sometimes even among competitors, for the sake of innovation and other benefits, the types of "collaboration" generally found not to harm competition and to further innovation were very different from TV Everywhere. Some types of collaboration were illegal because they replaced the competitive marketplace, driving low prices, choice, and innovation with an agreement among incumbents effectively not to engage in competition with one another in certain ways.

TV Everywhere evidence suggested it included *both* price-fixing and allocation, violating anti-trust laws, according to Marvin Ammori. First, TV Everywhere set the price for consumers to access much television content on-line. The price was the cost of a traditional cable TV subscription and an Internet connection plus access to "free" content if you watch advertising. In other words, consumers would need to pay three different ways. TV Everywhere also appeared to set the terms in the negotiations between distributors and programmers—requiring, for one thing, that programmers keep content off the Internet unless a viewer subscribes also to cable TV. Setting such terms among competitors for suppliers through horizontal agreement appeared problematic (Ammori, 2010b).

In a world without TV Everywhere, we could expect programmers to compete directly with distributors on the Internet (for example, Hulu, currently owned by programmers such as Disney and Fox, versus Comcast, a traditional distributor). TV Everywhere undid that competition, as people would not be able to cancel their cable service to watch popular programming exclusively on-line without also paying for cable TV. And without TV Everywhere, cable companies in different regions would need to compete with one another on-line—with a company such as Comcast competing against Cox, Time Warner Cable, AT&T, Verizon, Qwest, and the like. However, TV Everywhere tied content to a local cable subscription, thereby assuring no new competition (Ammori, 2010b).

According to the *New York Times*, "so as to avoid being accused of collusion, much of the discussions" by executives about TV Everywhere "have been on the telephone and in private, one-on-one chats during industry events." That is, to avoid being accused of collusion, the executives didn't stop having the talks—they just tried to eliminate the paper trail (Arango, 2009).

Cable industry participants attempted to stem *competition* undermining their industry's economics (of high prices and limited choice for consumers), because the point of TV Everywhere was not to innovate. It was to protect the cable business model. Media moguls were looking for a way to protect their investments from the ravages of the Internet. What was at stake was the last remaining pillar of the old business model not severely affected by the Internet: cable TV. Aware of how print, broadcast, and music suffered from business erosion, chief executives at Time Warner, Viacom, and NBC Universal made protecting cable a top priority. Some studies indicated that they could lose as many as 35 percent of their subscribers due to the Internet, a key concern as the majority of profits for big entertainment were now from cable TV (Arango, 2009). TV Everywhere could be seen as designed to preserve their existing, limited competition model for years to come.

As Ammori, concludes,

> We stand at a defining moment for the future of television and film. Existing and evolving Internet technologies may finally inject much needed competition and choice into the TV market by enabling Americans to watch high-definition programs on the Internet from anywhere or on the family living room screen. But the big cable, satellite and phone companies, which benefit from the status quo, are trying to put down this revolution in online video. The dominant distributors and studios have a long history of scrambling to kill online TV and trying to preserve the current market structure and prevent disruptive competition. Over the past decade, they have locked down and controlled TV set-top boxes to limit competing programming sources; they have considered imposing fees for high-capacity Internet use in ways that would discourage online TV viewing; and they have pressured programmers to keep their best content off the Internet.

(For more expanded argument on the cable industry and its anti-competitive and anti-consumer attempts to establish and control barriers to entry into its market by the Internet, see Marvin Ammori, 2010b.)

By 2009, the FCC signaled it would break the cozy relationship between TV networks and cable systems, making it easier for anyone who makes a video program to send it directly to TV set without first cutting a deal with a cable or TV company. In 1996, Congress ordered the commission to create rules to allow people to buy "navigation" devices such as set-top boxes from an electronics company rather than cable companies. The idea was to create a standard so any set-top box would work in any cable system. However cable companies dragged their feet in supporting open technical standards to reap further profits by renting boxes. The question now was how TV would connect to cable, satellite, and the Internet as cable TV shows were no different from other data sent over the Internet. TV programming could offer the same sort of open standards used by computers, rather than the closed systems desired by the media corporations by cutting out cable companies as middlemen. The FCC pushed for set-top boxes to deliver content from sources other than the traditional programmer to help drive its goals of broadband access and utilization.

Whither Ratings?

Advertising on television had become complicated; there was no getting around it. As the industry moved toward an on-demand, delayed-content delivery model that embraced addressable advertising, panel data no longer provided an acceptable level of accuracy for ratings. Panel-based ratings had been developed to measure the forced choice behaviors of the masses, leading to formulaic genres, spin-offs, and rigid time slots ensuring remorseless competitiveness. As DVD penetration increased, ad-skipping behaviors increased, with as many as 73 percent of the audience for TV drama skipping commercials. As a result, programming had shifted from linear to non-linear, video on demand, allowing viewers to pick a playlist, and portable devices had shifted viewing from the home (Taylor, 2009).

For the ratings industry, the buzz had switched from reliance on GRPs and CPPs and focused on niche cross-platform measurement across silos. The year 2007 marked the first year that DVRs became mainstream and were included in Nielsen ratings, as stakeholders were offered live-plus-7-days ratings for viewing watched up to seven days after recording. DVRs were in 35 percent of all households with playback accounting for six percent of viewing. However, of this six percent, between 55 percent and 60 percent skipped the commercials, according to Nielsen (Taylor, 2009). Prime-time viewing told a different story where as many as 24 percent of the key demographic (eighteen to forty-nine years old) now used DVRs.

The biggest impact in DVR growth was on commercials and whether advertisers received the audiences for whcih they paid as viewers fast-forwarded through the endless barrage of commercials. Nielsen and the major networks still perpetuated the propaganda that commercials were not skipped during play and that viewers liked commercials, but advertising demanded more precision data. Thus, 2007 marked the year of the first commercial ratings (second by second) and a demand for more measurement of audience engagement, as indicated by such devices as digital video recorders, video on demand, and interactive services. The increasingly fragmented, mobile, and device-laden consumer had changed the nature of TV consumption from a one screen to a three-screens model. Advertisers now wanted ratings, which included all three screens—TV, Internet, and mobiles—and they wanted more-measureable outcomes.

Possible power shifts in the ratings-industry players were now possible as older methods, still employed by Nielsen, such as the people meter, were seen as outmoded in failing to provide three-screen measurement. However, despite its limitations, it was the people meter that first registered significant growth in cable networks over their broadcast counterparts, who had lost the most under this new system, an important finding as cable power brokers now dominated the pipeline. Furthermore, the people meter still at least required panel members to press a button on a remote every fifty minutes to indicate they were watching. Realizing that the people meter could not provide Internet or mobile ratings, Nielsen had taken steps to protect its sampling-based panel methods by including these types of users in its panels and by updating its telephone-based ratings sample frame to include mobiles.

Another device that appeared to make the transition was the portable people meter. Despite its rejection by Nielsen as a possible partner, Arbitron and its PPM method embraced a platform approach in measuring radio, TV, and mobiles. It had made major inroads in Singapore (2003), Canada (2004), and Norway, Kenya, and Kazakhstan (2006) as Arbitron, together with Taylor Nelson Sofres (which was acquired by WPP Group in 2008) had worked together internationally since 2000 to make it a method of choice internationally. After being introduced into Philadelphia and Houston in 2007, by 2008 it had moved into twelve major markets in 2009 and would be in most major markets by 2010.

Early PPM reports suggested a reversal of findings for radio audiences' diary reports compared to the people meter audience findings for television. For radio stations using the PPM, niche stations suffered the most while mass stations played at malls and businesses gained strengths, putting radio in the position of becomeing even more homogeneous. Key genres to benefit from the PPM were light rock, oldies, news, and country whereas genres such as talk, classical, smooth jazz, and Spanish-speaking stations all lost audience, causing an uproar among minority-interest groups who accused Arbitron of understating minority audiences and demanding Congressional actions. Of course, the PPM had changed the definition of listening dramatically from written personal diary recordings made by the listener to measures simply of exposure, any panel member standing close enough to a radio signal to warrant its being picked up by a pager-type device carried by the member. The question of whether this type of measure indicated true interest or intent had yet to be answered, as radio played ubiquitously throughout restaurants, malls, and most public areas, including listeners more as a matter of chance than choice.

Clickstream data now possible through the Internet and set-top boxes offered second-by-second ratings, gave boosts to niche channels that were underreported in sample-centric approaches, and offered measures of engagement and three-screen data. That, along with DVR usage, extensive and stable out-of-home information, the ability to integrate seamlessly with on-line usage, and the ability to parse out actual ad performance, made the data unique and valuable to a range of customers.

However, as a measurement currency, it was still in its infancy, as there were many issues to be resolved. Among the issues were standardization of data-processing rules, such as the ability to know whether the television was on or off, and how to report time-shifted viewing; standardization of the metrics and nomenclature, to conform to the currency vocabulary of ratings, shares, households use television (HUTs) and persons using television (PUTs). Or would new measurements be needed? There was no agreed-upon national footprint, and efforts to weight the data to make it more national were not universally accepted. Could matching data points to actual spending and lifestyle information counteract a lack of demographic data? Industry leaders (Wurtzel, 2009) called for establishing a joint industry committee such as a non-affiliated, non-partisan advisory council either through an established industry or respected accreditation organization. This council, composed of programmers, agencies, processors, and suppliers, would help build consensus and guide the formation of a new measurement currency that worked for all interested parties.

For years, planning, buying, and selling TV commercial time has depended on one provider, one currency—Nielsen's. The traditional approach relied on a laboriously built and relatively small representative panel of consumers. But recruiting and maintaining those panels was not cheap. Many would-be TV ratings providers had been crushed under the competitive challenge of building expensive panels in the hopes the industry would support them.

In 2009, Nielsen began measuring Internet usage in its national TV ratings panels "to build a foundation for the inclusion of on-line viewing in our TV currency." Furthermore it was at work on its three-screen strategy. A host of potential set-top box data and two vying Internet ratings competitors offered a variety of types of ratings, but none had assumed the currency mantle. A number of factors affected the potential outcome as to whether Nielsen would continue its long-held monopoly, including continued upheavals in the credit markets and financial services industry, industry competition, ability to commercialize new products, impact of increased costs of data collection with the trends toward cell phone-only homes, the ability to expand into new markets, the ability to identify and integrate appropriate acquisitions, and, last but not least, patent purchase and litigation.

REFERENCES

Advertising Age (1950). It's official: Nielsen absorbs Hooperatings. March 6, p. 1.

Advertising Age (1955). ARB has new service for advertisers—TV ratings in 140 small markets. March 7, p. 3.

Advertising Age (1959a). ARB set to catch all TV viewing. September 19, pp. 42–43.

Advertising Age (1959b). ARB to compile county by county studies by computer. May 25, p. 3.

Advertising Age (1999). Why we don't count: A roundtable discussion for the millennium. May, p. 1.

Advertising Age (2006). Nielsen rejects Arbitron partnership. March 6, p. 14.

Advertising and Selling (1949). Roster, coincidental, and unaided recall: How they compare in terms of counting listeners. August.

Advertising Report (2001). Jupiter feels the dot.com loss. July 30, pp. 1–5.

Ammori, M. (2010a). Cable industry claims collusion as pro-consumer: Response on TV Everywhere. *Huffington Post*, January 5. http://www.huffingtonpost.com/marvin-ammori/cable-industry-claims-col_b_411748.html

Ammori, M. (2010b). TV competition nowhere: How the cable industry is colluding to kill on-line TV. January. http://www.freepress.*net/files/TV-Nowhere*

Appelman, H. (2000). Ratings that know what you're looking at and when. *New York Times*, June 7, pp. 1–6.

Arango, T. (2009). Cable TV's big worry: Taming the Web. *New York Times*, June 23. http://www.nytimes.com/2009/06/24/business/media/24pay.html

Arbitron Company (n.d.). Company histories. fundinguniverse.com. NPD Group. http://www.fundinguniverse.com/company-histories/The-Arbitron-Company-Company-History.html

Bachman, K. (1991) Arbitron buys RADAR. *Mediaweek*, July 2. http://www.allbusiness.com/services/business-services-miscellaneous-business/4742513-1.html

Bachman, K. (2000). Arbitron delays Fall '99 ratings book. *Mediaweek*, January 10, p. 16.

Bachman, K. (2002). Delay on portable meters. *Mediaweek*, September 9, p. 1.

Bachman, K. (2004a). Arbitron readies Texas PPM. *Mediaweek*, September 27, p. 13.

Bachman, K. (2004b). Burns asks if FTC can monitor Nielsen's LPM. *Advertising Week*, October 7, p. 1.

Bachman, K. (2005). Ads would grow with PPM. *Mediaweek*, July 25, p. 8.

Bachman, K. (2006). Four agencies queued for Arbitron's PPM service. *Mediaweek*, January 16, pp. 4–6.

Bachman, K. (2007a). Nielsen to roll out digital plus. *MediaWeek*, February 13. http://www.allbusiness.com/services/business-services-miscellaneous-business/4794722-1.html

Bachman, K. (2007b). Nielsen's digital plus could trigger lawsuit. *MediaWeek*, February 13. http://www.allbusiness.com/services/business-services-miscellaneous-business/4794832-1.html

Bachman, K. (2007c). ErinMedia loses funding pursues suit against Nielsen. *Mediaweek*, February 21, p. 1.

Bachman, K. (2009a). Univision refuses to encode signals in new PPM areas. *Mediaweek*, November 2, p. 1.

Bachman, K. (2009b). Cracking the set-top-box code. *AdWeek*, pp. 1–5.

Bachman, K., and Consoli, J. (2006). Back to square one. *Mediaweek*, March 6, p. 6. http://www.allbusiness.com/services/business-services-miscellaneous-business/4843725-1.html

Barlas, P. (1998). Rivals vie to be Nielsen of the net. *Investors Business Daily*, July 9, p. 15.

Bermejo, F. (2009). Audience manufacture in historical perspective: From broadcasting to Google. *New Media Society* 11(133): 133–154.

Beville, H. M. (1983). Interview conducted by the author in Douglaston, NY, March 10.

Beville, H. M. (1988). *Audience ratings, radio, television, cable*. Hillsdale, NJ: Lawrence Erlbaum.

Billboard (1991a). Arbitron council seeks sample boost. March 30, p. 19.

Billboard (1991b). Arbitron users divided over 3-book plan. June 15, p. 1.

Billboard (1993). Arbitron refocuses on radio after leaving TV race. October 30, p. 4.

Billboard (1994). Arbitron plans to increase sample size in 85 markets. January 29, p. 95.

Billboard (1995). Arbitron to use military and college area phone nos. April 22, p. 94.

Bloomberg.com (2009). TiVo examines "pure program ratings" using its Stop//Watch ratings service in May. July 30. http://www.bloomberg.com/apps/news?pid=newsarchive&sid=a_ZqcVp0YexQ

Bloomberg News (2009). ComScore announce media measurement 360: Next generation of global digital measurement. *Bloomberg News*, June 1. http://www.bloomberg.com/apps/news?pid=newsarchive&sid=aOBdYUkbC6F4

BMI News (2011). Nielsen signs off on radio ratings. January 5. http://www.bmi.com/news/entry/550155

Brassine, J. (2011). Ever-changing usage of the DVR and its impact on advertising. www.sunriseadvertising.com/white_paper.pdf

Broadcasting (1942). Coincidental survey is added by CAB. October 5, p. 60.

Broadcasting (1946). CAB suspends ratings service. June 24, p. 46.

Broadcasting (1950). National Hooperatings sold. February 28, p. 27.

Broadcasting (1959). Electronic brain for timebuying. May 25, p. 31.

Broadcasting (1964). Big shake-up at ARB. November 23, p. 58.

Broadcasting (1986). Nielsen speeds up overnight. February 24, pp. 36–37.

Broadcasting (1987). Arbitron, Birch lock horns in audience measurement battle. February 9, p. 96.

Broadcasting (1989). AGB tells networks it needs contracts to survive. June 30, p. 41.

Broadcasting (1991). Stations opting for only one ratings service. June, p. 39.

Broadcasting & Cable (1993) Arbitron drops TV Ratings. October 25 , p. 45.

Broadcasting & Cable (1994). Arbitron solution: Paid sample increases in 117 markets. January 24, p. 153.

Broadcasting & Cable (1996). Broadcasters hope they're SMART. April 8, pp. 25–27.

Broadcasting & Cable (1997). Cable networks get SMART. August 4, pp. 72–73.

Broadcasting/Telecasting (1953). Our respects to James William Seiler. November 30.

Bunzel, R. E., and Flint, J. (1991). Birch Radio to cease operations. *Broadcasting*, December 23, p. 11.

Business Week (1957/1958). ARB offers instantaneous TV program ratings. December 21, 1957, p. 45 and September 6, 1958, p.129.

Business Week (2005). The end of TV (as you know it). November 21, pp. 2–24.

Business Wire (1999). Nielsen Media Research to begin in local markets. December 8, p. 1.

Business Wire (2007). ErinMedia cuts staff, renews demand for fair and open competition in the U.S. ratings industry. February 20. http://www.businesswire.com/news/home/20070220006157/en/ErinMedia-Cuts-Staff-Renews-Demand-Fair-Open

Buzzard, K. (1990). *Chains of gold: Marketing the ratings and rating the markets.* Methuen, New Jersey: Scarecrow Press.

Buzzard, K. (1992). *Electronic media ratings: Turning audience into dollars and sense.* Stoneham, MA: Butterworth-Heinemann.

Buzzard, K. (1999). Radio ratings pioneers. *Journal of Radio Studies* 6(2): 287–305.

Buzzard, K. (2002). The people meter wars: A case study of technological innovation and diffusion in the ratings industry. *Journal of Media Economics* 15(4): 273–291.

Buzzard, K. (2003). Net ratings: Defining a new medium by the old, measuring internet audiences. In A. Everett and J.T. Caldwell (eds.), *New media: Theories and practices of digititexuality* (pp. 197–208). New York: Routledge.

Capitol Confidential (2011). Congress, internet privacy and Google. http://biggovernment.com/capitolconfidential/2011/07/22/congress-internet-privacy-and-google/

CCN Disclosure (2000). Media Metrix: First ever multi-county Internet audience measurement results released by Media Metrix. June 19, pp. 1–5.

Coffey, S. (2001). Internet audience measurement: A practitioner's view. *Journal of Interactive Advertising* 2 (Spring): 1–9.

Coffey, S. (2002). Internet metrics: The loyal audience. *OPA Whitepapers* 1(1): 1–14. http://www.on-linepublishers.org, see http://docs.google.com/viewer?a=v&q=cache:PLCgSplpB98J:www.ggcomm.com/OPA_P.et+metrics,&hl=en&gl=us&pid=bl&srcid=ADGEESiDOCdDAMrpIaoelPychlC16Ts91qLVjfjqCHxp5tPGwWzuKKJeyrZoJFxw8ONOC3GdmTWReofxZQSLxo6-z5Vc-_7d05ZUaXV95OYTpvBbEl84VQl11XpWQuR2VwxYODPiJCCq&sig=AHIEtbRvJBzyOFuwl8G7rpgKRT7YQS_mig

Communications Daily (1991). Improved peoplemeter. November 1, p. 1.

Communications Daily (1992). Local operations continue: Arbitron drops ScanAmerica services. September 3, p. 4.

Communications Daily (1993). Matter of concern: Arbitron throws in the towel. October 19, p. 1.

Conte, A. J. (1983). Measuring up: How broadcast ratings grew. *Advertising Age*, October 31, M–28+.

Converse, J. (1987). *Survey research in the United States: Roots and emergence, 1890–1960.* Berkeley, CA: University of California Press.

Cooper, R. (1983). Interview conducted by Ted Shaker in Arbitron History Tapes. New York.

Crossley, A. M. (1983). Interview conducted by the author in Princeton, NJ, March 18.

Danner, M., *et al.* (1985). TV looks AT itself. *Harpers*, March 26, pp. 3–5.

Dewar H., and K. Cooper (1992). Congress overrides cable bill veto, hands Bush first defeat. *The Tech.* On-line edition, October 6. http://tech.mit.edu/V112/N47/cable.47w.html

Dot.Com (1998). Company measures web user patterns. August 31, 5: 1.

Douglas, S. (1999). *Listening in: Radio and the American imagination.* New York: Times Books.

Electronic Information Report (2002). ComScore is net measurement king. July 29. http://business.highbeam.com/5085/article-1G1-89651117/comscore-net-measurement-king-doubleclick-bails-out

Electronic Media (1988a). Meters show viewers turned out commercials. March 14, p. 1.

Electronic Media (1988b). AGB studies VCR use. March 21, p. 20.

Electronic Media (1988c). AGB blames industry for its demise. August 8, p. 8.

Electronic Media (1993). Arbitron bows out. October 26, p. 10.

Ettema, J. S., and D. C. Whitney (eds.) (1994). The money arrow: An introduction to audiencemaking. In *Audiencemaking: How the media create the audience*. Thousand Oaks, CA: Sage.

Everett, D. (2001). Portable people meter's long walk to Wilmington. *Media Life Magazine*, January 1, p. 1. http://www.medialifemagazine.com/news2001/jan01/jan02/4_thurs/news6thursday.html

Fleming, D., and B. Bailyn (eds.) (1969). "Paul Lazarsfeld." In *The intellectual migrating: Europe and America, 1930–1960*. Cambridge, MA: Harvard University Press.

Friedman, W. (2009). Standard ops, Nielsen delivers live plus same day DVR ratings. *Media Daily News*, September 9, pp. 1–2.

Garvin, G. (2011). Sunbeam TV loses suit over Nielsen ratings. *Miami Herald*, February 14, p. 1.

Gertner, J. (2005). Our ratings, ourselves. *New York Times Magazine*, Magazine Section, April 10, pp. 1–4.

Goetzl, D. (2009a). Nielsen: Ad minutes added to primetime in 2008. *Media Daily News*, July 22, p. 1.

Goetzl, D. (2009b). Nielsen measures TV everywhere. *Media Daily News*, September 8, pp. 1–2.

Goetzl, D. (2011). Nielsen brings TV metrics to online ads. *Media Daily News*, September 7, p. 1.

Hansell, S. (2002). Technology briefing: Media Metrix sold to comScore. *New York Times*, June 7, p. 32. http://www.nytimes.com/2002/06/07/business/technology-briefing-internet-media-metrix-sold-to-comscore.html

Harris Commission (1963). Broadcast ratings: Hearings before a Subcommittee on Interstate and Foreign Commerce House of Representatives, 88th Congress (March 5–20). On the methodology, accuracy, and use of rating in broadcasting. Washington DC: U.S. Government Printing Office.

Harvey, B. (1983). Interview conducted by author in New York City, May.

Harvey, B. (2004). Better TV audience measurement through the research integration of set-top-box data. WAM – Worldwide Audience Measurement 2004 – Television Conference. http://www.esomar.org/web/research_papers/Conjoint-Analysis_857_Better-television-audience-measurement-through-the-research-integration-of-set-top-box-data-br-Phase-Two.php

hearusnow.org (2009). Cable dominates markets. December 25. http://www.hearusnow.org/mediaownership/25/

Higgenbotham, S. (2009). Battle for the home network pits PCs against set top boxes. GigaOM.com, June 23. www address http://gigaom.com/2009/06/23/the-battle-for-the-home-network-pits-pcs-against-set-top-boxes/

Hines, B. D. (1960). Brain offer political campaigners minute-by-minute progress reports. *Washington Star*. p. 2.

Hinman, J. (2008). Nielsen erinMedia settle antitrust suit. *Tampa Bay Business Journal*, April 1, p. 1.

Holahan, C. (2007). Ganging up on Nielsen. *Business Week*, February 6. http://www.thebostonchannel.com/r/10952761/detail.html

Hooper, C. E. (1949). Letter to William Brooks. May 4. Madison, WI: Hooper Collection, State Historical Archives.

Hooper, C. E., and Chappell, M. W. (1944). *Radio audience measurement*. New York: S. Daye, Inc.

Hu, J. (1998). Racing to the start line. http://C/NET.news.com, May 14, http://news.cnet.com/2009-1023-211162.html

Hughes, D., and Lublin, J. (2010). Arbitron CEO resigns after Hill testimony. *Wall Street Journal*, January 13, p. 1. http://online.wsj.com/article/SB10001424052748703672104574654392623606448.html

INTV Journal (1989). Peoplemeters raise ire, not the numbers. August/September, pp. 28–32.

James, M. (2007). Nielsen to expand its TV sample. *Los Angeles Times*, September 27. http://articles.latimes.com/2007/sep/27/business/fi-nielsen27Page?

Jhally, S. (1982). Probing the blindspot: The audience commodity. *Canadian Journal of Political and Social Theory* 6(1–2): 204–210.

Joyce, E. (2002). Clock ticking for Jupiter Media Metrix. *Clickz*, April 1, 2002 http://www.clickz.com/clickz/news/1708036/clock-ticking-jupiter-media-metrix

Joyce, E. (2003). VOD: The first skirmish in the battle. Internetnews.com, January. http://www.internetnews.com/infra/article.php/1577831/VOD+the+First+Skirmish+in+the+Battle.htm

Joyce, E., and Sanders, C. (2001). NetRatings to buy Jupiter Media Metrix, eRatings.com. *Advertising Report*, October 25, p. 1.

Kang, C. (2010). Public interest groups call for antitrust probe of TV Everywhere. *Washington Post*, January 4. http://www.blogrunner.com/snapshot/D/0/2/public_interest_groups_call_for_antitrust_probe_of_tv_everywhere/

Katz, R. (1999). For Nielsen foe SMART, it's final. *Variety*, May 31, p. 24.

Kawamoto, D. (1998). Cashing in on portal fever. *C/Net News*, May 14, pp. 1–2.

Kerschbaumer, K. (2002). Media Metrix-Jupiter merge. *Broadcasting & Cable*, July 5, p. 35.

Klaassen, A. (2005). PPM data paints new picture of radio audience. *Advertising Age,* 21 September. http://adage.com/article/mediaworks/ppm-data-paints-picture-radio-audience/46849/

Klaassen, A. (2007). Meet the little guys who are challenging comScore and NetRatings. *Advertising Age,* August 6. http://www.highbeam.com/doc/1G1-167355715.html

Krol, C. (2007). Online measurement debate produces more questions than answers. *B to B online,* December 10.   http://www.btobonline.com/article/20071210/FREE/71210008/online-measurement-debate-produces-more-questions-than-answers#seenit

Landreth, J. (2008). Interview conducted by author in Silver Springs, Maryland, Spring, 2008.

LawyersUSA (2006). How long does patent infringement litigation take? http://www.inventionstatistics.com/Duration_of_Patent_Lawsuits_Litigation_Length.html

Layfayette, J. (1999). SMART money wasn't there for ratings rival. *Electronic Media,* May 12, p. 3.

Leahy, S. (2005). Challenging Nielsen as a monopoly. *Media Life*, June 23. http://www.medialifemagazine.com/news2005/jun05/june20/4_thurs/news3thursday.html

Learmonth, M. (2007). Start-up rivals target Nielsen. *Variety*, February 17.

Leddy, C. (2009). TV Everywhere, can cable solve its Hula problem. *Cable Industry Insider*, October 22.   http://www.prnewswire.com/news-releases/hulus-success-pushes-cable-toward-ip-video-report-finds-65579902.html

Levin, G. (2007). Time shifting viewers stay tuned days later. *USA Today,* October 16. http://www.usatoday.com/life/television/news/2007-10-15-timeshift_N.htm

Lewis, F. (2001). It knows what you watched last Tuesday. *Philadelphia City*, January 18–25, p. 1.

Liedtke, M. (2009). Online ads: Getting back into high gear. *Ecommerce Times*, October 14, p.1.

Littleton, C. (2004). People meter pulls in protesters. *Hollywood Reporter*, May 11, pp. 1–4.

Loftus, J. (2006). Nielsen to adopt portfolio strategy for TV. Nielsen Media Research Web site, March 2. http://www.prnewswire.com/news-releases/nielsen-to-adopt-portfolio-strategy-for-tv-measurement-55211872.html

Mandese, J. (2004). Infinity dumps Arbitron. *Media Daily News*, June 25, p. 2.

Mandese, J. (2007). ErinMedia set deadline for backers. *Media Daily News*, February 13.

Mandese, J. (2008). Nielsen-backed group bids for set-top based TV ratings. *Media Daily News,* August 18. http://www.mediapost.com/publications/article/88695/nielsen-backed-group-bids-for-set-top-based-tv-rat.html?print

Mandese, J. (2009a). Primetime TV commercial prices plummet. *Media Daily News*, February 3, p. 1.

Mandese, J. (2009b). Nielsen probe finds people not pushing button properly. *Media Daily News*, April 30, p. 1.

Mandese, J. (2009c). Sunbeam suit sheds light on TV ratings monopoly. *Media Daily News*, May 1, p. 1.

Mandese, J. (2009d). Morris steps downs at Arbitron. *Media Daily News*, January 12, p. 1.

Mandese, J. (2009e). Nielsen launches systems for logging TV commercial data. *Media Daily News,* September 3, p. 1.

Mandese, J. (2010). C3 and MRC: Did Nielsen give credit where accreditation was due? *Media Daily News,* May 6. http://www.mediapost.com/publications/article/150039/

Maneer, P. (2002). Global customer satisfaction survey of TV audience measurement. ARF/ ESMOMAR/WAM Conference, June 26, Cannes France. http://www.warc.com/News/PrintNewsItem.aspx?ID=11739

Marchand, R. (1985). *Advertising the American dream: Making way for modernity, 1920–1949.* Berkeley, CA: University of California Press.

Marketing Vox (2006). Nielsen backs out of deal with Arbitron. March 2. http://www.marketingvox.com/nielsen_backs_out_of_ppm_deal_with_arbitron-021183/

Masnick, M. (2011). Nielsen sues comScore with patent it once was sued for infringing Techdirt. com. http://www.techdirt.com/articles/20110323/04095313599/nielsen-sues-comscore-with-patent-it-once-was-sued-infringing.shtml

Maynard, J. (2005). Local people meters mean sweeping changes on TV. *Washington Post,* April 28, p.1.

McArthur, H. (1953). It's like tasting soup. *Washington Star,* August 17, Section E, p. 1.

McArthur, H. (1955). What goes on here. *Washington Star,* April 24, Section E. p. 11.

McClellan, S. (1998). SRI seeks SMART investors. *Broadcasting and Cable,* November 16, p. 35.

McClellan, S. (2006). Maggio to seek set-top-box data for alternative ratings system. *Mediaweek,* June 26.

McClellan, S. (2007). Live-plus-three-day ratings hold surprises, quirks. *Adweek,* June 18.

Media Buyer Planner (2007). Networks gain a tad with live-plus 3-day commercial combo. June 1.

Media Daily News (2009). RCN offer co-branded TiVo DVR. August 4. http://www.mediapost.com/publications/article/111071/

Media Post (2004). Real media riff. September 30, p. 1.

Media Report (1988) Two nuked in ratings war. August 30, pp. 1–8.

Meehan, E. (1990). Why we don't count: The commodity audience. In P. Mellencamp (ed.), *Logics of television.* Bloomington, IN: Indiana University Press.

Meehan, E. (1993). The commodity audience, actual audience: The blindspot debate. In J. Wasko, V. Mosco, and M. Pendakus (eds.), *Illuminating the blindspots: Essays honouring Dallas W. Smythe* (pp. 378–397). Norwood, NJ: Ablex.

Mehta, S. (November 29 2007). A champion for cable 2.0 http://money.cnn.com/2007/11/28/magazines/fortune/waynedavis_1129.fortune/index.htm

Moshavi, S. D. (1992a). Arbitron ends ScanAmerica network service. *Broadcasting,* September 7, p. 37.

Moshavi, S. D. (1992b). Room for two: Accuratings hopes so. *Broadcasting,* September 7, p. 54.

Murdock, G. (1978). Blindspots about Western Marxism: A reply to Dallas Smythe. *Canadian Journal of Political and Social Theory* 2(2): 109–119.

Napoli, P. (2008). *Audience measurement and media policy: Audience economics, the diversity principle, and the PPM.* McGannon Working Paper Series. New York: Donald McGannon Research Center, Fordham University.

Napoli, P. (2010). *The local people meter, the portable people meter, and the unsettled law and policy of audience measurement in the U.S.* McGannon Working Paper Series. New York: Donald McGannon Research Center, Fordham University.

Newsweek (1959). TV ratings: The men behind them. May 18, pp. 66–68.

Nielsen 101 (2006). Local TV ratings methodology. June 30. Media Management Inc. http://www.brandeo.com/content/nielsen-101-local-tv-ratings-methodology

Nielsen, A. C. (1942a). Trends in mechanization of radio advertising. *Journal of Marketing,* January, pp. 218–227.

Nielsen, A. C. (1942b). Two years of commercial operation. *Journal of Marketing*, January, pp. 218–235.

Nielsen, A. C. (1949). New projectable ratings. Nielsen File, Broadcast Pioneers Library, Washington DC.

Nielsen, A. C. (1950). National radio index. Nielsen Collection, Wisconsin State Historical Society, Madison, WI.

Nielsen A. C. (1964). *Great prosperity through marketing research: The first fifty years of Nielsen.* Princeton, NJ: Princeton University Press.

Nielsen, A. C. Jr. (2001). Interview conducted by author in Deerfield, IL, August 11.

Nye, F. W. (1957). *"Hoop" of Hooperatings: The man and his work.* Norwalk, CT: Privately published.

Oppelaar, J. (2000). Web ratings gladiator. *Variety*, October 5, 38: S34.

Ozemhoya, C. U. (1990). Birch/Scarborough Research Inc turns into ratings giant. *South Florida Business Journal*, December 3, p. 15.

Pelligrini, F. (2001). Does America deserve a lower cable bill. Time.com, February 6. http://www.time.com/time/nation/article/0,8599,99740,00.html

Pellegrini, P., and Purdye, K. (2004). Passive vs. button pushing. ESOMAR/ARFWAM Conference, June, Beijing.

Perez, S. (2009). New internet meter will officially measure webTV audience. www.readwriteweb.com, November 30.

Petrozzello, D. (1996). Arbitron to offer audio measuring (portable people meter). *Broadcasting & Cable*, August 26, p. 23.

Phillips, J. (2007). The yin and yang of online metrics: Audience measurement and Web analysis. *Media Post*, 30 November. http://www.mediapost.com/publications/article/71918/the-yin-and-yang-of-online-metrics.html

Poltrack, D. (2006). TV enters the digital era, the era of the digital franchise program. CBS Study presented at MIT communications forums. March 8, Boston.

Printer's Ink (1938). The first fifty years of advertising, July 28, p. 348.

PR Newswire (1998). InfoSeek hosts great web ratings debate. June 11. http://www.thefreelibrary.com/ 27The+Great+Web+Ratings+Debate,%27+The+First+Independent...-a020783026

PR Newswire (2001). Ceredian completes reverse spinoff of Arbitron. March 30, p. 1.

Radio Business Report (2008). Arbitron exec bonuses tied to PPM. January 31, p. 1.

Ramos, E. (2009). New media people meters tune to local Hispanics. *Baltimore Business Examiner*, July 20, p. 1.

Rashid, F. (2011). White House asks for do not track legislation. *E Week*, March 3. http://www.eweek.com/c/a/Security/White-House-Asks-for-Do-Not-Track-Legislation-185776/

Rick, C. (2011). Nielsen, comScore row over patents. Reelseo, April. http://www.reelseo.com/nielsen-comscore-row-patents/

Rivkin, M. (2006). Gaming demonstrates a cross-platform, multi-platform solution for set-top-box data. http://www.thefreelibrary.com/Zodiac+Gaming+Demonstrates+a+Cross-Platform+Multi-Player+Solution+for...-a0144878258

Rosenthal, P. (2009) Coalition of media firms, marketers may form own group to challenge Nielsen measurements. *Chicago Tribune*, August 16. http://articles.chicagotribune.com/2009-08-16/business/0908140388_1_new-ratings-system-nielsen-media-research-audience-estimates

Saunders, C. (2002). ComScore nabs Media Metrix, *InternetNews.com* June 6. http://www.internetnews.com/IAR/article.php/1347911/comScore+Nabs+Media+Metrix.htm

Saxe, F. (1999). Arbitron study details net radio usage. *Billboard*, July 17, p. 99.

Schechner S., and Dana, R. (2009). Local TV stations face a fuzzy future. *Wall Street Journal*, February 10, p. 1.

Scherer, F. M. (1992). *High technology competition.* Cambridge, MA: Harvard University Press.

Scherer, F. M., and Ross, D. (1990). *Industrial market structure and economic performance* (3rd edn). Boston, MA: Houghton Mifflin Company.

Schumpeter, J. A. (1942). *Capitalism, socialism, and democracy*. New York: Harper.

Search Engine Reports (2000). The problem with ratings services. April 4, pp. 1–4.

Seidman, R. (2011). DVR penetration grows to 39.7% of households, 42.4 % of viewers. *New TV Technology*, March 23, p. 1.

Seiler Personal Papers (n.d.). James Seiler: Ratings innovator. *The Phoney Report*. Silver Springs, MD.

Seiler, J. W. (1947). Ratings on individual basis are urged. *Broadcasting/Telecasting*, May 12, p. 13.

Seiler, J. W. (1981). Early beginnings of radio audience research as recollected by James Seiler, December 21. James. W. Seiler Personal Documents, Silver Springs, MD.

Seiler, M. G. (2000). Interview conducted by K. S. Buzzard, August 10–12. Silver Springs, MD.

Shields, M. (2009). Nielsen: TV watching soars, but so does time shifting. *Adweek*, May 20, p. 1.

Shields, T., and Bliss, J. (2011). Comcast wins U.S. approval to buy NBC Universal from GE for 13.8 billion. BloombergNews.com, January 18. http://www.bloomberg.com/news/2011-01-18/comcast-nbc-universal-deal-said-to-be-near-u-s-fcc-approval.html

Shim, R. (2002). Nielsen begins monitoring TiVo usage. *C/NET News*, August 6. www.news.cnet.com/Nielsen-begins-monitoring-TiVo-usage/2100-1041_3-948580.html

Sieber, R. (1988). Cable networks. *Gannett Center Journal*, Summer, p. 71.

Sims, J. (1988). AGB, the ratings innovator. *Gannett Center Journal*, Summer, pp. 84–88.

Small, C. (1947). The biggest man in radio. *Saturday Evening Post*, November 22, pp. 15–18.

Smythe, D. W. (1977). Communication blindspot of Western Marxism. *Canadian Journal of Political and Social Theory* 1(3): 1–27.

Solman, G. (2004). Local people meter launch to spell new beginning. *Adweek*, March 22, p. 1.

Spangler T., and M. Farrell (2009a). Thinking inside the box. *Multi-channel News,* June 15.

Spangler, T. and M. Farrell (2009b). Set-top box data can vastly improve advertising. *Multi-channel News*, May 7.

Sponsor (1958). Behind the rating system: Arbitron. September 17, pp. 37–38.

Stark, P. (1992). Birch Radio folds; Arbitron to market Scarborough data. *Billboard*, January 4, p. 1.

Stark, P. (1994). Arbitron plans to increase sample size to 85 markets. *Billboard*, October 30, p. 4.

Sterling, C. H., and John M. Kittross (1978). *Stay-tuned: A concise history of American broadcasting*. Belmont, CA: Wadsworth Publishing Co.

Stine, R. (2010). PPM transforms radio's clock. *Radio World*, December 1, p. 1.

Supreme Court of the State of New York, County of New York (2010). Arbitron v. Spanish Broadcasting System. Index No. 6000366/2010.

Taylor, C. (2001). Jupiter offers vertical reports for nine areas. *Advertising Age*, April 9, p. 8.

Taylor, C. (2009). Nielsen data shows DVRs are great and awful for broadcast TV. *B/NET*, October 14. http://www.cbsnews.com/8301-505123_162-43744187/nielsen-data-shows-dvrs-are-great-and-awful-for-broadcast-tv/

Television Digest (1993) Arbitron throws in towel. October 25, p. 4.

Thompson, M. (1999). Ratings firms vie for global domination. *The Industry Standard,* October 15, pp. 1-3.

Todreas, T. (1999). *Value creation and branding in TV's digital age*. Westport, CT: Quorum Books.

Torpey-Kemph, A. (2000). Arbitron forms alliance with Lariat. *Mediaweek*, July 31, p. 51.

Trachenberg, J. A. (1988). Diary of a failure (AGB Research). *Forbes*, 142, pp. 168–169.

Trigoboff, D. (2003). Philly's new headcount. *Broadcasting and Cable,* June 24, p. 12.

Turner, T. (2004). My beef with big media. *Washington Monthly*, July/August. http://www.washingtonmonthly.com/features/2004/0407.turner.html

Turow, J. (1997). *Breaking up America: Advertisers and the new media world*. Chicago, IL: University of Chicago Press.

TV Bureau of Advertising (1995). The television ratings services: Interview with James Seiler. May.

TV Bureau of Advertising (n.d.). Multi-platforms: Internet measurement methodology. pp. 1–3.

TV/Radio Age (1984a). Ad agencies vary widely on ERIM competitor. October 1, p. 48.

TV/Radio Age (1984b). Viewer/purchase meter opens up new ballgame for ARB. September 3, pp. 57–58.

TV/Radio Age (1988). ARB prepared to lose $125 million on ScanAmerica peoplemeter service. June 27, p. 17.

U.S. District Court Southern District of Florida. (2005). ErinMedia vs. Nielsen Media Research, April.

U.S. District Court Southern District of Florida (2009). Sunbeam TV Corp. vs. Nielsen Media Research, April.

Video Age International (2004). People meter struggle through growing pains. October 1, p. 1.

View (1989) People who don't need peoplemeters. August 21, pp. 10–11.

Webster, J. G., and L. W. Lichty (1991). *Ratings analysis: Theory and practice.* Hillsdale, NJ: Lawrence Erlbaum Associates.

Wired (2004). Nielsen "people meter" draws fire. April 16, p. 1.

Womer, S. (1941). What they say of two leading methods of measuring radio. *Printer's Ink,* February 7, pp. 73–79.

Wurtzel, A. (2009). Crisis measurement. Audience Measurement 4.0 Conference, Advertising Research Foundation, June 23–24. New York City.

Yankelovitch, D. (1963). Advertising's 75th year. *Printer's Ink,* June 14, pp. 321–322.

Zamp wiki (n.d.). Web banner. http://www.zampwiki.com/?t=Banner_ad

INDEX

Ratings Analysis

Third Edition

James Webster, Patricia F. Phalen and Lawrence Lichty

Ratings Analysis: The Theory and Practice of Audience Research provides a thorough and up-to-date presentation of the ratings industry and analysis processes. It serves as a practical guide for conducting audience research, offering readers the tools for becoming informed and discriminating consumers of audience information, from broadcasting to cable to the World Wide Web. In its third edition, this essential volume:

- illustrates applications of audience research in advertising, programming, financial analysis, and social policy
- describes audience research data and summarizes the history of audience measurement, the research methods most often used, and the kinds of ratings research products currently available
- discusses the analysis of audience data by offering a framework within which to understand mass media audiences and by focusing specifically to the analysis of ratings data.

Appropriate for all readers needing an in-depth understanding of audience research, including people working in advertising, electronic media, and related industries, *Ratings Analysis* also has much to offer academics, critics, policy-makers, and students of mass media.

Hardback: 978-0-8058-5409-1
Paperback: 978-0-8058-5410-7
eBook: 978-1-4106-1735-4

For ordering and further information please visit:

www.routledge.com